To be a Pilgrim

A comprehensive guide
Information, instruction
and inspiration for pilgrims

Barbara Butler and Jo White

Kevin
Mayhew

First published in 2002 by
KEVIN MAYHEW LTD
Buxhall, Stowmarket, Suffolk IP14 3BW
Email: info@kevinmayhewltd.com

9 8 7 6 5 4 3 2 1 0

ISBN 1 84003 847 0
Catalogue No 1500473

Cover illustration from an original painting
by Anne Gregson

Cover design by Angela Selfe
Edited by Katherine Laidler
Typesetting by Louise Selfe

Printed and bound in Great Britain

Christians Aware

Christians Aware is a network of individuals and groups, including Baptists, Methodists, Orthodox, Roman Catholics, Society of Friends, Anglicans and United Reformed Church members in Britain and around the world. The organisation's links include communities in Africa, Mauritius, the Middle East, India, Sri Lanka, Japan and the Caribbean. Approximately 2,500 people are involved directly and many more through their churches and communities.

Christians Aware offers varied opportunities for listening, encounter, learning and reflection, so that understanding and trust may grow between people, including Christians and those of other faiths, who may then work together to overcome injustices.

Christians Aware is an educational and religious charity and a member body of Churches Together in Britain and Ireland and Churches Together in England.

Acknowledgements

The publishers wish to express their gratitude to the following for permission to include copyright material in this book:

Inderjit Bhogal for 'Borders and Binoculars', taken from *Theology on the Hoof,* originally published by Penistone Publications.

Revd David Bryant for his article 'Yorkshire Abbeys'.

Cambridge University Press, The Edinburgh Building, Shaftesbury Road, Cambridge, CB2 2RU, for the extracts from *The Book of Common Prayer,* the rights in which are vested in the Crown and reproduced by permission of the Crown's Patentee, Cambridge University Press.

Church Action on Poverty, Central Buildings, Oldham Street, Manchester, M1 1JT, for the extract from the *Report on Pilgrimage Against Poverty.*

Churches Together in Britain & Ireland, Inter-Church House, 35-41 Lower Marsh, London, SE1 7RL, for the extract from *Holy Land Pilgrimage,* 1992.

Julie Myerson for her piece, 'Boy Growing'.

Katy Hounsell-Robert for her articles 'A Journey to Santiago de Compostela' and 'In the Footsteps of St Augustine of Hippo'.

SCM Press, 9-17 St Albans Place, London, N1 0NX, for the extracts from *Where Three Ways Meet* by John A. Robinson (1987); *The Cost of Discipleship* by Dietrich Bonhoeffer (1959) and *Exploration into Goodness* by Frank Wright (1988).

SPCK, Holy Trinity Church, Marylebone Road, London, NW1 4DU, for David Adam's poem about Holy Island, taken from *The Edge of Glory* (SPCK).

June B. Tillman for her poem 'Ayers Rock', © 1988 June B. Tillman.

Paul Valleley for his piece 'Wilderness Weekend'.

The publisher has made every effort to trace the owners of copyright material and we hope that no copyright has been infringed. Pardon is sought and apology made if the contrary be the case, and a correction will be made in any reprint of this book.

Contents

Foreword

This book contains fascinating and very varied accounts of pilgrimage, some lasting a day or less, others lasting months, some to holy places, others to places of tragedy such as Auschwitz and Hiroshima, while other forms of pilgrimage have no particular destination. The Celtic monks, for example, set out to wander wherever the Spirit prompted them. When Kevin set out from Ireland in his coracle and landed in America, his original purpose, according to the ninth-century writer of *The Voyage of St Brendan,* was not to reach America, nor to convert any people he might find there, but 'to wonder at the glories of God's creation'.

Pilgrimage is normally a journey to some sacred place, but it can also be a journey undertaken to any place of importance to the pilgrim, or even to no particular place, as in the case of the Celtic monks, but whether to a sacred place, a profane place, or no particular place, pilgrimage entails journeying for a particular purpose. It is a universal phenomenon. Section Three gives an account of pilgrimage-making in every major world religion.

Why do people undertake pilgrimages? Probably for as many reasons as there are pilgrims. In medieval times pilgrimage was undertaken as a penance for sins, as an act of reparation, to touch the relics of the saints whose remains were thought to be irradiated with heavenly power which could cure us of our ills, both physical and spiritual. Some might go on pilgrimage because life at home had become impossible; others might go just for the adventure of it; while thieves might find it easier to practise their art on pilgrim strangers rather than at home. In the Netherlands, up to the nineteenth century, an alternative to prison was to be sent on pilgrimage!

I have been on two walking pilgrimages, one from Weybridge to Rome, walking every inch of the way; the other from my birthplace in Ayrshire to Jerusalem, walking most of the way.

It was only a long time after the first pilgrimage that I discovered the real reason why I had set out, a reason I was not clearly aware of at the time. In this book I found the reasons pilgrims give for their journey to be very varied, but there is a convergence of purpose in most of the accounts.

Someone has written, 'Pilgrimage is the poor person's substitute for mysticism.' The 'poor person' is everyone. All of us have to find some kind of meaning in our existence. If we reflect at all, we become conscious of conflict within us, conflicting desires, conflicting ideas, conflicting relationships, bewilderment at the complexity of life. There is a very striking passage in the autobiography of Bertrand Russell, mathematician, philosopher, pacifist and leading atheistic humanist of the twentieth century.

> The centre of me is always and eternally a terrible pain – a curious wild pain – a searching for something beyond what the world contains, something transfigured and infinite – the beatific vision – God – I do not find it, I do not think it is to be found – but the love of it is my life – it's like a passionate love for a ghost. At times it fills me with rage, at times with wild despair, it is the source of gentleness and cruelty and work, it fills every passion that I have – it is the actual spring of life within me.

One way of finding direction in our inner confusion of conflicting desires and ideas is to externalise the inner conflict in some way. One way is to set out on a journey. The destination may not be clear, the journey may be circular, or it may have no specific destination. These outward journeys can enable us to understand more clearly the meaning of our bewildering and confusing inner journey. Our destination, or the purpose of the journey, becomes a symbol for the destination/purpose of our life journey. Every decision taken on the pilgrimage is determined by this chosen destination/purpose – for example, the direction taken each day, the distance we travel, where we stop and why, the luggage we carry, what we eat and drink, where and for how long we sleep each day, the clothes we wear, the money we take, or don't take.

It is interesting to note the answers which so many explorers, pioneers, inventors, creative artists have given when asked, 'What led you to undertake this task/way of life?' They tend to answer, 'I just had to undertake this project/search', echoing Luther's reply to his accusers, 'Here I stand, I cannot do otherwise.' Pilgrimage is a way of finding the meaning, the purpose in our lives. Towards the end of his life St Augustine wrote, 'Lord, you have created me for yourself and my heart is restless until it rests in you.' We go on pilgrimage because of our restlessness, and through the journeying we can understand better the source of our restlessness. This is confirmed both explicitly and implicitly in most accounts in this book.

In human life it is desire that draws us, energises us, directs us. Desire is not something we create in ourselves, nor is it something we possess: it is something we discover and can allow to possess us. But desire, which is the creative source within us, can also become a destructive force for ourselves and for others. Desires can tear us apart and destroy others, too. The legitimate desire for security, for example, within an individual, group or nation can become destructive for other individuals, groups and nations, as our nuclear defence systems clearly show.

By undertaking a pilgrimage, we can become more aware of the distinction between the creative and the destructive desires within us.

Many of the contributors to this book agree that it is the journey itself which matters more than arrival at the destination. Many of the stories also agree that the change in outlook which the journey effects is of much greater value than the pilgrimage itself. Pilgrimage must have a purpose, even if the purpose is simply to wander. While on pilgrimage, every decision made is influenced by this purpose. Reflecting on this, the pilgrim may then ask, 'What is the purpose of my own life? What is this inner restlessness pointing me towards? What is it that I really desire?' The journeying day by day, especially on a walking pilgrimage, can begin to show us the folly of our ways and help us to become more conscious of what we really desire.

On a walking pilgrimage, even if it is only for a day, one becomes painfully aware of the weight of the haversack. This leads to a conclusion so obvious that it can seem ridiculous even to mention it. Most of our individual, regional, national and international conflicts could be avoided if we could accept and act upon this conclusion. The conclusion is:

> Luggage is for the sake of the journey:
> the journey is not for the luggage.

What a valuable piece of luggage to take home from the pilgrimage, freeing us from the illusion that I am what I possess, that my security lies in my possessions or in my achievements. The illusion can lead me to become what I possess, cling to, defend and kill for my possessions with all the strength of my self-preservation instinct, for my true self (my purpose/destination) has disappeared under my heap of possessions. Nations go to war for the preservation and accumulation of their possessions, concealing this truth beneath thick-spun webs of words about freedom, human rights, democratic values, even sometimes 'doing the will of God'.

Another simple truth for life which soon becomes clear on a pilgrimage, and which is amply confirmed in the accounts which follow, is:

> The more we cling to any created thing as though it were our ultimate good, the more imprisoned we become by our own attachments.

The more fussy I am about my likes and dislikes, the more miserable my pilgrimage is likely to be. For example, is my attitude to the weather, scenery, food, sleeping accommodation and cleanliness such that unless every element is exactly to my taste, my day is ruined? If so, my pilgrimage will be a misery, and unless I learn from it, the rest of my life will also continue to be miserable.

All pilgrimages offer the opportunity to meet strangers, and, as the following accounts show very clearly, these encounters can become the most valuable part of the journey itself and of its after-effect. These encounters with people of different cultures, background and religion can help me to see how my own racism, sexism, the way I relate to my religion or lack of it, how I relate to my political views, ideologies and 'isms', can close me off from communication with others. Encountering anyone who does not share my views – and that may include all but a select few of the human race – becomes a source of strain and sadness. Being open to and becoming friendly with people of other cultures, other faiths, and of no faith can set us free from the prison of our own ego.

This book ends with a very practical Appendix, including the addresses of organisations giving further information. Even for those for whom physical journeys are no longer possible, the book will be of interest, because it can help us to become more aware of the pilgrim nature of our own life and better to appreciate its richness.

GERARD W. HUGHES SJ

He who would valiant be
'gainst all disaster,
let him in constancy
follow the Master.
There's no discouragement
shall make him once relent
his first avowed intent
to be a pilgrim.

PERCY DEARMER (1867-1936)
after JOHN BUNYAN (1628-1688)

Drawing by Jane Walton-Loxton

Introduction

We have called our book *To be a Pilgrim* because this, we believe, is the hope of every person, and has been since the dawn of humanity. People have a natural drive – it is within us all – to move, mentally, spiritually and also physically. The hope is that there is always something else, in a new adventure, a new place and through meeting new people.

Every faith has its pilgrimage traditions and its special places. We, as Christians, have focused on Christian pilgrimage, but we have not forgotten the pilgrimages of friends of other faiths. We have also included pilgrimage which is not strictly from a faith tradition at all, but would qualify to be called pilgrimage in its widest sense, including the physical challenge of some journeys.

The outer journey of going to new places and of meeting challenges and overcoming hardships mirrors the inner journey of prayer, meditation, contemplation and simply being alone with God.

There is also the journey of life, which cannot be avoided, but which may become a pilgrimage when it is approached with courage and hope in the future.

The forest is sometimes associated with the inner journey and the journey of life because it may often be dark, it may provide security and comfort, but it may equally have hidden dangers, perhaps wild animals or holes to fall into along the way. It is easy to become lost in a forest, because paths may not be clear but rather covered with leaves and twigs. Often the way in life may be unclear. The fears people face differ greatly, but every person faces fear at some time. Fears which many people articulate include loneliness, disablement and death. There is also the fear of the loss of creativity and the loss of personal identity.

On any journey of pilgrimage the true pilgrim is ready to forsake everything and to take great risks to travel, and thus to be enlightened, changed and challenged. The true pilgrim does not have the security of knowing that he or she is on the right path, but is ever open, ever questioning, ever listening to God and to the people around.

There are few people, perhaps, who are able to recognise the many crossroads they come to, and who are brave enough to stand there, in good and bad weathers, in good and bad times, providing a link between the various ways, cultures and faiths. The few people who are able to do this are those who bear the pain of being the bridge of meeting, at the crossroads, in the cross.

The pilgrim in all the main world faiths traditionally faces worry and uncertainty. He or she is leaving a secure place and perhaps a family and friends, and moving off into an unknown future. The pilgrim is vulnerable and exposed, with the constant need to meet strangers, to share new cultures, difficult climates and lands. There are always new experiences, some good and some bad. There are great fears, especially of loss, even loss of life itself.

The pilgrim has never avoided the risks of a journey, and in the Christian tradition has experienced God with him or her every step of the way. This has not meant, however, that God would save the pilgrim from the many perils of the way, but rather that God would be there, no matter what happened. God would be there in the rejoicing but also in the sorrow. A friend went off to Central Africa to be with the people and to work, knowing that the greatest danger there would be death in a road accident. He was out driving with his wife in a bush area in Northern Zambia when the car hit a tree and turned over. He remembers thinking, at the time when the car turned over, 'All is well. God is with us.' He did not mean by this that God would save them, but that, whatever happened, God would be there.

St Cuthbert is an example of a great early Christian pilgrim, who took risks every day of his life, knowing that God was there, and who never seems to have avoided difficulties, no matter how much pain they caused him. He was born around 625 CE in the Scottish border areas and the Venerable Bede provides most of the early written information about him. We can read about the young Cuthbert who joined Melrose Abbey as a monk and later became the prior. He later moved to Lindisfarne Abbey as the prior. After the Synod of Whitby in 664 CE he retired to Inner Farne where he stayed for almost ten years. He then, reluctantly, became Bishop of Lindisfarne, but only for two years. He retired to Inner Farne where he died in 687 CE. About 100 years after his burial in Lindisfarne Abbey the Viking raids began and the monks carried his body away on a journey which only ended when he was buried in Durham Cathedral.

There are many legends about the life of St Cuthbert but none are of any importance compared with the real person who somehow comes through to us from so long ago, a person who did not take an easy or straightforward path in life, but who rather could see many paths, and managed to hold them all in tension. He was a true bridge person. He stood at the crossroads between monastery and people. He was a happy monk, and a happy hermit, but he spent a lot of his time in the homes of the poor, sharing the conditions and the unbearable problems. In the tradition of Anthony of Egypt and of Pope Gregory, he stood at the crossroads between being a pastor and being a hermit. He linked earth and heaven; he was both Martha and Mary. He held the Celtic and Roman traditions of the Church in himself, and he struggled for unity and understanding. The outcome of the Synod of Whitby made him feel a failure in his lifetime, but he was ever the faithful pilgrim, standing at the crossroads of life, loving God and his neighbour, accepting solitude and work, living his faith through love. He was a great pilgrim and a great inspiration.

We hope this book will provide stories, resources and inspiration for pilgrims to venture forth into unknown places and conditions where there is uncertainty and insecurity. We have included many aspects of pilgrimage and many pilgrim people. We hope that the exposure to new ideas, situations, people, cultures, climates and places will lead to joyful surprise and enrichment, and on to new pilgrim paths.

BARBARA BUTLER AND JO WHITE

Photograph: Barbara Butler

Moors above Calderdale

SECTION ONE

Inner Journey

Drawing by Jane Walton-Loxton

Introduction

There is something in each one of us that seeks God; that longs for him. Someone once described it as having a God-shaped hole in our hearts that can only be filled when we recognise God at the centre of ourselves. There is so much searching taking place in people's lives: reading horoscopes, trying things that we often know won't do us any good, holding special stones, wearing coloured bangles, rearranging our rooms, buying things we don't need, having casual sex, taking illegal drugs, drinking too much alcohol, trying to get in touch with dead loved ones through mediums – the list is endless. But rarely do any of these satisfy us for long.

People may not know what they are searching for; they may not put a name to it. Perhaps we could just call it God.

St Augustine wrote, 'Truly our hearts are restless until they find their rest in you, O God.'

If pilgrimage is about a conscious choice to seek the holy, then we can find the holy within ourselves and in where we are. Often it's a case of turning things round, changing our attitude to something. Often we can't change the other person or the situation we are in, but we can change our attitude to it and to them. The case of the glass being half-full or half-empty is often cited, but we like the one describing a marriage partner: 'We've been married a while now and I think he's really boring. He never surprises me, never arrives late to collect me, has pretty much the same views all the time. It's funny really because when I first met him, what really attracted me was how stable he was. I could rely on him. If he said he would do something, then he would. If he said he'd meet me at a certain time, then that's the time he'd be there, not ten minutes late. He rarely changed his mind on things; you could trust him.'

It's all in the way we look at things! On the mornings when we are wakened early by the singing of a million birds, we want them all shot, but quietly. When we are working in the garden, there's little better than the sweet melody of a flock of birds all lined up on the phone wires and singing just for us! When the day is hot, it is wonderful to sit in the shade of a tree, but when we are trying to take a picture of a view, we may feel tempted to want all the trees that are in our way cut down.

Looking inside ourselves can be difficult. We may think we know what we'll find and not want to look. We say 'may think' because so often when we actually look we find some things very different from our expectations. As adults we need to revisit our childhood memories to try to understand why we behave and think as we do. It is only then that we can be in control of our behaviour. If we don't understand why we respond to things as we do, we can rarely take control. Not that there's necessarily anything wrong in the way we behave; it's just that it should be a choice and not automatic. If you're the person who cannot say 'No' to anything, you'll understand what we mean. Or perhaps you never say anything when something happens that makes you unhappy, but every now and then you just have to have a good row 'to clear the air'.

The 'inner journey' can be painful, and can continue for a long time, though often people will tackle one bit at a time. Perhaps we say to ourselves that we want to get to grips with a particular aspect of our behaviour or personality. This can come out in religious-speak as wanting to get closer to God. Wonderful. That's really what we all want to do: 'To know you more clearly, love you more dearly and follow you more nearly.' But what stops us getting closer to God? Well, it's different for all of us, but let's just look at some of the possible reasons.

There's something we feel guilty about

- Are we right to take the responsibility for the guilt on our own shoulders?
- Have we already talked with God about this and been forgiven by him but not by ourselves? If he can forgive and forget, why can't we?

- Is it something we are still doing? Do we plan to stop?
- Is it something in our past? Was it actually right behaviour for back then? Do we need to make amends for whatever it was? If we can't make amends to that particular person what would be an appropriate thing to do?

We are afraid God won't want us closer
- Perhaps we are not used to being wanted.
- Perhaps we are unsure what being loved will be like.
- Perhaps we think God's too busy to want or have time for us.

We are wondering what God will expect of us
- Will he want us to change something in our lives that we don't want to change?
- Are we anticipating a confrontation with something we are doing at the moment?
- Perhaps we've got something on our minds that we think God will challenge us further about, and we do not want to take any more steps on that yet?

As we can see, not only are there many different reasons stopping us getting closer to ourselves and thus to God, but there are a hundred thousand little questions – mind fields – waiting for all of us who take that step closer. You see, we never quite know with God.

So often we don't know where to start, not just about the practical aspects of which book to read, who to talk with, where to stay, but about how actually to start to get closer to God. To take that step further than usual, try to imagine a very long, deep lake with steep banks. It's surrounded with nicely cut grass, and the water comes level with the grass. Every day we walk across the lawn towards the lake to stand and admire it. We look across to the other side and wonder how we could ever cross this wide, deep lake. We don't want to fall into the lake because we can't swim. One day we hear that it is actually easy to cross because there are large stepping-stones at all points along the lake bank that extend right across to the other side. We just can't see them until we tread on them. Each day we walk a little closer to the water's edge. We can't see these stones, but the attraction of the other side grows and grows. Eventually we take a deep breath, hold our noses tightly, and put one foot on the surface of the lake's water. Immediately we feel the solid rock under us. We move the other leg over the water and step forward again and put that foot on the surface of the water, and again we feel solid rock under us. The rocks are solid and not slippery. It's up to us now to choose our path to the other side.

So it often is with making those steps to get closer to God. We will never know if the stepping-stones are there until we put out a foot and our trust.

Keeping a prayer book is a good idea for many people. Not just to write down prayer requests and answers, but also to make a note of what we hear God saying to us or of our response; of the ideas that come to mind during quiet times that often don't feel as if they came from us at all, thoughts that question our established thinking or patterns of behaviour, that ask those uneasy 'Why' questions, and leave us to think through the 'How' answers. Sometimes these thoughts and ideas make little sense at the time, but looking back sometime later, or sharing them with a trusted counsellor, often gives them real clarity.

The examples we have used in this chapter reflect those times when we go searching for the holy, either at home or away, when we take time out of our busyness to search out those stepping stones of faith that may bring us closer to the holy. They are not always easy journeys but their impact on our futures may be enormous. They can be literally life-changing.

Susan Hughes writes of a moorland weekend in West Yorkshire, organised by Christians Aware, held in a remote area reflecting the wildness of geography, sociology and history, and bringing out the wilderness within the person. The weather was damp and very foggy for the whole weekend, so a real atmosphere was built up. The first day's walk was focused on a reservoir originally built at the head of a new remote valley to feed the water wheels of mills in industrial Yorkshire in the mid-1800s. It was in use for some 50 years until the mills transferred to coal power, and was then deliberately breached following a new Act of Parliament that required all reservoirs capable of storing water to have watermen on site. To see such an enormous piece of work in such a wild and now inaccessible area that has been deliberately smashed spoke starkly of failed plans, broken promises, time passing and things changing.

Going on Retreat

Henry Evans

In the context of this book, you might say that a retreat is an amalgam of at least two pilgrimage experiences. There is, first, the much-looked-forward-to rest and refreshment and relaxation that a cosy inn or youth hostel provides, and also the welcome breather on the mountain top to get one's breath, look back on the way you've come, and take a peep at the way ahead. In Archbishop Michael Ramsey's words, a retreat is the Christian's opportunity to realise one's self as 'one who belongs to eternity'.

These days, retreats for lay people need little commendation. Retreat houses are fairly well booked up, the retreat lists in the annual *Retreat* magazine get longer, and more houses for retreat (especially smaller ones) are opened. Weekend retreats (Friday evening to Sunday lunch or tea) are the most popular, but if a week's retreat – Monday lunch, say, to Friday lunch – can be managed, or even longer, so much the better.

Again, there is a huge variety of retreats to suit all tastes. There are the so-called 'theme' retreats – prayer and . . . painting, dance, calligraphy, nature study. Then there are retreats for beginners, for younger people, for older people; retreats, too, which help people to understand their own personality and relate this understanding to their spiritual journey. There are the individually guided retreats, especially ones conducted with the insights of Ignatian spirituality. The variety now is large: there is something to suit everyone. Quiet days in retreat houses or with the Quiet Garden Movement are welcome tasters for the real thing.

To illustrate the place of a retreat in the context of life's pilgrimage, let's imagine that a weekend preached retreat for a layperson has been booked. After arrival, the first meal and introduction to fellow guests, the retreatants will gather for the first address by the retreat conductor, which is probably the most important of all the addresses, as he or she helps participants to make the best possible use of some hard-won time in a busy life.

A summary of the first address will go, perhaps, something like this.

You have been invited by our Lord to draw aside with him from 'the muchness and manyness' of life, as someone has put it. The conductor will carefully explain the programme (usually printed out beforehand), the geography of the retreat house, the kind of worship to be provided, where suitable books can be found. In this way retreatants are enabled to withdraw quickly from the busyness and burdens at home.

A silent retreat is to be strongly commended. Archbishop Ramsey called himself 'a total silence man'. For two reasons, he said. 'First, silence is not just a matter of not talking, it's a matter of depth, and there is a deep quality of silence that is only really obtained if the silence is continuous.' Second, he felt it was 'a fallacy that people are initiated into silence if the silence is interrupted by little spaces of conversation. The right invitation into silence is silence.'

An experienced retreat conductor will carefully explain that people have found that God seems to speak most clearly in the silence; that people tend to avoid the silence means they are afraid God might speak, or they are afraid of what comes bubbling up from their depths in the silence. Hence it is important that an experienced conductor is available and that there is nothing to fear, because, in the words of the book of Daniel (2:22), '(God) knows what is in the darkness'. Silence is not to be feared, but welcomed, as a place where 'heart speaks to heart'. Silence is not a negative being; rather 'silence is golden'. A retreat is a happy opportunity to experience 'the silence of eternity/interpreted by love'. So the silence is to be joyful, not solemn. Retreatants are encouraged to smile – even wink – at each other! Silence is to be sensible too: a loud whisper is permissible if you want the salt at table

– or if someone is standing on your toe! At meal times, a silence which could be embarrassing is avoided by the playing of a tape, or the reading of a book by the conductor.

In the retreat introductory address, the conductor will make some fairly obvious points. He or she may use words beginning with 'R' – 'R' for 'Retreat'. First *rest*: the retreatant has nothing to do for a whole weekend – no demands, no meals to plan, no meals to cook. There is to be a minimum of 'doing'; one has time to 'be', to remember again that one has been created by God and that one is loved by God. So it's a time to *relax* into God's presence, to feel the warmth of the sunlight of his love – a time to allow God to do the doing. One has time, as someone has put it, to *register*: to stop and stare at the 'giddy wonder' of God's creation, to savour the sounds, the tastes, the sights, for in the rush of life we usually do a lot of looking but not much 'noticing'.

A retreat, too, is a time to *read*, to dip into some of the great masters of prayer and pilgrimage, an opportunity to read the biography of one who did find the Way. So it's a time of *reflection*, a time to look back with thanksgiving and sometimes remorse; it's a time to see where one is perhaps being led by God. Quite often a phrase or some fresh ideas emerge from an address or a prayer. It's as if God the Holy Spirit is using that to give one a new perspective on one's life, to give new hope. It's a time, too, to *repent*, to take stock, to say 'sorry', to begin again. Retreat houses are often places of great natural beauty, but they are also 'rubbish dumps' where past mistakes can be dumped and left behind for good, and wrong turnings rectified. In the exercise of repenting, it is an opportunity, also, to *relate* one's heartaches or hang-ups or bereavements to the retreat conductor, to receive godly counsel, absolution (sacramental or otherwise), and so a new beginning in the journey.

Towards the end of the retreat, a need will arise to 'make real and effective' that desire for a new beginning in the making of one or two (or more) simple and alterable '*resolutions*' for the future. Maybe that will include an attempt at a more disciplined prayer life, and perhaps an attempt at a reconciliation in a relationship that has gone wrong. The final 'R' is surely a deep need to *rejoice* in God's goodness, care and protection; to realise afresh that one is loved and that all *is* well.

A retreat should give one a new awareness of the reality of one's own unseen Compassion in Life's Pilgrimage and a new and lively expectation of the End of Life's Pilgrimage – the House of many Mansions.

Henry Evans was the Warden of Launde Abbey Retreat House, Leicestershire.

The Contemplative and Religious Vocation

A Sister, Sisters of the Love of God

Through Baptism all Christians are called to a life of total commitment to the service of God, but the living out of this will vary in many ways as the response to 'Lord, what will you have me do?' is prayed. When we ask that in all openness, and wait upon God, we may be surprised and even horrified to find that we are being called to be a Religious. Every Christian has a 'vocation' so why not continue in our daily lives worshipping and working with the local Church? Why set out to be different? What is it that draws us continually to contemplation within the Religious life, and what is distinctive about it today?

We inherit the Church's long tradition of contemplative monastic life in a form that requires no outward ministry beyond prayer, and it is this tradition that gives shape to our life in a modern Community; so it does not need to be 're-invented' with every Congregation and Order. There is the accumulated wisdom of 16 centuries dating back to the Desert Fathers, and it is from this that we draw our life. It gives the characteristic features of attentive silence, a life steeped in scripture, rhythms of prayer and worship, in solitude and corporately, work and recreation together – a life bound by the Vows of Poverty, Chastity and Obedience.

In the Community life there is a balance between the corporate and solitude. It is both a joy and a cross, a recognition that we may not have chosen each other, and are very different from each other, but are drawn by God to live out and experience his unconditional love. As members of the Body of Christ, we celebrate the liturgical prayer of the Divine Office which punctuates the day, and is like a scaffold to our life and the life of the Church. This contrasts with the individual prayer in the cell, but both are part of the complete oblation. The hiddenness and withdrawal of the life gives a respect and love for the cell, and we experience the unique and particular love that God has for each of us and all creation. It is here that we are 'shaped' by time specifically for God alone, and by letting the Holy Spirit speak in and through scripture as we meditate upon it. Some will centre on the Orthodox Jesus Prayer – 'Lord Jesus Christ, Son of God, have mercy on me' – a prayer that has been used for centuries by countless numbers of the Church in the East and the West. It is here, during these times of prayer and meditation that we are made aware of, and see more clearly the needs of the world; and recognise that we are a tiny microcosm of the whole. Individually we can hold those needs, and the many intercessions that are received by the Community, to God, as we do corporately when we come together at the daily Eucharist.

Our silence is a witness and response to the holiness and presence of God, and is a continual act of reverence and thanksgiving – we receive and give God's peace. In it we are made aware of our own restlessness, false judgements and fears, and these can be 'converted' as we see them in the light of God. 'Be still and know that I am God' (Psalm 46) and 'For God alone my soul in silence waits' (Psalm 62:1) both remind us of this. In silence we seek support and keep open the channels of love that will extend our hospitality and mutual trust of each other and those who visit the Convent, whether it is in the preparation, welcome and care of our guests, catering for the Community, looking after the Convent and Sacristy, gardening or administrative work in its various forms.

We embrace a limitation of personal mobility for the sake of freedom in God, and through it seek to make possible a more complete offering of our life as we remain centred and present to him. It is a constant reminder of our hidden life of prayer to which we are called within the Body of Christ. Through contemplation we strive to participate in Christ's reconciliation by opening our whole being to God in the common life. This will not always be easy as self is stripped, but there is the spirit of love that unites us in Christ making us one in him.

Each life is given to God in an act of formal consecration (Profession) and is bound by the Vows of Poverty, Chastity and Obedience. The Vows are received by the Bishop on behalf of the Church, and remind us that we are all part of the whole Body of Christ. 'You are not your own, you are bought with a price; therefore glorify God in your body and in your spirit which are Christ's.' (1 Corinthians 6:20). Profession is the acceptance of the offering to God by, with and in Jesus Christ, in the unity of the Spirit, and the Vows are the foundation of our life. Profession redirects to God the natural life of each one in its ownership of things, in the exercise of all creative powers, and in the complete control of all self-interest. Therefore, monastic Poverty is more than a common ownership of possessions; it emphasises an entire dependence on Christ. Chastity likewise is more than perpetual celibacy; it is the whole being set on Christ. Obedience stresses a free response of love. The initial time before making our Profession will be several years, as the 'whole' of the person and the Community need to be sure that this is God's calling. It is a time of listening to God and Community, a time of preparation and training, a time of waiting on God, a time of giving generously in the common life to which we have been called, and a time of building and perfecting relationships with one another in the living Church of Christ in mutual love and obedience. The Vows are made for life, and whether that be long or short, we are ever looking to the end – '. . . and let us run with perseverance the race that is set before us', looking to Jesus the author and perfecter of our faith who said, 'I am the way the truth and the life' – seeking always that he must increase and I decrease.

Religious is a traditional term for a member of a religious order – brothers or sisters living in community and bound by vows of poverty, chastity and obedience.

A *cell* is neither just a bedroom nor a prison cell but the private room where the monk or nun withdraws for prayer.

The Sisters of the Love of God is an Anglican Contemplative Community.

Stepping to Your Own Drumbeat

Christopher Walton

'Why should we be in such desperate haste to succeed, and in such desperate enterprises?' wrote Henry Thoreau. 'If people do not keep pace with their companions, perhaps it is because they hear a different drummer. Let them step to the music which they hear, however measured or far away.'

I was going to suggest that this was an article for novices. But then I thought that a word which conjures up an image of monks and nuns might put beginners off from the start (my apologies to all whose vocation is the religious life). What I wanted to do was to open up doors for those who are new to the idea of hermitages or poustinias.

A hermitage or poustinia is 'a place apart', where individuals can, through solitude, come closer to God. Throughout Christian history, many people – the great, the holy, and the ordinary – have taken this inner journey.

Henri Nouwen, in his *Genesee Diary*,* which includes the quotation above from Thoreau, explores the notion of solitude: 'The measure of your solitude is the measure of your capacity for communion.' He develops this in his book *Reaching Out*,† in which he argues that without the experience of intentional solitude, we will not be able to live in relationship with people or with God, nor be at one with ourselves.

My own journey, through the mountains and storms of energetic Charismatic inner-city ministry, and of following the call of the God of justice and peace, brought me to the experience of contemplative prayer. I have found the need to

---

* *Genesee Diary, Report from a Trappist Monastery*, Henri Nouwen, Doubleday & Co., New York, 1976.
† *Reaching Out, The Three Movements of the Spiritual Life*, Henri Nouwen, Doubleday & Co., New York, 1975.

get away to a place apart to be alone, if I am ever going to hear the music of the different drummer.

Spending time in solitude is not necessarily easy, but it is rewarding. Coming closer to God takes us on an inner journey, and on that journey we encounter the demons within. The testimony of many who have undertaken this journey is that, through this encounter, we can discover and establish a quiet place deep within, where God's call, and his energy to live now according to the ways of his kingdom of peace and justice, can be heard and experienced.

At the retreat centre where I work, we are building a new hermitage to allow those who feel the need for a place apart to undertake the inner journey. The story of this building is a story of ordinary, faltering people who catch visions, try to live to the sound of a different drummer, but who don't get it all together. It is also the story of the grace of God who, despite our flaws and sins, keeps near.

The retreat centre, Ringsfield Hall, was started in 1972 by Peter and Sally Langford, then in parish ministry in east London. Their vision was for a residential centre where children from the inner city could experience and study the countryside, but which could also be a Christian retreat house.

In the early 1980s, Peter built a hermitage, hidden away in one of the wooded areas of the 14 acres of the grounds. Over the years, the hermitage had fallen into disrepair, and when my colleague Ross Ashley and I arrived it had been removed. We had both come to an awareness of contemplative prayer; so were sad that it was no longer there.

But Peter and Sally Langford, now retired from parish ministry, have returned to live in the area, and have asked whether they can build another hermitage.

The building will be a safe, simple, comfortable place, set apart in the woods. It will have heat and light, and facilities for preparing simple food and drinks. It is offered for a few hours, a few days, or longer. Help or guidance is available, if it is required.

Each person's need and experience of solitude is unique. Relying on other people's experience can never be a substitute for trying it yourself. Our relationship with God is a journey in which every step is a new discovery, however long we have been travelling.

So, after all, our small hermitage is a place for novices.

Christopher Walton is a former Baptist minister. He is co-director of Ringsfield Hall, a retreat centre in Suffolk.

Moorland Retreat

Susan Hughes

I knew God had been calling me to be alone with him for a long time. I needed to get away from the clutter of my life and listen to God and hear him speak. Jesus went alone into wilderness. I wanted to take a friend in case I didn't like what God was going to say to me. No one would, or could, come.

Ten of us gathered on the Friday night. We were warmly welcomed, after long journeys out of the swirling, grey mists and cold, dank, dark moorland by a hissing, crackling fire, hot lentil soup and the quiet hum of people getting to know one another.

Over a sumptuous meal the conversation developed as each chose what they wanted to reveal, each contributing and listening in what was clearly a safe environment. Alan, the local ranger and leader of our wilderness walk, gave us a slide presentation of 'The Seasons of Calderdale Valley', where we'd be walking over the next two days. He used no words to show the climate extremes – the beautiful blossoms against blue sky to bleak, boggy moorland. It was the start of our listening discipline.

We discussed what wilderness might mean to us – alone in the desert or alone in a crowded city! And so, in the boy scouts' bunks, we large adults slept imagining the echoes of excited cub scouts talking about their camp escapades.

On Saturday morning we guiltily tucked into eggs, cereals and fresh bread – hardly Jesus' experience of the wilderness! Then someone found a switch for hot water showers! Outside, the clouds enveloped us. We were hoping to see God's beautiful land of Yorkshire.

We set off for a 9½-mile hike, unable to see more than a few feet in front of us. God was saying very clearly to me, 'Never you mind what is in front or even to the sides – I want

Photograph: Barbara Butler

Stoodley Pike, Todmorden

you *here* – just where you are now. Don't worry about what is ahead or around you – just walk with me!' We prayed and then Alan led us down cut paths, over soft spongy peaty earth, stepping on tufts of grass to avoid the boggy land which stank and sucked our boots down if we slipped, over damp walls, rickety gates. The wind beat our ears and noses cold, our bodies in waterproof coats became hot from the effort of it all.

Our luxury was to sit in the shelter of farmhouse ruins for refreshment breaks. We stopped several times to meditate on Jesus' experience of wilderness. All the time we saw parallels between the ups and downs, the difficult and easy passages in our path, and in our lives and our spiritual journey with God. In our contemplative walk we had time to put our lives in perspective and find room for God to come first, as God asked us to 'be still – be here, now, for me'.

And so in the silence of the wilderness where there is no path,
we ask for your vision, Lord,
where you lead us.
We must trust in you to lead
us over overbearing mountains (others' expectations),
through rough, tufty terrain (our daily concerns),
through thick, sucking, stinking fog (those we love who are over-
whelmed with their circumstances),
over, past, deserted buildings,
up through the cloud to your kingdom,
in us here and now.

On the Sunday we experienced the breaking of bread on a Yorkshire moorland. Refreshed and renewed in spiritual strength, we gladly returned home to continue our journey with our Lord, in our very different settings and circumstances. Thank you for all who made it possible.

Tuning in to the Still Small Voice

Janina Macdonald

The silence seeped into me as I leaned my back against the warm rock and watched the rich colours of the distant mountains change with the shifting sun.

I closed my eyes briefly and strained to catch a sound, any sound, but all I could hear was the beautiful, never-ending silence.

I was on a retreat in the middle of the sandstone desert in the south Sinai, accompanied by six other people, a spiritual leader with in-depth knowledge of the Sinai, a cook, two Bedouin guides, and one camel.

When we had first arrived at our campsite, it was immediately clear that this retreat was going to be completely different from any we had participated in at home. Our everyday cares and commitments melted away as we took in our unfamiliar surroundings – the wide, sandy valley framed by low, golden sandstone hills, the distant mountain peaks outlined against the bright-blue sky, and the traditional Bedouin tent set up for worship services.

That night we sat round the campfire, listening to the crackle of the flames, and enjoying its warmth and the star-filled desert sky above us.

The next morning, our spiritual leader, the Venerable Malcolm Colmer, Archdeacon of Middlesex, told us we were going to have as much space as possible to use this retreat as we wanted. There would be opportunities each day for silent worship, and there would be group services, Sinai-related talks, desert walks, and a chance to speak privately and pray with Malcolm. But all these activities were optional; we could plan our days as we wanted.

Each night, after dinner and cups of hot sweet tea and conversation, we kept silence. In the morning, one of our group broke it with a gentle hymn, preparing us for another day.

On the last day, as I sat savouring the desert quiet, I thought about the verse Malcolm had read to us at our morning service: the story of Elijah and his experience on Mount Sinai: 'And after the earthquake, a fire; but the Lord was not in the fire; and after the fire a still small voice. And it was so, when Elijah heard it, that he wrapped his face in his mantle, and went out, and stood in the entering in of the cave.' (1 Kings 19:12-13a)

My proximity to the place where Elijah heard God speak, and the experience of being in a similar environment, gave the verse depth and meaning. I began truly to understand how important it was to be patient enough to listen for that still small voice, something I had failed to do in my worship at home, caught up as I was in the bustle and noise of my daily routine. As we sat round our last evening campfire, Malcolm suggested that the next morning we each bring two rocks, one symbolising something we wanted to leave behind, the other symbolising something we wanted to bring home with us.

The following morning, after we had finished packing up camp, we met for the last time in our worship tent. Each of us placed a rock symbolising something we wanted to leave behind us in a circle in the sand in front of Malcolm. After a service and a short prayer, we helped each other bury these rocks. The others we kept.

Our jeeps arrived about an hour later to whisk us away to a hotel on the Red Sea coast, signalling the end of our beautiful week. The feeling of sadness among us as we climbed into the jeeps was almost tangible. I sat in the back, against the window, and, as we pulled away from our campsite, I kept hold of my rock, and thought of the still small voice of Sinai.

The journey was organised by Wind, Sand and Stars, 2 Arkwright Road, London NW3 6AD.

A Meditation Pilgrimage

Jeanne Mynett

Halfway through my second sabbatical year in India, in early 1989, I made the flight to Colombo in Sri Lanka to spend some time in this Buddhist country and to learn something about Buddhism and meditation. It proved to be a life-changing journey for me. Already in India I had become fascinated by the Hindu religion I experienced all around me – the colourful temple worship, the multitude of gods and goddesses worshipped at the humblest to the most ornate shrines, the simple life of the sanyasin, the renouncer, and of the ashrams, the disciples gathered around their spiritual master. I had begun to read and learn most of the vision and philosophy that lay behind these outward forms of religion, and saw how this could enrich my Christian faith. For example, I came to appreciate the vastness of the Divine which manifested in all these thousand names and forms. And I had also just begun the practice of meditation, the turning of the attention inwards to achieve a deeper awareness of, and openness to, the Divine at the heart of myself, stilling the body and outer involvements so as to become present to the space within.

On my arrival in Sri Lanka I immediately sensed the different flavour of the Buddhist religion there, so much more austere and removed, manifested in enormous white or painted figures of the Buddha seated absorbed in meditation, graceful and serene, and in the brown-robed monks whom one saw in the streets and on the buses. I met up with a Christians Aware acquaintance, Sriyani. When she discovered my interest in learning more about Buddhism, she arranged for me to travel up to Kandy in the central hill country of Sri Lanka to meet the meditation teacher, Godwin Samaratna, and to stay at his meditation centre outside Kandy at Nillambe.

So early on a Thursday morning I took the beautiful train journey up from Colombo to Kandy, and then travelled by van with Godwin to the meditation centre high up in the hills at the top of a tea-estate, with magnificent views over the countryside below. The centre was simple and welcoming, consisting of several low buildings built from warm yellow/grey stone, set amongst open areas of grass, trees, bushes and flowers. At that time the centre was still small, generally with only between six and twelve meditators, mostly westerners, though there was a monthly influx of local Sri Lankans for the Poya (full moon) holidays.

When I saw the daily timetable of the centre I almost turned and fled: it appeared so rigorous (though now I know it is one of the least rigorous for Buddhist meditation centres in southern Asia):

Rise – 4.45am
Group meditation – 5-6am
Tea and yoga
Breakfast – 7.30am
Working meditation – 8-9.30am
Group sitting and walking meditation – 9.30-11am
Individual and outdoor meditation – 11am-12 noon
Lunch, rest and library time – 12 noon-2.30pm
Group meditation – 2.30-4pm
Tea and yoga or free time – 4-5.30pm
Watching the sunset – 5.30-6.30pm
Buddhist chanting and group meditation – 6.30-7.30pm
Soya coffee and biscuits
Evening discussion – 8-9.30pm, followed by bed.

However was I going to survive these long hours of meditation? And when I was shown to the women's quarters, I saw that my bed was to be a narrow concrete bench in a double room on which lay a thin coconut fibre-filled mattress. No creature-comforts here – and no electricity, only candlelight. The cooking of simple vegetarian meals is still done mainly over wood fires, and water for bathing is warmed only by the sun.

Despite all this I stayed for nearly five months. Godwin taught Vipassana, or insight meditation, largely through meeting individually with each meditator, and nothing was harsh or forced. I found that even the longer meditation periods passed quite easily and without much restlessness, as I explored what came up in my mind, surrounded by the hum of insects, the song of birds, the rain or the sunshine. There was more 'noise' and distraction from within than without. Godwin taught that Vipassana meditation is a way of exploration of the mind, of thoughts, of emotions and of bodily sensations. Everything that comes to one's awareness in meditation may be explored without judgement. It is easy to leave behind all ready-made forms of reference in favour of gaining insight for oneself. Godwin explained that the Buddha was a teacher and guide, but that each meditator must ultimately follow their own direct experience. The aim of meditation, we were taught, is not to achieve a particular level of calmness or a special spiritual state, but to become freer and more stable in oneself by coming to know oneself and to heal one's inner wounds, thus being able to act in response to the world and its challenges rather than simply reacting to everything. One would not be taken unawares or carried away either by the centres of one's mind and emotions or by one's own desires and expectations.

Along with the formal meditation practice there was urged the constant practice of 'mindfulness' throughout the day, of being alert and aware of what is going on within and around one. There was no rule of absolute silence at Nillambe, but there were small notices which read, 'Do not speak unless you can improve on the silence.' A great stress was placed on respecting the silence of others. But when the monsoon rains tied us to sitting in the kitchen at teatime Godwin encouraged us to talk, so as to learn to use speech constructively. In the end the idea was to achieve a real awareness of each moment and action one was engaged in, and the ability to be in that moment or action and not miles away, or caught in the past or future.

There was no systematic teaching about Buddhism at Nillambe, but little by little I did learn about Theravada Buddhism and the Dhamma (the way) taught by the Buddha, and was often challenged by its very different perspective. I found it difficult to locate its meeting points with Christianity, unlike my experience with Hinduism. For example, all my Christian life I had been seeking to know and come into relationship with God 'out there'; but now the question was turned round, to who is the 'I' who is seeking to know God? It is well known that in Theravada Buddhism no belief in God is postulated. What I found harder to get my mind round was the teaching that there is no object – like 'soul' or essential personal self – that we can discover; rather that we are an on-going flow of different body-mind processes. That shook me. Did 'I' really not exist then? Certainly sitting in meditation that was what one really experienced – the ever-changing flow of thoughts, sensations and emotions, all arising and passing away from moment to moment. Was any of it worth holding on to, or defining oneself by? My solid senses of 'I' began to feel somewhat shaky! And in similarly exploring and discussing other conventional religious ideas which I held on to, I began to see how as humans we viewed everything through culturally defined and reinforced contextual frame-works, like window-frames both directing, and ultimately limiting our vision and understanding. Seeing this for myself, I feel I have become very much more open to others' ideas and beliefs about God, self and all manner of other spiritual questions and experiences.

Turning the same attention and awareness to the world at large, by living in this very simple lifestyle and different culture, and with new perspectives on life, I learned to question the values of our western culture and lifestyle, so geared to achievement, to doing, to acquiring things, to fixing things to our own desires and conveniences; putting so much emphasis and concern on ourselves and our own plans, rather than just flowing with life.

And in exploring the practice of loving-kindness meditation, where Godwin guided us to direct thoughts of friendliness, kindness, forgiveness and acceptance both to ourselves and others, one came to the experience and understanding that in not hating and resisting negative parts of ourselves, negative emotions, painful situations, difficult people, but rather in dealing kindly with them, their power over us was much diminished. So, would it be possible to live in a different way when I returned to my home and life in England? For is this not the essence of pilgrimage: to travel away from home, to open oneself to new and possibly world-shaking experiences and understandings, to see through a broader vision, to come to a greater self-understanding, and appreciation of self and others, to learn to embrace the stranger within and without? And then to return and seek to integrate the new understandings in one's everyday life.

Postscript
I have continued over the last 11 years to divide my time between life in England and life at Nillambe, deepening my experience of meditation, and reflecting more and more on the deeper issues of life. The meditation centre at Nillambe has grown considerably, with meditators coming from all over the world. Sadly, our teacher, Godwin, has died. Like so many others, I owe a tremendous debt to him and his teaching of the gentle way of meditation.

SECTION TWO
Journey of Life

Photograph: Barbara Butler

Yorkshire Sculpture Park

Introduction

Where can I go from your Spirit?
Where can I flee from your presence?
If I go up to the heavens, you are there;
if I make my bed in the depths, you are there.
If I rise on the wings of the dawn,
if I settle on the far side of the sea,
even there your hand will guide me,
your right hand will hold me fast.

Psalm 139:7-10

'Life is one long journey' is such an old saying that it's almost trite to put it here – but in a way that's exactly what the pilgrimage of life is all about. It just seems too easy to recognise that whilst there is a goal and ultimately an end, even if we may view that as a door, it's the travelling itself that's important.

When we are swinging along on a sunny day and all feels well with the world, then that's fine; but when we open our eyes and look around us at the needs and concerns of those we love, the people where we live, the places where we work, the world we read about in the papers, we know it's not that simple or easy.

Sometimes, as Jane writes later in this section, just getting through a day is a pilgrimage, which, without the strength of God, would probably be insurmountable. 'We're never given anything we can't handle.' 'You only have this extra burden because you're special and can cope.' What god are people thinking about when they say this? A god who piles up the load just so that people get to breaking point? There is a video of the Oprah Winfrey Show. It's hard to remember what the subject being discussed was but the gist of what Oprah was saying was, 'If you don't hear God speak the first time, he speaks louder, first in a breeze, then in the wind, then a storm comes, and finally you get a hurricane. Why not try to discern him in the whisper!'

There's something here about God always being there, and of being in a time and place where we will listen or turn to him. How often do we hear someone's testimony of how they first came to faith and the story involves a time of real difficulty and darkness when at that very time they turned to God, or they just knew his presence? Perhaps when all's well we can just breeze along without really thinking of God, but come the day of disaster we cry, 'Oh God, help!'

The other aspect of timing that always makes us think is how people react differently to the same thing at different times, or the same message from different people. We can talk till we're blue in the face to someone about our faith and they just nod politely but are not moved in their faith at all. Some other time we hardly speak and the person will fall on their knees in an overwhelming show of instant recognition.

This is similarly true when we have bad or difficult times in our lives. This can range from disappointments to major tragedies, and everyone responds in their own unique way. For some people these times are quickly passed and moved on from, whilst for others they can become dominant. The old expression of people making mountains out of molehills is true – but so also is the other way round. Some people cope with mountains better than others manage molehills. And then again, at another time and in other circumstances, the same capable person manages very badly.

How often can we see God simply being there through times of trouble? At the time it is a disaster but so often when it is over there is a feeling that something good might yet come from the experience, or, at the very least, that it could have been worse. When we look back at our lives, we may come to know that God has been there with us in the midst of whatever we were involved in, even though we were not conscious of his presence at the time.

The famous 'Footprints' prayer expresses this so well. Put briefly, the prayer is that while looking back on his life a man asks God why he was not there at the times of greatest trouble.

God asks him to look at the footprints he walked. Where there are two sets – the good times – God walked alongside him. But where there is only one set – the bad times – this is where God carried him.

Then there are the day-to-day things that usually pass us by, like a rainbow in the sky, a wildflower meadow on a sunny day, the way a cat instantly purrs the very first time she settles to suckle her new-born kittens, or a million other things that we so often take for granted which just now and then thrust themselves before us with such incredible clarity that we have to stop and stand for a second in awe and wonder.

It takes very little effort to see God's 'work' when we look upon a much wanted and loved-before-she-was-even-born new-born healthy baby. We count the number of her fingers and toes and marvel at the size of such perfect nails. We say, 'Isn't she just perfect.' Hannah's story later on about falling in love and her preparation for marriage as well as June's about the wonder of each new day following her successful heart transplant operation some ten years ago both share in this sense of spectacle.

Finally there are those rare times when we are able to know God's presence in the hard times. Not looking back and knowing he was there, but actually seeking and being conscious of him in the dark days. Being aware that God is in everything, not just the easy, the happy and the good.

John Robinson, who died of cancer, wrote, 'For God is in everything and everything is in God, impersonal as well as personal; not merely the obviously beautiful and good, the intentional and meaningful, but the waste and void, the nebulae, earthquakes, sunsets, cancers, tapeworms.'*

In his last sermon Robinson said, 'For God is to be found in the cancer as in everything else. If he is not, then he is not the God of the Psalmist who said, "If I go down to hell, thou art there also", let alone of the Christian who knows God most deeply in the Cross.'

* John T. Robinson, *Where Three Ways Meet* (SCM Press, 1987).

So often when hard times are upon us we don't lift our hearts, souls or minds to God. Just as it's almost impossible to lift our heads in the darkest days, so it is to lift our hearts. And yet it is in this looking to God that we see he's already looking at us: standing close, holding and supporting us. Some of the stories of pilgrimage at the end of this chapter have been chosen especially to reflect these hard times and how individuals have been able to see God in them and how they continue to lift their hearts to him.

To some extent or other we all have hard times, and whilst it is simplistic to say we just have to deal with them and get on, it's not always that easy. Sometimes we get stuck. Sometimes we need help to get up and get on. We may need to ask for that help, and that in itself may be beyond us at that time. The writer of Proverbs 24:16a wrote, 'For though a righteous man falls seven times, he rises again.'

So it is in the rising again that we make our pilgrimage. And as we rise and learn to ask for help, to start to deal with the issue, to begin to pick up the pieces and get on, the real pilgrimage begins.

Frank Wright wrote, 'It is a false and ultimately damaging religion which simply asks us to recognise the light, the holy, the pious, and so makes us unconsciously project the evil, dark side elsewhere. True religion admits the necessity both to recognise that evil and dark side and to integrate it into personal freedom and goodness. . . . God is not confined to that artificial world, his is the real world.'*

It's the one with a faith in God who knows that whatever happens God is in it. It may not make any sense to us. It may look like God's got it terribly wrong this time. But we know that we can't see what God can see. It's like viewing a small part of the tapestry from the wrong side. It's not just about looking for the big picture, but looking at the picture the right side round.

* Frank Wright, *Exploration into Goodness* (SCM Press, 1988).

If we can develop that faith in God that allows us to see him and feel his presence in all things, then we will truly never feel alone. It's a bit like the man who gets mugged on the street and who defends himself so successfully that the mugger not only goes away empty-handed but thinks twice before he tries to mug anyone else. We need to develop and build up our spiritual skills to use in the hard times.

This is our daily pilgrimage. Building up our spiritual muscles to enjoy our relationship with God when life is 'easy', and to use them to carry on when times are 'hard'. The Psalmist was so right when he wrote, 'Blessed is the man who does not walk in the counsel of the wicked or stand in the way of sinners or sit in the seat of mockers. But his delight is in the law of the Lord, and on his law he meditates day and night. He is like a tree planted by streams of water, which yields its fruit in season and whose leaf does not wither.' (Psalm 1)

The Beginning of a Life

Salwa El Raheb/Booth

Books, magazines, antenatal classes, family and friends' accounts and advice; from the moment you announce that you are expecting a baby you get a constant reminder in any or all of the above-mentioned forms on how different your life will be with the new arrival.

All the preparations, the anxieties, and finally here I am holding the little baby that was part of me for the past nine months. Having just returned from hospital with my little treasure where she spent the first few days of her new life, all baby knows at this stage is that all-familiar smell of the Mummy thing, the source of food and comfort. It's time to introduce her to her new home. I proudly show her the newly painted nursery. Will she take to it, I wonder. But baby can't see very much to identify her surroundings and where is that Mummy smell? So baby decides she really prefers to be in company so, at her request, the cot moves to our bedroom.

So what were the first six months like? Well, if you're lucky, a member of your family might offer to help you with the baby until you're back on your feet; then they leave and you are faced with life on your own with your tiny baby and feeling really lost. But you won't have the time to dwell on that as your baby starts making demands on you. Yes, baby's first discovery is noise and that she can make lots of it. She discovers a good use for it as well, mainly drawing the world's attention to her needs and her existence. Noise, feeding time. Noise, time for a change. Noise, time for another change. Noise, 'I want company'. Noise, 'Just practising'. Time for a calming bath and a little nap. Then it's time to do it all over again and again. Forget the days when you went to sleep at night and woke up refreshed in the morning because your baby's body clock does not recognise day and night yet. In your deepest sleep you will hear a little 'sound wave' which is inaudible to anyone else, and in an almost hypnotic state you rise and attend to your baby's needs. It's the same story for the first few weeks: sleepless nights, changes and feeds, tears and colic and colds and baths and dribbles and burps and feeds and changes . . . total dependence. Baby's life and whole existence revolves around you, your smell, your touch; you are the source of food; you are baby's only contact with the outside world still.

One day, while you perform a certain aspect of the routine, your baby looks at you with recognising eyes and a smile: 'Ah, I can *see* the Mummy one.' Yes, a smile slowly creeps to her face. For the first time you are sure that your baby recognises you and the whole world smiles on you.

From then on it's a life of constant change as your baby starts learning new things every day – and new noises. Baby starts interacting and now there's a two-way communication line, if a very basic one. You watch and wait patiently for baby's firsts and you tick them off one by one in your mental diary. I am sure that years later I'll still be doing it.

Boy Growing

Julie Myerson

Eleven and a half years ago I had a baby. He burst out of me like a slippery torpedo – surprised, black-haired, fists flailing furiously. He grew into the sweetest, brightest child – funny, quick, curious, happy, eager (but never too eager) to please. 'I love you, Mummy,' he used to sigh, for no particular reason, as we walked along hand in warm, delighted hand.

And though he did undoubtedly love me, I knew it wasn't just that. I knew that what he really meant was, 'I'm happy, Mummy. I like this world, I love living this life of mine.' As I say, he was a sweet child – I should know, I am his mum. Sweet and small and manageable – all the best and most endearing aspects of his father and me, I liked to think, sheared off and rolled into one.

And now, suddenly, my baby is big. I say *suddenly* because, just as books, relatives and older parents always warn you, it has all taken no time at all. Really. Early life – childhood, teens, twenties – drags along as if you had all the time in the world, but make a baby and suddenly there you are hurtling towards the grave. Time evaporates when you're concentrating, and nothing concentrates the mind and body like children.

The baby moves on to solids, takes a first tottering step, says 'Cat', and before you have time to appreciate it, to linger on the moment, he's big enough to carry your shopping. This is why parents fill photo albums so manically – to be certain it all happened. Parenting devours time, gulping it down greedily. Blink and the scowling, black-haired infant is a tall, tough-man, grown-up child.

And my boy, my baby, where is he? Well, he's still there, but these days it's like I'm staring at a once-familiar line-drawing where the lines are growing steadily more blurred. He's not yet 12 and hasn't reached puberty – not physically anyway – but there's no doubt that he's moved into some strange emotional limbo land. He's just, well, not so straightforward any more – or do I just mean he's not quite so much mine?

That frank, affectionate openness has gone. He's often cross, opinionated, argumentative, obsessed with justice (for himself), quick to flare. 'Come back,' I want to say, 'I love you. Remember how you used to be happy with what you had: family life, spaghetti, colouring in.'

But each day, he looks beyond me, to a different horizon. Each day he wants more. He looks to his father for stuff he knows I can't provide (the soothing, male certainty of facts, the benison of explanations, the thrill of new, shiny equipment, physical contact that's not just about cuddling) and he looks beyond us both at times. Hardly a moment goes by without something new coming between us, something else for me to take in. Such as: he's strangely good-looking. The back of his head has changed, is less instantly recognisable. He doesn't always say what I think he'll say. His room smells eerily of something other than child. His cat mopes ceaselessly around him as if she knows something I don't.

And – God – listen to him, he thinks I know nothing. He tells me not to bite my nails, not to swear – then calls me a 'stupid bloody woman' if I interrupt his innings to call him in to tea. Any request to pick up his clothes, tidy his room is met with 'Yesss' hissed under exasperated breath. He's getting clever. He understands history, politics, seems undaunted by concepts I have somehow always ducked. He challenges me about everything, sends me up – and less gently than his father. He takes up an amazing amount of space in the house, seems to need more food only half an hour after finishing supper, goes to bed late, travels on the tube alone. Last week he got a spot.

And yet. He still won't eat green beans, let alone broccoli. He still mooches about in my bedroom as I put on my make-up, telling me about who said what to whom and what he thinks about this or that. We still go naked in front of each other without either of us noticing (and I keep making a mental note that soon this must stop – but when?). He tries earnestly to interest me in Warhammer, in the politics of Nintendo, asks me which actor I seriously think made the best James Bond – Connery, Dalton or Moore? He reads adult novels a lot of the time, but couldn't resist the new Harry Potter as soon as his younger sister finished it.

He still comes to me if he feels ill or gets a splinter in his toe. Until quite recently he worried about vampires coming in his bedroom window and would take my hand if he thought no one was looking. And then one day (when?) he just didn't. He still wants a cuddle when I kiss him goodnight – though I suspect it's more to delay the moment of lights out than because he craves contact. Yes, his motives are slipping and sliding. 'I love you, Mummy,' he still says, but only if I give him money for chewing gum or a Nintendo magazine.

And now, secondary school. Having sewed the last name tape on the last item of his new uniform, I root out his dusty old baby book in order to look up the immunisation dates demanded by the school medical form. There, among the laboriously plotted centile charts and catalogues of tetanus and whooping cough jabs, I see the words '25 February 1989: his first smile'.

'You smiled early,' I tell him. 'Three and a half weeks. That's really early.'

'What's that mean?' he grunts.

'Just that you're, well, a bit exceptional really.' (Of course he is, he's my boy, isn't he?)

He says nothing. Looks at me with a mixture of exasperation and pity.

Next day I walk him to the tube – first day of term, first day of the rest of his life. 'By the way, Mummy,' he says, 'I meant to tell you, please don't make me porridge for breakfast any more.'

'But,' I say, as we cross onto the leaf-strewn pavement by Holy Trinity, 'you love porridge.'

'No,' he says, 'I hate your porridge. I've been meaning to tell you. I always have. I just ate it to please you.'

Photograph: Barbara Butler

Sculpture by Henry Moore

He's my boy, my baby. When we brought him home from the hospital and laid him on our bed, his little body wrapped in its white cellular blanket so marooned and fragile – I wept. 'But what is it?' Jonathan said. 'Why are you crying?'

'I just never want him to go on a motor bike,' I said.

'Got your tube pass?' I ask him now for the second time. He nods patiently. 'Goodbye, Mummy.'

'Goodbye, boy. Take care. See you later.'

I struggle to stop myself saying anything else, but there's no need. He has already turned and is moving away from me, a dignified child-man in a black suit and tie and rucksack. I keep my eyes on him as long as I can, frozen where I stand, unable to move. I keep watching till I can't make him out any more, till he's just another dark head bobbing in the crowd.

Julie Myerson is the author of four novels including *Sleepwalking* and, most recently, *Laura Blundy*.

Love Is . . . ?

Hannah White

Dean and I have been together now for two and a half years. We first met when I was working in his local pub during my summer vacation from university. Quite simply he chatted up the barmaid. He stood in the pub one night and said to someone he didn't know, 'Who's the barmaid, the good-looking one?' only to discover he was talking to my brother! He then tried to persuade my brother to put in a good word for him. My good little brother came home and told me what he'd said! Eventually I agreed to go on a date with Dean and he took me to the cinema to see (of all things) *The Wedding Singer* and then on to a Pizza Hut. From there it just seemed to carry on. As it got towards the end of the summer holidays and I was going back to university, he suddenly proposed. I woke up one morning at his house to find an engagement ring on the bedside table, with a cup of tea, and him asking me to marry him. I said yes, and then went back to university two weeks later.

Luckily university isn't far from home and we saw each other most weeks. Then I returned home for summer again before I was due to spend a year on placement in London. Dean had already said he wanted to move to London with me and so we found somewhere to live and a job for him and moved to London together. With the placement finished, we moved back to university for me to finish my degree course. Unfortunately he hasn't been able to find a job here, so he's moved back with his parents and now we're back to visiting each other again. But only until I graduate and then we'll be back together again.

It all sounds easy, doesn't it? It's not been quite that simple really. We hate being apart. It hurts, almost physically, when one of us leaves the other, and the week can seem like for ever. But we know that it's just for a short time in the scale of things. We are also – and I can confidently speak for him here – madly in love with each other, and of course that helps too. We both trust each other implicitly and are very lucky really in that we are not just in love but are best friends too. I think that really matters, more so probably than anything else. We have been able to pull together to sort things out. Problems have always been for both of us to deal with, and no secrets are ever kept. If we know where we are up to with everything, then usually everything runs smoothly. Communication is crucial, and telephones and e-mail essential.

Love has a very silly effect on normally sensible people. At university I am calm, sensible, intelligent even (well, some of the time). When we're together we dissolve into giggles together, buy silly toys, use pet names, kiss in the street, and are generally mad as hatters. It has also made us both learn a lot, not just about each other but about things that you would never imagine you'd be interested in until you are with someone who is. I now know more about *Star Wars* than George Lucas; I have a six-foot-tall cardboard cut-out of Chewbacca sitting at the top of the stairs, R2D2 in the kitchen and Yoda in the front room. I have even been to science fiction conventions! Dean has been to local political party functions; knows all about British politics, Nordic politics, and European politics. I've never been artistic, so when Dean first sent me beautiful drawings I sent him cards back but now I'm drawing funny creatures doing stupid things and he loves them. I still think a three-year-old could draw better. My father once told me that when he and my mother were first together they had a house full of Snoopies. That makes me feel a little better for having *Star Wars* figures, Playmobil toys, bubblegum characters, cuddly dinosaurs, Winnie the Pooh toys, and magnetic letters on the fridge door. We've just bought a nativity scene for Christmas and even that is made from Playmobil (similar to Lego)!

We are currently planning our wedding. When Dean first proposed I said I wanted to graduate before I got married, so we're finally doing it next year. So far we've booked the church and the reception. I'm collecting articles about flowers, hair and dresses. It's all really exciting. It will be a great day, and although little will change in a practical sense, except my name, it means a great deal to both of us. Somehow just living together isn't enough. We both want that piece of paper that says we belong to each other for ever, just as it matters to me that we get married in a church.

I'd recommend love to anyone. It's hard to find, almost certainly appears when least expected and will change your life for ever. But I wouldn't have it any other way. I see 70-year-old couples in the street holding hands and still looking happy, and hope that will be us in 50 years' time. But I'd like to think that even then we'll still have magnetic letters on the fridge, even if we pretend they are for the grandchildren!

Pilgrimage Is a Learning Process

Lee Krogulski

Lee's pilgrimage story is one that began in her teens and will probably continue, for her, for ever. It is the story of one who feels she doesn't fit in wherever she is. No place is really home. She is not comfortable with any one group of people, but always slightly at odds, always a little different, never quite the same.

And yet Lee is at home with God. In him she has her 'ground of being'. Her pilgrimage is simply turning and travelling to him, learning to be still and patient, and to be open to his life-giving Holy Spirit.

As Lee herself points out, who among us is not handicapped in one way or another?

My faith is a source of great strength and comfort to me; without it I'm sure I would be an empty and deeply unhappy individual. I remember a time when I was living in Manchester, I was in my early twenties, and I'd just come home from one of the city centre nightclubs. It was while I was in the club that I experienced an overwhelming sense of loneliness and emptiness. The club, incidentally, was the favoured haunt of transvestites and transsexuals, and I myself, being transsexual, used to go there often. I arrived home about 2am and just sat outside in the cold, crisp night, and looked up at the countless stars. The tears started to well up, and then the dam broke. This was followed by a torrent of insults and rage at this silent God.

Why was I born like this? Why aren't I like everybody else? The loneliness and isolation I felt at that time was so acute that it felt almost like an invisible knife cutting into my heart.

Looking back now, I know the Lord did respond and thankfully did forgive me for the insults I hurled at him. From that point on, my life gradually began to change for the better. Of course, this didn't happen overnight and there have been many falls, doubts and struggles along the way. Nevertheless the pilgrimage is a learning process as well as an exciting adventure!

I have since then experienced his glorious nearness, his guiding hand and wise counsel. The Spirit of Jesus lives in everyone's heart and this same Spirit struggles to gain expression, to share and sanctify each and everyone's life. In my despair I turned to my Creator: I stormed the very gates of heaven.

I now believe suffering can be our greatest friend. It forces us to take a good look at our lives, to stand back and observe from a different perspective. If life were perfect here, there would be no desire to seek God or better ourselves. As C. S. Lewis wrote, 'Pain is God's megaphone to a deaf world.'

Transsexualism is a phenomenon that nobody really understands. It can be a hard life, not really fitting in – a handicap really. As one grows in the spiritual life, one also begins to understand oneself better and for that matter be gentler with oneself. It suddenly dawned on me one day that we are all alone, all handicapped in a way, because we are all cut off from our Creator. This changed with the life, death and resurrection of our Lord Jesus Christ, who opened up the way for our return to fellowship with the Father.

Our task, therefore, is to respond to that call. This responding means to turn back, or to repent, as the Bible urges us to do. We have to practise this in our daily lives, by learning to develop a relationship with the Lord, allowing him into all aspects of our day-to-day life. I am learning to do this by daily prayer and meditation on God's word which is an integral part of Christian fellowship; to take time out each day, learning to be still and patient, to wait upon him, to allow myself to be open to his life-giving Spirit, like a flower opens up to bathe in the life-giving rays of the sun.

After a lengthy discussion on gender identity, Andrew, my good friend of long standing, remarked that despite the difficulties and disappointments I've lived with, there is still a lot of laughter in my life. And he is right. I heartily thank God for this gift, to be able to laugh at oneself and to try and not take life too seriously. For faith brings with it the intuitive knowing that ultimately everything is in God's hands, and everything will work out for the best.

I remember telling someone when I was 16, that it was my destiny to be a woman; more importantly, I believe the destiny of all people is a grand and glorious pilgrimage back home. Back to that ocean of God's beauty and peace, where there is eternal laughter and joy. Where our earthly experiences, joys and sufferings will be viewed as but a dream, and like all dreams we will awaken into that reality of our true destiny, which is life, which is light; which is love.

Thrown into Total Chaos

Roy Brierley

Roy's story of his heart attack tells us of the care and concern that was shown to him by family and friends during his recovery period, his wife and daughter taking on extra work and responsibilities to cover for his enforced absence. It tells also of Roy's care for his family, especially his wife, even when he was very poorly.

Look at how Roy sees his illness as being a third way, an option he had never considered before; not a pilgrimage that he was seeking or had even given much thought to previously, but one that in the end he has come to value, not of itself, but because of the care and love that he has received, and the feelings of activity and pleasure that he enjoys while continuing to travel.

It's funny, no matter how much memory we lose, some things we never forget; one is the day I had a heart attack.

All through my life I was told there were two paths to choose from, but no one told me about this one – my whole life was thrown into total chaos.

At the time, in 1991, a Heart Group in this area – Calderdale – had not been set up, and the doctors gave very little advice. I had a busy post office I ran on my own; my wife ran the private shop side and knew very little about my side. The Post Office does not have people on hand to step in and help, and Enid, my wife, had to open the next day, 18 March 1991, as normal. She was frantically ringing the Post Office and other postmasters who got together, and help was given which was a great relief to both of us.

I told Enid in the event of my death to get rid of the post office as quickly as possible. At this time I did not know if I would be able to get back to working ever again.

On 1 April 1991 I was allowed home and the doctor gave me a sick note for three months. Enid worked the post office and my daughter looked after the shop side. I did the books and all the counter work and so Enid could ask me things she didn't know. It worked.

Over the first month I did very little as my heart needed time to recover. The second month I started to walk around the house at first and then the garden, then to the end of the road, and onwards – always remembering I had to walk back!

The biggest thing about having a heart attack is the loss of confidence, and it took ages for me to regain it. I had the funny idea that when I went for walks on my own, I should stick to road walking; then if I went down, surely someone would see this lump on the pavement or the side of the road and stop!

My customers were great and sent cards, flowers, best wishes, and there was advice from two fellow heart sufferers. One told Enid to get a certain book from the library – it was great and the information in it inspired me to go on. The other customer told me he had a heart attack twenty years ago, but he had returned to work digging holes in the road for the water board; this man died in his nineties.

After four and a half months the doctor allowed me to resume work. Within two years I heard about a heart support group that was being set up in the area. I was there post-haste to be at the first meeting when the Calderdale Heart Group was being formed, and I was a part of it and it felt good. Exercise groups were set up, talks, a walking group and much more.

I sold the business a year ago, nine years after my heart attack, and am now retired. I am still very active and enjoying life. There is life after a heart attack and there is lots of help even if you do finish on the third path.

A Daily Pilgrimage

Jane's pilgrimage (not her real name) covers just one day. In her case that one day has been repeated with monotonous regularity for the last ten or so years since she was diagnosed with lifelong severe clinical depression. Having spent most of those ten years in hospital wards, she has now moved to a sheltered community hostel where she still has full-time medical help on hand at all times of day and all night.

I wake up in the morning thinking, 'Oh no, not another day.' I guess that's where my pilgrimage starts each day, though it feels more like an obstacle course than a pilgrimage. I try to feel God with me but often I feel so empty. I know in theory that he's there getting me through the day, but sometimes I feel alone and black. The effort of getting dressed, having breakfast, going out or whatever I'm doing that day, is very difficult. I send up arrow prayers to God for courage and strength to get through. Some days I just can't believe God loves me, but even so I do see his protection, keeping me safe when I go out, helping me cope with things I'm scared of, helping me to be civil to people when I just want to run away and hide myself from them, or even to shout and scream at them.

It's hard to keep a smile on my face when I want to collapse into tears and when I wish I'd never been born, but God does help me get through, even if I don't realise he's doing it at the time. Sometimes he seems a million miles off (though if it wasn't for him I would be dead by now) and I cry out to him in mental agony and torture.

But time does pass and gradually I realise I am getting through the day, however difficult it is. When it gets to the evening, I feel relieved that the day is nearly over. However, this thought then produces the realisation that another day will follow. Tomorrow.

I go to bed with a sinking feeling in my stomach, knowing

I will have to start all over again when I wake up. I lie in bed praying, pleading with God for a good sleep and for the strength to get through the next day, and to cope with myself and with whatever God wants of me.

Every Day Is Wonderful!

June Buckley

June's pilgrimage tells the story of a woman who has had new life put into her in a very real way. She makes absolute use of this new life and she describes how she celebrates it in many different ways today. Since her new pilgrimage began, she has travelled to many different countries, including Australia, successfully competing in her chosen sport of walking and running. As she herself writes, she is so busy now she doesn't have time to 'work'.

Every day is wonderful! I've said that many times when someone makes comments such as 'It's a dreadful day' or 'What a terrible morning' – referring, of course, to the weather.

My reply that 'Every day is wonderful' certainly brings some strange looks.

To me, everything *is* wonderful; I wake up in the morning with the thought, 'I am here.'

Just over ten years ago I came round after a heart transplant operation and felt immediately better. I had been warned that even after the operation had started something might not be quite right with the new heart. However, looking at the spaghetti mass of wires around me, I knew something had happened.

The care from the nurses, from the hospital, from surgeon all the way to the ward orderly was truly fantastic. A porter said, 'It's a pity you couldn't have seen the hospital staff on the day of operation, as the whole place had a smile on its face.'

The hospital chaplain came once visitors were allowed into my room. She asked how I felt, to which I replied, 'Absolutely fine but very humble.'

'Why?' she asked.

'Why has all that money been spent on me?'

'It has, so prove it's been worth while.'

I've tried since then to do just that.

Training for the British Transplant Games and as a member of the Great Britain team in the World Games takes up time. Living in the Pennines and walking is superb exercise too. Our garden is quite large and working in it is enjoyable, plus the garden parties and flower festivals we have held to raise money for 'Take Heart', Leeds and Calderdale Heart Care. I work voluntarily at the local primary school, the nearby BHF shop, Calderdale Talking Newspaper, our Church and guild. I give talks to various clubs and groups and would-be transplantees and encourage people to carry donor cards.

I haven't time to work.

I am eternally grateful to my Dutch donor and her family, the medics, my family and friends. I am so lucky.

The Rough Valley

Janet Dickenson

Sometimes our pilgrimage takes us, like Christian in *Pilgrim's Progress*, through the Slough of Despond. My life seems to have been punctuated with losses, from the ending of my parents' marriage when I was 13 and the subsequent moving away of my mother, to my own divorce, the death of my 19-year-old daughter, and the deaths of both my parents. I could be sorry for myself if I dwelt on all these bereavements, but most of the time I accept, along with Job: 'The Lord gave and the Lord takes away. Blessed be the name of the Lord.'

In fact, Job and some of the Psalms have been a particular inspiration to me at times when I have walked through that valley. The most memorable text at the time my daughter died, when I was not sleeping well (and at night you can't easily go out for that country walk which blows the cobwebs away and the tears from your eyes), was this passage from the Psalms: 'Crying may go on all night, but joy comes in the morning.'

It did! Every time I looked for it, there was joy! The new leaf of spring, seen for the *first* time as I awoke from the dark night of my early teenage years, was my first glimpse of God. As I recovered from my grief at my daughter's death in 1993 this is what I saw:

A glimpse of heaven

In the sky I saw a glimpse of heaven,
a band of sunset, red, from sky to earth,
a crimson cross along the west's horizon.
Death brings us new birth.

In the sky, I saw a glimpse of heaven,
the face of God on the edges of a cloud.

Compassion tinged with judgement – or vice versa,
a silver lining on our world of doubt.

In the house I saw a glimpse of heaven,
a place of peace and love for all to share.
A triumph-song to cast out death and darkness,
new life of Jesus breaking through despair.

In the church I saw a glimpse of heaven,
just a glint of light through dirt-stained glass.
The weight of centuries-old tradition lifted,
shattering our cosy silent pews.

In my life I saw a glimpse of heaven,
began to feel the wounds of past decay,
to pull the pieces back into a body.
New life of Christ pulsing through the vine,
through us, the branches.

From heaven to earth
a crimson cross of love
stretched out.

Each day, as I open my curtains to the world and look out on
the beauty of the Pennine valleys, I remember that glimpse of
heaven. It really did look as if the sky had opened up and that
red cross made by the sunset was opening up a new spiritual
world to me. It did! So I travel on in my pilgrimage, with friends
and strangers. Whoever God brings to me for a travelling
companion, I know he also is by my side as I walk.

We're Never Too Old

Liz Nunn

My dear old mum said to me after I had been moaning at her for doing too much work, 'We're never too old, so be quiet, dear.' At that moment I did not realise how much that sentence was to mean to me in the distant future. It is true, dear friends, that we are never too old to feel empathy, to feel anger, or to feel pity and compassion, but feelings are useless unless we do something about them.

I am 80 years old and lived the first 38 years in London, so in the years I should have been having fun and travelling I was called up or living in a shelter at the bottom of our garden. I always promised myself that one day I would go to India with my dad as he wanted to see the country his Indian friends had talked about in the trenches of the First World War. Sadly Dad died so my visit to India did not come to fruition until I was 61 years old. By then I was a widow with four children and a long-term foster child. I knew a Hindu family in Bombay, and I had met a priest from South India. I went with the expectation of helping in a clinic for two months – that is all my intentions were. For three months I enjoyed the sights of Bombay, Madras, Bangalore, Kerala, and meeting Father Bede Griffiths at Shantivan. At the end of December I arrived at 'Reaching the Unreached' where I was hoping to help in their clinic. On my second day there a baby girl died in my arms. She was less than eight pounds in weight and was 2½ years old. A few days later a boy of 4 years spilt boiling rice from his shoulder to his hand on the Saturday but did not come to the clinic until the Monday. I dressed the arm once or twice a day for eight weeks and never once did he make a sound. When it was time to leave I was wondering what life was about. I had dressed every kind of wound and helped children with every kind of illness. I had learned about the horror of infanticide, of leprosy and many other tropical diseases. I wanted to stay, yet I wanted to leave to see my family again and know this was not the norm. But it was the norm in Tamil Nadu and other places in India.

I had much more to learn, as I realised in Bangalore. I thought I had reached Christian adulthood, and my past life in youth work had been just a game to prepare me for India, but there was much more I had to experience. In Bangalore I stayed for a while in Kristu Jyothi College, then with a German Sister who was an expert in leprosy. I had also become friendly with a Muslim family and stayed with them for many weeks. From Brother James Kimpton who ran the 'Reaching the Unreached', and from my Hindu, Muslim and Christian friends, I learnt their tolerance of each other's religions. It is in our nature that some of us should be fanatics about the faith we were brought up in, but I found an interfaith understanding from these dear friends for which I am forever grateful.

In Bangalore the students were going on the streets in their spare time to teach the street children to count, and to read and write. This, they told me, was so necessary for street boys who collected rubbish from garbage bins and rubbish heaps to sell for re-cycling. The men were cheating the young boys, some of whom had never been to school, but by learning the 3Rs they would be able to ensure they were being treated fairly. Being of an inquisitive nature, I asked to accompany them and meet these boys. The long and short of this experience, together with the experience of the clinic in Tamil Nadu, made me feel awful and an inadequate mum. True, I had brought up my four children and cared for many short-term foster children, but if that was all that I could do in my life, I felt sorry for myself. Sitting thinking one evening in my Muslim friend's house, I remembered my parents and how good they had been to me, how happy and connected we had all been in spite of poverty. Then my mum's words came back to me: 'We're never too old.' As these words sunk into me, tears choked me as I also remembered the stories I had heard of these boys, some so young they had no memory of a home. I had to do something . . . but what?

Before I knew what God was asking me to do, I went on a seminar to learn more about the Indian Rite Mass. It was interesting, but not so interesting was the contaminated water I drank on the last day. I became very ill and do not remember much about it. It was no use trying to help in the cities with the street children; I did not know any of the many languages they spoke and in the long run I would be a hindrance as I was now 63 years old. After another couple of months I returned home. I had been in India for 11 months.

Before leaving my new and very special friends, I asked their permission to try to spread awareness of the children's problems in the western world and raise funds to help their work. They gave me their blessing and so did Father Bede.

Returning home was a nightmare. True, it was wonderful to see my children and grandchildren again, but a loneliness took a hold of me which remains today. The only people who understood were other folk who had children with no one and nothing. They all helped me but I had no financial backing, so I had to start without it. In October 1984 we became a registered charity. I had contacted some well-known people and the Essex Youth Service my husband and I had worked for. We also had an inter-faith committee which I thanked God for every day. In the winter of 1984-5 a group of Essex young people went to India with me and the county officers. I had only expected them to be aware of the developing world. They were, and on their return raised £17,000 within ten months. We were on the way. Many other youth groups followed and raised funds on their return. Our committee was wonderful to me, for the next year I had cancer, and an operation and laser treatment left me very tired. The rock who held the charity together through thick and thin was a Muslim friend; he was the most wonderful friend I or the street children ever had.

I was able to visit India now and then. The youth groups

continue to do so today although we had to merge with another Trust in 1999. Altogether we raised nearly £200,000, thanks to the committee and the various youth groups.

I moved to Scotland to be near to my eldest son, Dennis, and just dreamed of my special friends in India. Then last year I reached the age of 80. Knowing about the ache in my heart, Dennis took me to India to see my friends again while I could still manage the journey with his help.

To write that it was wonderful is the understatement of the century, but now there is even greater need – for babies born with HIV. At long last the dream I had in 1983 is coming true: a village outside Bangalore for street boys is being built. They also have street girls being cared for by the Sisters. I have now returned to my lovely rented home by the sea, and have been suffering a guilt feeling of being loved and cared for. What to do? Oh, what to do? Then, looking at the photographs from India I came across one of my mum. How had this got into the wrong album, I thought. I remembered her words and then felt sick because I knew what they meant. In my mind I heard my mum saying, 'You're not too old', and my dad saying, 'Thank you for going to India for me'.

So, God be with me, I am starting again. This time it will be called 'The Lotus Child Fund'. . . . I wish to say that none of us is too old to follow our feelings, and I know people will pray for me.

SECTION THREE

Pilgrimage in the Faith Traditions

Painting of an oil lamp
Jyoti Sahi

Introduction

We have seen that journeying is natural to all people and has been part of life on earth since its beginnings. People have always moved from their places of birth and everyday living to new places, sometimes because they had to, to find food for themselves and their animals, or because they became displaced people and refugees. However, when the moving out and ever onwards has been spiritually motivated, in search of something new and inspiring, something beyond the pilgrims themselves, and frequently something they would never, except perhaps fleetingly, reach, it has and always will be enriching and life-giving at the same time as bringing out the stark realities of life and of death.

There is the story, written about by Olive Shreiner in her *Story of an African Farm*, of the hunter who, when he was hunting for wildfowl, reached a lake where an enormous shadow fell over him and he saw a dim reflection in the water. He was overcome by a great desire to hold the huge white bird whose reflection he had fleetingly glimpsed in the water. He set off in search of the bird, which was truth. He left the security of his home and entered a time of loneliness and danger as he travelled across unknown lands and up mountains, until the years passed and he was very old and dying on a bleak mountainside. A white feather fluttered down, and he died holding it.

Many people of faith quite deliberately leave their ordinary everyday lives and routines and communities behind in order to enter a new world with a new community, new experiences and new and unknown challenges.

Traditionally, the pilgrim in all cultures and faiths faced worry and uncertainty, because he or she was leaving a secure place and perhaps sometimes family and friends also, and moving into an unknown future; sometimes people did not know whether they would ever return home. The early Celtic Christians deliberately set off on their journeys with the intention of wandering for God, not knowing the direction or the destination. The pilgrim was vulnerable and exposed, with constant physical challenges arising from the journey itself and also the constant need to meet new people in new places, climates and lands. There was the challenge of being faced by new cultures with new experiences, some good but others very hard. Pilgrims experienced great fears, especially fears of loss: of comfort, lifestyle, friends and sometimes of life itself. Even today with twenty-first-century conveniences, including lightweight food, easy-to-carry rucksacks and mobile telephones, it is not always easy to walk the way as a spiritual seeker. Aware pilgrims will have many enrichments and challenges and sometimes the spiritual experience they are seeking. They will also be accompanied by the hovering image of the inevitability of the end of the journey and of all things, of death.

Shikoku is an island to the South of the main island of Japan. It has 88 temples linked to the life of a Buddhist saint, Kobo Daishi, and from ancient times many Japanese people have walked the 1000-mile route in honour of the saint. An American, Oliver Statler, made the pilgrimage in the early 1970s, and wrote down his experiences. From his writings we learn that it is impossible for anyone who walks along this way to ignore the reality of death because the route is lined with the graves of pilgrims who died during their walk. Those who were not able to afford a gravestone had their bodies thrown down a mountainside and into a ravine.

The challenge to go into the unknown was well put by Meister Eckhart when he said, 'Put on your travelling shoes and jump into the arms of God.' People of faith who make this leap are likely to experience the chill of fear followed by the thrill of uncertainty about how they will react and cope with the new. Those who are open and ready to experience the new and to learn from it will have something very special to take with them if they return to their normal or usual lives.

There will also be those who go along for the fun of it, or even because they feel obliged to go to please someone else. They may be those who do not wish to change and who may gain little, but journeys often bring surprises.

When the BBC challenged a large cross section of British people, including children, to give up their normal, comfortable lives and to go and live on a Scottish island for a year, they were asking them in a certain sense to be pilgrims, to give up their normal routines, homes and work, and to live in a new and much more basic way, farming, killing their animals for food and making most of the things they needed. At the end of the year most of those who had stayed for the full time said that they could never be the same people who set out. Many talked about having made a spiritual journey.

In Japan, one form of Buddhist pilgrimage is to go away from all the comforts of life into the forest, to walk, climb and camp in the most basic conditions where none of the normal rituals of life, including conversation and the cleaning of teeth, are allowed. In this way the pilgrim is in new surroundings in a state of disorientation, so that, with perseverance, new insights may be possible after which nothing will ever be the same again.

When Muslims go to Mecca they are required to dispense with their normal clothing, wear white sheets and to walk barefoot. Those who have made the journey or 'hajj' say that they have become aware in a new and stark way of the teaching of Islam that every person is the equal of every other person in the eyes of God; there is no special privilege for anyone, no matter how famous or rich they may be in the eyes of the world.

We were on a train in South India when we met a group of Hindu devotees of Lord Ayyappa, all dressed in similar black robes and carrying very little to emphasise their equality and dependence on God.

Every great faith has its traditions and present practice of pilgrimage to its special places. We write as Christians and most of the pilgrimages in this book are written from a Christian faith or cultural perspective. In this section we offer an insight into pilgrimage in the main world faiths. At the end of the section we include a multi-faith pilgrimage which took place at the time of the Millennium. We have given a very short introduction to the world faiths, because this may be helpful for readers who will probably be mostly Christian in faith and culture. This section includes Christianity, as one of the main world faiths.

Zoroastrian Pilgrimage

The most ancient of the great world religions is perhaps the Zoroastrian religion and journeying is at its heart. Zarathustra, the great prophet of the faith, is thought to have lived in north-eastern Iran around 1200 BCE. He called for the worship of the wholly good God, through the medium of fire, and for all people to live in harmony through making wise choices in life and through mutual respect. By the time of the great Persian Empire in the sixth century BCE Zoroastrianism was the official religion of the huge area from North India to Greece and Egypt. It was a benevolent and generous time, when other faiths, including the Jewish faith, were encouraged, and it lasted until the conquest by Alexander the Great in the fourth century BCE. Many ups and downs followed, until the seventh-century rise of Islam when Zoroastrians became a subject people and were forced to retreat to desert areas. In the tenth century, many of them went to India. The long journey to India took a large group of the people to a new life of freedom, mainly in the area around Mumbai (Bombay), where they are known as the Parsis, the people from Pars or Persia. The harshness of the lives of the Zoroastrians who remained in their original homeland continued, with a few brighter times, through the eleventh-century invasion of the Turks, to the establishment of the Islamic Republic under Ayatollah Khomeini in 1979, when the Parsi diaspora grew, this time to the USA, Canada, Britain, and Australia.

The story of the other wise man is a story of a Zoroastrian journey which highlights the truth at the heart of any spiritual journey: that what is important is not the destination but the act of getting there, not the goal but the going.

Who seeks for heaven alone to save his soul,
may keep the path, but will not reach the goal;

while he who walks in love will wander far,
yet God will bring him where the blessed are.*

The story is of the journey of the magi or Zoroastrian priests from their home in the Persian mountains to Bethlehem during the reign of King Herod, following a star and in search of a new king. The magi are Caspar, Melchior and Balthazar, with the fourth, Artaban. Artaban prepares for the journey by selling his house and buying three jewels, a sapphire, a ruby and a pearl. He sets off to meet the other three magi, but on the way he stops to help a sick man and the three leave without him. He therefore arrives in Bethlehem having given his sapphire away; the other magi have already been there and have seen Mary and Joseph and the baby Jesus. Artaban finds the place terrorised by Herod killing the young children. He is able to save the life of a child by giving the ruby to the soldiers. He never gives up, but follows Jesus and his family to Egypt, to the foot of the pyramids and to Alexandria. He goes on around the suffering world for 33 years, helping the refugees, the ill, the bereaved and those fleeing from war. He arrives in Jerusalem and follows the crowds on the way to Golgotha where he spends the pearl in rescuing a young girl from slavery. He dies as the storm breaks. His journey of love has given him the peace of God.

* From *The Story of the Other Wise Man* by Henry Van Dyke, published in 1990 by Enthea Press, Columbus, Ohio.

Jewish Pilgrimage

Judaism began as a nomadic religion, first with the life of Abraham who journeyed for God, and then with Moses who led the Exodus and long journey for the freedom of the people of God. After Moses' time the people continued to journey, carrying the Ark of the Covenant, where God was always present, with them to Shiloh and on, with King David, to Jerusalem. In the sixth century BCE, after the destruction of Solomon's Temple by Nebuchadnezzar, the Jews were exiled to Babylon. Seventy years later they began their pilgrimage of liberation back to their homeland, where city and temple would eventually be rebuilt. Indeed, the final temple built by King Herod was one of the wonders of the world. The later history of the people is the history of the traumatic destruction of this third and last temple in 70 CE by the Romans, the re-working of a spirituality which had to exist without the focus of temple worship, the diaspora of about 2000 years and the formation of the state of Israel in 1948. With this history it is not surprising that exile and lamentation are central to Jewish living and writing, perhaps the most famous being Psalm 137, which refers to the Babylonian exile.

> By the rivers of Babylon, there we sat down, and there we wept, when we remembered Zion . . . How shall we sing the Lord's song in a strange land? If I forget thee, O Jerusalem, let my right hand forget her cunning. If I do not remember thee, let my tongue cleave to the roof of my mouth: if I prefer not Jerusalem above my chief joy.

Some of the main festivals of Judaism are linked to journeying. The Passover marks the beginning of the Exodus, and is a festival of exile, of longing and of the promise of return, as participants were and are reminded that the festival will be

By the Rivers of Babylon
Woodcut by Jyoti Sahi

'Next year in Jerusalem'. Sukkot, the Feast of Tabernacles, marks the temporary living of the people in Sinai.

Just as the exile of the people became linked to suffering and sin, so the return to Zion became linked to the uplifting and restoring of the people. Throughout the long years of the diaspora the people struggled to reach Jerusalem, and often lamented their inability to do so.

When Jews moved from all over the world to be part of the new Israel after the Second World War and Shoah, which had surely marked their worst period of suffering in the entire history of the people, they were especially aware of being restored to wholeness. Today, when religious Jews visit Israel they go first to pray at the Western wall, all that remains of the destroyed temple of Herod. The remaining wall upholds the memory and traditions of the people perhaps more powerfully than if the whole temple was still standing. There is little wonder that the people find it hard to contemplate the sharing of Jerusalem as an international city, the holy city of Christians and Muslims as well as of Jews, but nonetheless, as people of God, this is what they are reasonably being asked to work towards in the twenty-first century.

In the absence of the temple, the synagogues all over the world are much more than the meeting places of the people. They house the Torah, the law, a link with the Ark of the Covenant. People who are not in Israel still celebrate the Passover Festival with the promise that it will be 'Next year in Jerusalem'. They go on pilgrimage to Jerusalem, and also to places where the people live or have lived, and where they were persecuted. Following the Shoah many people go to visit Auschwitz, where over 6 million Jews died. They also go to Yad Vashem, the memorial of the people in Western Jerusalem.

A Jewish historian who made the pilgrimage to Auschwitz decided that he would do a circular tour in that part of Europe and he therefore took a one-way ticket to the place of persecution and death for so many. It was only later that he realised just what he had done.

Rabbi Lionel Blue tells a story which illustrates the uncrushable nature of the Jewish spirit. He tells of meeting a rabbi who had somehow survived the Holocaust. How had he managed to keep his faith alive during such dreadful times, Lionel asked him. 'Mr Blue,' was the reply, 'before the war I believed in the holiness of God and the essential goodness of humankind. Nothing that has happened to me has changed that belief. We are not people of passing fashions!'

Some Jewish people have recently made pilgrimages to the places they were uprooted from during the Second World War when they were taken off to concentration camps where many of their friends and family had died. One of them was Rabbi Hugo Gryn, whose daughter Naomi made a film in 1989 of the visit they both made to Berehovo, the small town beneath the Carpathian mountains where he was born and brought up until life was changed for ever by the war and the persecution of his people.* What shines through the film and the book is the normality of life in Berehovo before the horror took over. Hugo Gryn wrote, 'As I was growing up, there was a sense that Jews had lived in the region for ever.' He described the love and security of his early life, the centrality of the Great Synagogue and the ceremonies and worship of the people. He told of how he came to realise 'that Torah is the finest merchandise' and of how the last time his family was together was for the celebration of his Bar Mitzvah in 1943. Then followed the horror of the train journeys and the camps and eventually the liberation of the few. The book includes a photograph of Berehovo's Jewish Elementary School which was taken in 1942-3 and included Hugo Gryn's younger brother. All the children in the photograph were selected for death on their arrival in Auschwitz a year later.

When Jewish people from the West visit Israel for the first time they usually speak about the contrast in the lives they

* Hugo Gryn's story is told in *Chasing Shadows*, published in 2001 by Penguin Books.

have lived and those of their families and friends in Israel. They speak of their own comfortable lives in contrast to the pioneering lives of the Israelis, most of whom have done national service. Many of them feel a great sense of solidarity with the Israelis, who they see living a frontier life.

Christian Pilgrimage

Christianity inherited the great tradition of Jewish pilgrimage, and this has always been an important aspect of the living out of the faith, whether through contemplation, the journey of life, or recognition of, and journeys to mark, special times, places and people. Most of our book is about Christian pilgrimage, so this section is short.

Jesus did not ask his followers to go on pilgrimage to particular places, and said that people should develop closeness to God through prayer and action. However, the Gospel challenge suggests pilgrimage in asking disciples to take up the cross and follow Christ. Some of Jesus' own journeys are seen as encouragements to pilgrimage, perhaps most obviously the walk to Emmaus after the resurrection.* In the early years of Christianity the Christians were persecuted, often hidden and not able to move about easily, however. Their journeys then were in the mind.

Pilgrimage to the Holy Land began after Constantine became Christian and the eastern and western Mediterranean was united under him. When the Council of Nicaea was called in 325 there was much discussion, including discussion about pilgrimage, which some thought was more likely to corrupt than uplift. It was also felt to be dangerous for people to think that God could be found in Palestine more than anywhere else. The hesitations and warnings failed to stop Christians going to the Holy Land in fairly large numbers, and in the early years they took great risks to do so. The tradition has continued ever since, though following the rise of Islam and the later split in the Christian Church, it became very dangerous for a long time, and local and national pilgrimages grew in importance. The crusades were seen as pilgrimages, but were a long way from the early and later peaceful and spiritual

* Luke 24:13-24.

journeys. Through the ages, however, pilgrims have gone to the Holy Land for special times in the Christian year or perhaps for special times in their lives. The shrines have grown up, and for some the collection of memorabilia has become part of the experience. Many churches have been established and religious communities have grown. Later in the book we include a walking pilgrimage from Nazareth to Bethlehem which took place in 2000 and follows the long tradition of going to the Holy Land, though this pilgrimage was to meet the people who live there now and not just to be where Jesus was.

Gradually, sacred places grew up all over Europe, including Rome and Santiago de Compostella. We have included pilgrimages to both places in other sections. Walsingham in Norfolk became a pilgrim place in the eleventh century when a local woman had a dream of being taken to Nazareth to the house of Mary and Joseph, and arranged the building of her own house of Nazareth. The tradition of taking relics from the tombs of saints grew up, and soon churches had to have a relic. Soon there was the tradition of pilgrimage leading to healing and to bringing the pilgrim a step nearer to salvation. With the Reformation, and especially the dissolution of the monasteries, pilgrimage became less important in many parts of Western Europe for a while. The Orthodox had developed their own pilgrim centres, including Constantinople, with relics and icons. There was also the tradition of journeying to the tombs of saints. When Constantinople fell to the Turks in 1453, the Orthodox pilgrimage tradition continued but became more local. The Orthodox saw pilgrimage as a way of life in the imitation of Christ, often dressing the part.

Pilgrimages gradually returned to the Christian way of life in post-Reformation Western Europe, and by the nineteenth century, as travel became easy and more of the world was opened up, Christian pilgrimages became popular again, including those to the Holy Land. More special places were discovered, including Lourdes, where the 14-year-old Bernadette had visions of the Virgin who helped her to find a spring which was reputed to have healing powers.

In the twentieth and twenty-first centuries Christian pilgrimage has continued to be popular. People go on pilgrimage for a whole range of reasons. We have included some of these in other sections of this book.

Muslim Pilgrimage

Abraham, Moses and Jesus are early prophets of Islam, which developed in the seventh century CE, which Muslims mark as the time when the Prophet Mohammed, born in 570 CE, was given the final revelation from God when he was living in Mecca and Medina. The divine message was recorded in the Qu'ran which was written in Arabic.

Pilgrimage to Mecca (now in Saudi Arabia) – the 'hajj' – is one of the 'Five Pillars of Islam', one of the main duties of Muslims ordered in the Qu'ran. The other pillars are the proclamation of Allah and of his Prophet Mohammed, fasting, the giving of alms, and prayer five times every day.* The hajj, which means 'effort', is obligatory for Muslims who are in good health and who can afford to make the journey once in a lifetime, and it takes place during the month Dhu L-Hijja, the twelfth month of the Muslim year. There is also a lesser pilgrimage, the 'umra' to the Ka'ba, which may be performed at any time of the year. The umra does not take the place of the hajj.

The hajj stems from the time in 622 when Mohammed and his followers fled from Mecca, where he had been unpopular in preaching against polytheism and the worship of idols, and had made the journey to Medina from where he worked for the successful conversion of Mecca, after which only Muslims were allowed to enter the purified Ka'ba and the sacred area round it. Mohammed went on pilgrimage to Mecca just before his death, thus offering the model for all other Muslims to seek to follow. The hajj also commemorates the sacrifice of Abraham when he was asked by God to sacrifice his son Ishmael. The festival of Idd ul-Adha, is the occasion when animals are sacrificed and the food given to the poor, to mark Abraham's sacrifice.

* For full explanation of the Five Pillars of Islam see Chapter 5 of *How to Understand Islam* by Jaques Jomier, published by SCM Press Ltd, 1988.

The Qu'ran 2.125: 'We made a covenant with Ibrahim and Isma'il that they should sanctify my House for those who go around it and who use it as a retreat, who there bend and prostrate themselves.'*

The hajj is a vivid reminder of the international community and equality of all Muslims in the world. It brings great blessings on those who manage to take part in it. All Muslims are hopeful that they will go on the hajj at least once, and many make great sacrifices to do so. Even today, however, only a small percentage of the Muslims in the world manage to make the journey. In the past, the journey to Mecca would take many months or even years to complete and sometimes people died on the way there or back. Even today the hajj is a sacrifice for the pilgrims. Sometimes people save up to make the journey for many years and make hard physical efforts to complete the journey and rituals.

The ceremonies for the hajj are described in detail in the 'Hadith' which records the practice of the Prophet and is the model of living for all Muslims. The ceremonies refer back to the rites of the 'Farewell Pilgrimage' of Mohammed in 632, the year of his death.

The area around Mecca is a holy area. When the pilgrims reach the edge of the holy area, they change their clothes. Women cover their bodies in white sheets, except their faces and hands. Men cover their upper and lower bodies with two sheets, and wear sandals. Rites of purification include the cutting of hair and nails and elaborate washing ceremonies. From this moment and until the end of the hajj, the pilgrim must not put on any other clothes or shoes, cut nails or hair, have sexual relations, fight, hunt animals or argue with anyone. In Mecca the pilgrims move from the edge of the sacred area to the centre, the Masjid al-Haram, for the ceremony of the circling of the Ka'ba, the earthly house of Allah, when they hope to kiss the black stone. There is a ceremony of the

* A translation of the Qu'ran is published by Penguin Books.

pilgrims running between two hillocks, in memory of Hagar who ran in search of water for her child.

The hajj proper begins on the seventh day with a sermon, and then, on the eighth day, the pilgrims move east from Mecca. On the ninth day the central part of the 'hajj' takes place when the pilgrims stand at Arafat in front of a small hill called 'Jabal al-Rahma' for a time of sermons and prayer before going back within the Meccan boundaries. On the tenth day they move to Mina, to throw small stones at pillars representing the devil. They also make ritual sacrifice of an animal, in honour of Abraham. It is at this point that Muslims from all over the world take part symbolically and are part of the hajj. From Mina the pilgrims go back to Mecca for more ceremony and afterwards they may cut their hair or shave their heads and the state of 'ihram' is over. The next three days are spent visiting friends and many people also go to see the tomb of Mohammed in Medina.

For most of the Muslims in the world the pilgrimage to Mecca remains always a dream which never becomes reality. For those who do make the journey, the experiences, as on any pilgrimage of faith, are as many as the people. Many Muslims are acutely aware of the need for inner change as they move along the route to Mecca, and especially as they arrive in the holy area and move from the edges of the sacred space to the centre. Naser Khosrow wrote a poem which is a challenge to those Muslims who may simply perform the rituals of pilgrimage to keep the spirit of pilgrimage rather than the letter.

> The pilgrims returned with reverence.
> They were thankful to Merciful God.
>
> But among the crowd of this caravan
> I had a dear and sincere friend.
> I asked him how he accomplished
> this very difficult and fearful trip.

I asked him:

While he was in Arafat,
while he stood so close to Almighty God,
did he have a chance to know Him?
Was he not eager to learn a bit of the knowledge?

He replied NO!

The poem continues in this vein and ends with the challenge to the Muslim pilgrim and to all people of faith who are travelling on their own personal or group pilgrimage.

Oh friend, you have not performed the Hajj!
And you have not obeyed God!

You went to Mecca and visited the Kaaba!
You spent your money to buy the hardships of the desert!

If you try to go on Hajj again,
try to perform it as I have instructed you.

The famous pilgrim, the black American activist, Malcolm X, moved from the Nation of Islam to become an orthodox Muslim and made the journey to Mecca alone. He was a spiritual pilgrim and was not disappointed in his journey. He had become famous in working for black awareness through separation from white American society, but on the hajj he found himself thrown into the company of Muslims of all races and conditions, and had to reassess his values and work with the realisation that his experience was one of unity and brotherhood for people of all backgrounds and races, something he had never known in America. The film of his life shows his amazed wonder as he reaches Mecca and the sacred area, and joins the crowds of people from all over the world.

Muslims have developed a tradition of pilgrimage to other holy places including Jerusalem, where the Prophet is said to have ascended into heaven from the sacred stone in the Dome of the Rock, a mosque dating from the seventh century.

A Shi'ite tradition has also grown up of making pilgrimages to the tombs of imams. Shiism is the main minority sect of Islam and is marked by its love for Mohammed's family and their descendants.

The Sufi tradition of Islam, which some think grew directly from the Qu'ran and others suggest has gradually developed over the years, has stressed the importance of faith, religious experience and even ecstasy. Sufis, clerical and lay, have often been mystics who came close to God, and ideally to a state of complete trust in God, through spiritual practices. Unlike most Muslims, many Sufis have sought God through art and music. Some of them have been content to move in heart and soul, without making the physical journey to Mecca.

The movement of the spirit towards the community and towards God is clear in the traditional initiation ceremony of a particular group of Sufis in Turkey which is carried out in the hall of the lodge. There is a throne, holding candles, at one end of the hall and the brothers sit on sheepskins. The new entrant to the group is brought in and instructed, and then the head-dress and belt are put on. The belt has three knots which represent the rejection of lying, stealing and fornication. The new member then shakes hands with everyone, a drink is shared and a prayer said. The ceremony ends with dancing.*

---

* Taken from the account in *Mystical Islam: An Introduction to Sufism* by Julian Baldick, published in 2000 by Tauris Parke Paperbacks.

Hindu Pilgrimage

'Hindu' comes from 'Sindhu' which is the Persian name for the River Indus. The Aryan people moved into the Indus Valley area around 1500 BCE. The Persians called the people 'the people beyond the Sindhu' or 'Hindu.' The word 'Hindu' originally meant Indian and, as the people could not, and still cannot, be separated from their religion, came to describe the religion. The religion is based on right conduct, which may be different for different people, but which is for all times and which was originally for all the world. Hindus, however, are allowed great freedom in faith, with a whole range of sacred texts, and also in worship. They may worship God in whatever form and way they choose, and there are millions of deities and religious practices. Gandhi said of his religion, 'Hinduism is a living organism liable to growth and decay and subject to the laws of nature. One and indivisible at the root, it has grown into a vast tree with innumerable branches.' God is understood as the one ultimate reality, the Brahman, or as a trinity of Brahma representing creation, Vishnu representing preservation, and Shiva representing destruction. God may also be seen as a personal God. Hindus aim to become free of the cycle of births and deaths, and to achieve unity with the one supreme God. Each person has a spark of God which may grow or diminish through the actions of life.

Pilgrimage is central to the Hindu life, and the pilgrim is traditionally seen as like the lotus flower, moving from the mud into the light and becoming beautiful in the process. The stages of life are highlighted in Hinduism, so that the seekers are very aware of moving through the period of training and education to the life of householder and active worker, to retirement and the beginnings of detachment, to the final stage of hermit or 'sanyasi', focusing on union with God.

The journey inwards through meditation is well developed

in Hinduism. Yoga or union with oneself, with other people and creatures and with God is the goal of all seekers. There are several limbs of yoga, which are paths to the same goal of uniting the spirit or self or Atman within to the God within, and they are suitable for different temperaments. Pantanjali classified the yogic system and defined it as 'the stilling of thought waves'. The chanting of 'Aum', the best name for God and identical with God, conveys something of the character of God. The chanting focuses the senses, the will, the intellect and the emotions on the name of the Lord.

An important aspect of any pilgrimage is devotion to God, 'bhakti' in Sanskrit. This has led to the development of many songs and poems. This personal devotion has been very important in allowing any person, and not just the Brahmin group, to move closer to God. Many places of pilgrimage, though not all, allow people of all castes and of no caste to go there.

The physical pilgrimage is always obvious in India, where people are constantly on the move to the hundreds and thousands of sacred places. Natural features of the landscape are often pilgrim places. There are seven holy rivers, of which the Ganges is the most important because it is said to begin in Shiva's hair. Benares is perhaps the most famous place for ritual bathing. In *The Mahabharata* the whole of India is seen as a sacred place, where God is specially present.* Journeying is an essential part of the faith path. 'Yatra' comes from the Sanskrit and means to swim or to get across. Pilgrimage is also called 'tirayatra' or the journey to a sacred place. The journey is an expression of faith and a sign of holiness; the aim, as in all of life, is to come closer to reality, to God.

Puri, on the coast of Orissa, is sacred as the place of pilgrimage to the Lord Jagannath, which many people think was a tribal deity taken over by Hinduism as an image of Lord Krishna. The beautiful stone temple was built in the twelfth

---

* *The Mahabharata* is a Channel 4 book by Garry O'Connor, Hodder & Stoughton, 1989.

century CE. Every August the Lord Jagganath goes on procession around Puri, and thousands of pilgrims are there to see him, thus giving rise to the word 'juggernaut'.

A famous place of pilgrimage is Vrindavan, which is on the River Jumna to the south of Delhi. Thousands of pilgrims from all over India go to Vrindavan particularly at the time of the monsoon in July and August. They bathe in the river and collect water to take home. They enjoy the sacred dramas which are celebrated every year when the local children take the parts of Krishna, Radha and the cowherds, for Vrindavan is celebrated as the birthplace of the Lord Krishna. The dramas, which are also liturgies, are about the life of Krishna. The divine presence is invoked through the image of the god.

Another well-known place of pilgrimage is Mount Kailash which is the sacred home of Lord Shiva and his wife, the goddess Parvati. The tradition is that Brahma collected and saved God's tears of joy and poured them into a lake in Tibet which he called Manasarovar. Manasarovar is 940 kilometres from Khatmandu, and Mount Kailash is a further 40 to 50 kilometres west of the lake.

Vibhooti Acharya joined the pilgrimage to Mount Kailash and wrote of her experiences.

Arriving at Manasarovar in June 1998 . . . snow-covered mountains surrounded us on all four sides. I felt tiny. . . . The colours were changing quickly and dramatically from blue to lilac to purple and blazing red as the sun began to set. I could have stood there and watched for ever. . . . I felt connected, one with nature. . . . We gathered together, over 200 people from all over the world in a large tent. Puja, worship, was performed, led by the three principal Sants from India, equivalent of living saints. Ganesh, remover of obstacles, was worshipped, then Siva, Lakshmi, the sun, moon, stars, planets and the holy waters of Manasarovar. . . . I was becoming focused on the Self, Spirit or God. . . . We started the three-day Parikrama on foot from Darchen.

. . . We focused ourselves through prayer God and started the yatra. The altitude was already affecting our heads . . . the slopes were getting steeper and it was becoming more of an effort to push ourselves up each section of the mountain. We had to stop more frequently. . . . We had been advised to save every breath and thought and focus ourselves on our goal. . . . As we continued . . . our shoulders were weighing us down. . . . We were losing control of our body and mind. . . . We couldn't carry anything, not even our own bodies. . . . Just for a moment, I found myself searching within me for the reason why we were doing this. . . . I looked up in desperation, hoping to find some guidance. There, in front of us, was a long line of coloured flags flying high up on a mountain top. This had to be Drolmapass, the summit. . . .

When I got to the top, my soul came to meet me; it felt as if it had always been there, dancing, awaiting my return. . . . My spirit was elevated, soaring over the mountains, themselves some 19,000 feet high, and yet I felt so small and humble.

The climb down was long but less laborious. . . . We bowed down, with our heads resting on Mother Earth who had carried the burden of our weight in such a difficult time. Lying there in my Mother's lap, with my Father Shiva in the shape of the mountain wrapping his arms around me, I sobbed uncontrollably like a little child. . . . I couldn't believe that it was possible to feel so empty and fulfilled, so heavy and yet so light and free, so united and so disconnected all at once. I couldn't believe it was possible to feel so much love and pain in one single breath.*

* Vibhooti's experience of pilgrimage is taken from *Meeting Hindus*, edited by Gwyneth Little and published by Christians Aware, 2001.

Photograph: Barbara Butler

Japanese Buddhist temple and garden

Buddhist Pilgrimage

Buddhism began in the sixth and fifth centuries BCE in India with the enlightenment of Gotama who thus became 'Sakya-muni', the muni of the Sakya clan. He had been born as Prince Siddhartha, in about 567 BCE in Kapilavatthu at the foot of the Himalayas. Six years later, after days of meditation, on a full moon night in May, as he was sitting under the Bodhi tree, he realised the truths which he later taught, and thus reached enlightenment. He was persuaded to share the way to his enlightenment, and so his teaching, 'dharma,' became the foundation of Buddhism or 'Buddha dharma'. It has its followers in the two main schools of Theravada, or traditional Buddhism, and Mahayana, or more liberal Buddhism. There are many schools, developed from the different collections of the Buddha's teachings. The Buddha's teaching was developed out of Hinduism, but took the seeker in a different direction. He saw everything as transient and associated with the suffering which arises when permanence is sought. He believed that there could not be a soul or an eternal God. The teaching is encapsulated in the Four Noble Truths, the truth of transience and of the suffering caused by its denial, and of how to escape this through the Eightfold Path towards enlightenment. The Eightfold Path is right view, right thought, right speech, right action, right livelihood, right striving, right mindfulness and right concentration. People may, through the Eightfold Path, change and become fulfilled and useful. Buddhist commitment is through the three Jewels or Refuges, the Buddha, the Dharma, and the Sangha, the community of the bhikkhus or monks.

Buddhism spread in the third century BCE under the Emperor Asoka. This was a time when philosophy, art, image-making and pilgrimage flowered. The development of Mahayana Buddhism came between the first century BCE and the second century CE. One outcome of this movement was the change from the individual journey towards enlightenment to the journey followed by a turning back from enlightenment to help others. Those who turned back became known as the 'bodhisattvas'. The buddha-nature became understood as the nature which emptied itself for others.

As Buddhism moved beyond India it went north into Tibet, east into China, Korea and Japan, and south-east into Sri Lanka, Burma and Thailand. The south-eastern movement remained Theravada, and the other movements became Mahayana Buddhism.

Buddhist pilgrimage is very important in both the Theravada and Mahayana traditions, and it normally takes pilgrims to places associated with the Buddha or where there are said to be relics of the Buddha. There are also pilgrim sites where cuttings of the bodhi tree, where the Buddha became enlightened, are growing. Mountain tops, like Adam's Peak in Sri Lanka, are also pilgrim places. Adam's Peak is a place of pilgrimage for Buddhists, Hindus, Muslims and Christians. The pilgrims walk through the forested lower slopes and up the steep and rocky paths. They sleep overnight in caves and greet the rising of the sun before moving off to the summit of the peak.

Anuradhapura is one of the ancient centres of Buddhism in Sri Lanka. Between the third century BCE and the eighth century CE it was a beautiful city with extensive religious monuments and large Buddhist communities of monks and nuns. A bodhi tree was planted here, taken from the tree of the Buddha's enlightenment. The tree is said to be the oldest tree in the world, lovingly tended for 2000 years. Anuradhapura is a place of pilgrimage for Buddhists from all over Sri Lanka and the world. The pilgrims are always there, often dressed in white. Sometimes they spend all night near the holy Bo tree.

Elizabeth Harris, a Christian, spent several years in Sri Lanka and has written about the Buddhist pilgrims to the tree in Anuradhapura.

Pleasant open parkland lies between the dagoba and the Sri Maha Bodhi, the sacred bo tree. Since I was there towards noon on Poya (full moon) Day, groups of pilgrims were eating their main meal on the grass. There was little talk, as packets of rice and curry were opened. Quieter still was the atmosphere in the enclosed area around the Bo tree, shaded and swept clean. Here a number of women in white and orange were sitting in relaxed positions. Those in orange were nuns keeping the Ten Precepts.

The stairs to the ancient tree, propped up by metal supports, were packed. At the top, the white, tiled flower ledge was overflowing with petals, as more and more came to offer and chant verses of reverence. The space where people could attach flags was weighted down and yet more were being handed to the person in attendance. In a lower room, where, nearly four years ago, I had been deeply moved by the painting of the Buddha against a cosmic background of mountains and sky, men, women and children were kneeling.

Elizabeth has described the Perahera, an annual festival in Kandy in Sri Lanka, when thousands of Buddhist pilgrims go to watch the procession of the most sacred relic in the country, the tooth of the Buddha.

The focus of the procession is the ancient tusker elephant which carries, on his decorated back, a casket in which the tooth, or a replica, lies.

Outside, people are finding their plots on the pavement and spreading out sheets of plastic ready to wait for three or four hours. . . . Balloons, artificial flowers, candy, nuts, ice-cream, psychedelic sheeting and toys are being sold among the crowds. . . .

The boom of the canon at an auspicious hour marks the beginning of everything. Processions from five places converge. . . . The procession is headed by whipcrackers. . . . After this come fire-throwers, dressed in black, wielding flaming sticks, dancing with burning thongs attached to their heads or carrying iron wheels with flares attached. They dance, roll on the ground and do acrobatics with the fire perilously near to their skins. Then come the elephants, drummers, dancers and dignitaries. . . . Carnival, feudalism and religion mix. . . . In the dark, the elephants, beautifully caparisoned and lit with strings of coloured lights, are a wonderful sight. About seventy have been marching and there will be more. . . .

Before the procession began the pilgrims went to the Temple of the Tooth, to kneel in front of the tooth and to place offerings of flowers in front of the holy place. . . .

Jain Pilgrimage

Jainism emerged from Hinduism in the sixth century BCE through the witness of Mahavira, who spent much of his life as a wandering teacher and ascetic. He was the last of the 24 tirthankaras or bridge builders, who became enlightened and were removed from the cycle of reincarnation. Jains, who mostly live in Western India, follow Mahavira in self-purification through austerity and fasting. They practise non-violence or 'ahimsa'.

Journeying is important to Jains. Some monks and nuns constantly travel, carrying begging bowls, walking barefoot, wearing simple white clothes, and preaching non-attachment to the world. They carry long brushes with which they sweep away any insects in their path to avoid treading on them. Some monks go to the extreme length of being 'sky clad' or naked.

Some lay Jains spend a lot of time on pilgrimage. Many travel by bus or train, and some walk on pilgrimage to Mount Abu in Rajasthan or Parasnath in Bihar. Jains regularly go on pilgrimage to the 58-foot statue of Gomateshvara at Shravan-abelagola in Karnataka. Every 12 years or so, thousands of pilgrims gather and the central part of the ritual is the bathing of the statue with water, sugar-cane juice, milk and sandalwood.

Natubhai Shah has written about pilgrimage in his faith tradition.

Pilgrimage is an important part of the Jain way of life. Jain scriptures have laid down the pilgrimage as an annual obligation for the Jains as it is believed that pilgrimage encourages the devotee to the path of spiritual progress and austerities, and ultimately to liberation from the karmic bondage – to an eternal life of perfection.

Jain places of pilgrimage are numerous, scattered throughout India, and are known as *tirtha-ksetras* or *yatra-dhaamas*. Their serenity, devotional and spiritual atmosphere lead the pilgrim to the activities, from external to the internal sacred space, towards self-realisation and liberation. It is, perhaps, why the Jains places of pilgrimage are generally found on hilltops, in secluded places or in forests away from the habitation. They are associated with any of the five auspicious events *(kalyaanakas)* – conception, birth, renunciation, omniscience and liberation – in the lives of *tirthankaras* (spiritual path founders) whom Jains worship as an example and follow their teachings. Some places of pilgrimage may be associated with other saints *(siddhaksetras)*, miracles, myths *(atisayksetras)*, and monuments, temples and images *(kalaaksetras)* and, often, all of the above characteristics may be present at one site.

Pilgrims travel to these sites either by vehicles or on foot individually, with the family or in a group, but, over the past two decades, the old tradition of *sangha-yatraa*, walking to a pilgrimage destination covering a few miles to hundreds of miles, has been revived and proved very popular, as it trains the pilgrims for spirituality. Along the way the town or village Jains welcome the pilgrims, the ascetics deliver the sermons, the wealthy pilgrims donate to local temples and hence it has become a welcome event to promote the community spirit.

There are many guides available describing the journey and facilities to these holy places. Prominent among them are Pava in Bihar, Sammet shikhara in Zarkhand, Satrunjay and Girnar in Gujarat, Delvara, Jesalmir and Ranakpur in Rajasthan and Sravana Belgola in Karnataka. The recently built Jain Centre at Leicester attracts many Jain devotees throughout the world and is likely to be a place of Jain pilgrimage.

Because of time constraint, I usually travel to the place of pilgrimage by vehicle, but had an experience for a few days of *sangha-yatraa* to Jesalmir in 1996, which was a spiritual journey that I will never forget. It was a barefoot pilgrimage of 196 pilgrims, including 20 monks and nuns, from Sanchor to Jesalmir in Rajasthan covering about 200 miles and lasting for about a month (I was only with the pilgrims for three days). During this spiritual journey, the pilgrims made the night halt at temple guest houses or in tents where there are no guest houses. They observed six rules scrupulously: travelling barefoot, avoidance of sensual and carnal pleasures, eating food only once a day, avoiding consumption of raw or green vegetables, sleeping on a mat on the ground, and observing the vow of righteousness.

It is normal for the meritorious act of a *sangha-yatraa* to be sponsored by a family. The above pilgrimage was sponsored by my friend, whose family members and relatives looked after the needs of the pilgrims personally. One of the family members fasted in rotation on each day of the pilgrimage. The senior monk delivered sermons every day. A makeshift temple was created at each place of halt, where the *pujaa*, recitations and the rituals, including the meditation, were the daily spiritual activities. The food was cooked at the site and it required a meticulous planning and organisation to look after the needs of all. At the end of the pilgrimage, the sponsor gave gifts to each pilgrim. The pilgrims awarded the honorific title *Sanghapati* 'lord of the assembly' (considered equivalent to monastic initiation) to the sponsor. The *Sanghapati* and his wife were honoured by placing a garland around their necks (*maalaaropana*), and the honour of placing the garlands went to the highest bidders. The substantial amount thus raised went as donation to the temple-fund.

Most of the pilgrims travel by vehicle to various Jain holy places either individually or in sponsored groups (*sangha*), where the observance of the six rules of *sangha-yatraa* are not compulsory. I went to Satrunjay, considered to be the holiest Jain pilgrim place, by vehicle in 1998. It is a hilltop temple city where the first *tirthankara* achieved liberation. The ridges on two hills, 2000 feet above the sea level, have more than 3300 temples and shrines of varying size, beautiful and ornate architecture and pious atmosphere. Most of the pilgrims climb the hill barefoot, bathe at the top of the hill, and perform *pujaa* at the main temple. Monks and nuns, laity adults and children were seen climbing the hill with devotional feeling, some singing the hymns, some in silent walking meditation. No food is allowed on the hill, but on finishing the *yatraa*, pilgrims are served free snacks at the foot of the hill. Many devotees stay in the town at the foot of hill, which has hundreds of free guest houses, and climb the hill daily for a number of days. Some stay up to four months for the rainy season, for spiritual progress, and carry out various types of austerities for shedding the karma attached to their souls.

Pilgrimage rejuvenates the devotees physically and spiritually, and is an important aspect of the Jain way of life, encouraged by all for relaxation and spiritual progress. It increases the community spirit, motivates the pilgrims to do philanthropic activities, including donation to temple funds, and is considered to be a meritorious activity that helps the progress on the spiritual path towards inner sacred space and self-realisation.

Dr Natubhai Shah is a retired medical practitioner who has a PhD in Jain religion. He was responsible for the creation of the beautiful Jain temple in Leicester, and is the author of *Jainism: The World of Conquerors* (two volumes). He is the chairman of Jain Sangha of Europe, Chairman of the Ahimsa for Quality of Life, and the Secretary-General of the World Council of Jain Academics. He has been involved in the interfaith movement for many years, represents Jainism at the highest level, and was awarded 'Jain Ratna' by the Prime Minister of India on 8 April 2001.

Sikh Pilgrimage

The Sikh faith was founded by Guru Nanak who was born in the Punjab in 1469 CE. He came to feel that the faith path was neither Hindu nor Muslim and went on to reject exclusivism in religion, including the caste system. He said that moral character was much more important than birth. He wrote his own hymns, and stressed the need for each person to know God, who was everywhere, and to develop a good way of life. He offered a spirituality which was rich and life-affirming for all.

After Guru Nanak's death around 1540 the Sikh community grew in the Punjab area. Nanak was followed by nine living successors who taught in the vernacular and developed a strong religious community which faced many aggressors. Gradually, many Sikhs have come to feel united in faith, culture and also as a people. The last living guru was Guru Gobind Singh (1675-1708 CE), who founded the order of the 'Khalsa' or community of the baptised, and gave the distinctive external appearance to the Sikhs of the turban, together with the five sacred symbols – the uncut hair, the comb, the steel wrist band, the shorts, and the sword. He declared that after his lifetime the Sikhs were to see their scriptures as their guide, so that the next and continuing guru was the book, the Guru Granth Sahib. The Guru Granth Sahib is installed in the gurdwara, the centre of worship and of community life.*

Guru Nanak did not advocate formal physical pilgrimage but some of the gurus who followed him did. Sikhs today do go on journeys to places associated with the gurus. The most important place of pilgrimage is Amritsar in the Punjab. The fourth guru, Ram Das, excavated the pool there in the sixteenth century, and his son later built the Darbar Sahib, a place of worship and pilgrimage which now contains the famous Golden Temple and an original copy of the Granth Sahib.

* See *Meeting Sikhs*, edited by Joy Barrow and published by Christians Aware, 1999.

A Sikh who lives in Leicester has spoken about her first visit to the Golden Temple in Amritsar. This was the highlight of a pilgrimage in which she had travelled to many Sikh shrines in India and met many Sikh people. She had to go through the women's entrance to the Golden Temple, but, as a foreign visitor, she had to produce her passport. She had left the passport with her husband and was almost refused entry to the temple, but at last her husband was found and all was well. She described her feeling of near panic at the possibility of not being allowed into the temple she had travelled so far to visit. She also expressed her relief followed by joy when everything was sorted out, and she could enter the temple area. She told with great love of the atmosphere of peace, prayer and community which she experienced and which has never left her.

Bah'ai Pilgrimage

This religion was founded by Bahau'llah in the 1860s CE. After his death it was led by his son Abdu'l Baha and then his great-grandson Shogi Effendi. When Shogi Effendi died in 1957, the Universal House of Justice was elected. Bahau'llah preached of religious reform and unity in Persia, and from there the faith, though it remains small, has spread all over the world.

Bahais believe that God is utterly transcendent and that there are individuals who reflect and manifest the attributes of God and who reveal the divine purpose for people on the earth, who may make progress in religion. They recognise the main religious leaders of all the faiths. They pray in each other's homes and in meeting houses. They have special houses of worship in a few countries.

Bah'ais go on pilgrimage to shrines in Haifa and Akka associated with the life of the founder of the faith.

Interfaith Pilgrimage

On some special occasions people of many faiths join together in pilgrimage. The Westminster Interfaith Group, founded by Brother Daniel Faivre in 1982, has pioneered much of this work in London, aiming to promote greater understanding, co-operation and respect between people of different faiths.

Brother Daniel wrote, 'I am convinced that Christians cannot reach their full stature in Christ unless they become, like Jesus, partners in dialogue with all people of faith, and, with them, are totally involved in all those activities that are essential for the building of the kingdom of God on earth.'

Westminster Interfaith has organised a pilgrimage for peace every summer for many years. Eric Bramsted joined the Millennium Pilgrimage.

A Millennium Interfaith Pilgrimage for Peace
Eric Bramsted

To mark the Millennium, Westminster Interfaith decided to have five columns converging on central London for their annual pilgrimage: two from the north, and one each from the east, west and south. We were asked to organise the southern column, and decided to make this our annual walk.

At 9.30am, 60 of us assembled at Balham Mosque with which we have strong links, and Iqbal Khalfey, a very active member of this community and also on our committee, gave a brief history of the mosque, and an account of its many activities, including its private primary and secondary schools. This growing Sunni community has opened a second mosque in Tooting, which we have also visited several times. He showed us the worship area and answered many questions. As we left we were given a very informative pamphlet 'Understanding Islam'. Rev Nagase, a monk from the Buddhist Peace Pagoda in Battersea Park, brought a large and very fine purple prayer banner. He began our procession by steadily banging his drum, as he has done on so many previous Westminster Interfaith pilgrimages. We were under way.

Nearby in Balham High Road is the small Hindu Radha Krishna temple, which was founded by two women and is now led by several women. With increased numbers we filled the temple and joined the last part of one of the weekly services, which included a devotion to Hanuman, the monkey god (friend and ally of Rama) and aarti. We enjoyed traditional hospitality, and everybody received an apple from a huge bowl as we departed.

We then walked about a mile to the very large Jewish residential nursing home, with about 400 residents, in Nightingale Lane, and were given a very warm welcome in their hall by some of the residents, the director and his staff, and Rabbi Berkovits. We arrived in time for the kiddush, the blessing of wine and the two loaves of challah bread by the rabbi, which followed the end of the Sabbath service. The rabbi spoke eloquently about the value of interfaith visits and dialogue whilst we partook of delightful refreshments, most welcome as it was a warm day and we were thirsty. He then showed us the adjacent synagogue and answered a number of questions very wittily. Two Muslims said they were delighted by our visit as they had never been to a synagogue. We now had our maximum number of about 100, and we estimate that with comings and goings about 150 people took part in the South London column.

Next we made our way in glorious sunshine across Clapham Common to Trinity Hospice and ate our lunch in their lovely garden. The Anglican chaplain, Rev Peter Wells, spoke to us about the history of the hospice, dating from Victorian days and the oldest in the country. He stressed the increasing multi-faith nature of the hospice which has a team of chaplains from many faiths, and was therefore especially glad to see us. He then showed some of us the chapel and outlined future plans to locate the place of worship in a room designed for all faiths.

As we were leaving the garden, we noticed two of our pilgrims who were on their knees on a lawn saying the obligatory Muslim midday prayers and were moved by their devotion.

Some took a bus and some walked to All Saints' Anglican Church, very close to Battersea Park. Rev Ivor Smith-Cameron and Rev Alan Gadd, the former a founder of our Interfaith group, and both very active members of it, are the leaders of a multi-ethnic congregation. The cultural diversity of its members is reflected in the images and decoration of the church – for example, there is a large prominent picture showing a black Christ on the cross. Also the church is square with the worshippers sitting round the walls. Prayers, readings, sermon and communion take place in the middle. No wonder one visitor said he couldn't believe he was in an Anglican church. Ivor Smith-Cameron shook our hands as we arrived and Alan Gadd explained how the church had grown in this way, and that the worship area is much used by local community groups when there are no services. At each stop we gave a bunch of flowers together with a pilgrimage booklet to our hosts, as a small token of appreciation of the warm welcome and the hospitality we had received. When a committee member came forward for this presentation the lady responsible for the lovely refreshments provided for us was called for out of the kitchen to receive it. Adelaide responded by singing a religious song in Ghanaian and a famous one from South Africa, and many people joined in. Finally she led a great crocodile dance as more and more of us joined her and we followed her in song and clapping. We left reluctantly, but we knew we had to join the other columns at the Peace Pagoda.

Finally, after the speech by the Mayor of Wandsworth and the procession round the pagoda, and during the tea break some of us visited the Buddhist shrine in the small building where Rev Nagase lives. We noted the picture of the remarkable Japanese monk who founded the Buddhist order which is committed to building peace pagodas in different parts of the world, but who died some years ago. We held his memory and example and the work of the monks in our prayers. This was the sixth faith community we had visited.

All the columns then marched together for the last stage to Westminster Cathedral. On arrival we headed for the side chapel where Cardinal Hume was buried, to honour his memory. He had been a strong supporter of Westminster Interfaith from its inception, and it was fitting that Brother Daniel, who had been its initiator and leader for so many years, placed a wreath of flowers on his tomb. We stood in silence and remembered with gratitude his many spiritual gifts and his active commitment to interfaith dialogue. In the cathedral hall we were warmly received by Bishop Guazelli of the Westminster Diocese, who introduced representatives from seven faiths who read prayers or readings from their scriptures which moved us with their religious insights.

Finally we were served a sumptuous hot and cold vegetarian meal by members of the Roman Catholic Church in Hounslow, to which Alfred Agius belongs – he was the main organiser of the pilgrimage. As we ate so pleasurably, we relaxed after a long, tiring but most rewarding day, and exchanged news with many friends and acquaintances.

Photograph: Barbara Butler

Maasai moran, or warriors, celebrate the end
of a journey with a dance

A Maasai Journey

The Maasai people are natural travellers, roaming the huge area between Kenya and Tanzania with their three million or more cattle, which their traditional religion tells them were sent to them by God. A Maasai creation story tells that when God created heaven and earth he linked them together by a rope, down which he first sent a man and a cow. The man then prayed to God for a companion and God sent a woman to join him.

The cattle are the wealth of the Maasai, and cattle herding is the most important work they do, followed by the herding of the sheep and goats. Almost everything they have and eat comes from the cow, sheep or goat. The manyattas, the simple homes they live in, are made from twigs and mud and cow dung. The houses easily collapse when the people move on to new places in search of greenery or water for the cattle. The Maasai walk long distances daily, hunting, herding and gathering wood and water. They continue to wear their traditional dress and to walk everywhere.*

A traditional Maasai story, passed down by word of mouth from generation to generation, tells of the value of being unselfish and brave, of listening to God and thus inheriting the blessings of God.

The story is of Maasai 'moran', or warriors, and of a prophet. The warriors went to the prophet and asked him to prophesy on how they might go out and find cattle.

The prophet advised them to go out and to follow a long footpath until it divided into two, when they were then to choose the narrow path, and not the wide one.

As they continued their journey they would find two swords sharpening themselves. The swords would ask them to help them to become sharp. They were then to help and to go on with the journey, leaving the swords in their places.

* *Maasai Days*, Cheryl Bentsen, Collins, 1990.

Further on they would find fruit fallen from a tree which the prophet advised them to gather up and leave in a tidy heap. They were not to eat any of the fruit.

As the journey continued they would come to a stewing pot full of good meat which they must stir and then leave to cook, not eating anything themselves.

They would come to a settlement where they would meet a group of girls who would be smearing themselves in red ochre. The girls might invite them to join in with the smearing of the ochre and they could do this, but then they must leave the girls and continue the journey.

They would enter a forest in the rain, and must continue the journey, but very quietly.

They would find a manyatta which would run away from them. They were advised to be patient until the manyatta came to a halt, and they were then permitted to enter through the gate, to go into the home and to find a stool. The stool would run away and they must again be patient, until the stool came to a halt, and then they should sit on it. The family might ask them if they would like good or bad milk and they must request the bad milk. They would then be given the choice of sleeping in a good house, with good protection from the elements, or in a bad house, with holes in the walls and fleas. They should choose the bad house.

In the night time they might hear the sounds and feel the shaking of a thunderstorm. They should not be frightened.

The moran began the journey, following the advice of the prophet, but as they set off one of the moran broke a shoe and sat down to repair it. He asked his companions to wait for him, but none of them would do so. They all started the journey and left him alone.

The warrior repaired his shoe and then tried to follow the others, but when he reached a diversion in the path he remembered the advice of the prophet that he should follow the narrow path. He obeyed the prophet and went down the narrow path, meeting all the challenges along the way and following the advice of the prophet on every occasion.

Finally, he heard the thunderstorm and a sound of banging, as if someone was hitting the ground with his foot. He was called to come out of the house by an elder and was asked what he wished for. He anwered that he, a true Maasai, wished for cattle and goats. He was told to remove the branch used as a gate to the homestead. When he did so the cows came out in great numbers until he had to say that there were too many for him. He was asked to remove another branch and out came many goats and sheep. Finally. a third branch was removed and many calves came out. He was told to take all the animals to his own home as they were now his. On arriving home he met his brother who was amongst the big group of warriors who had not succeeded in their pilgrimage. They were astonished that he had so many animals whilst they had none. He offered to give them some of his animals and also explained how he got them.

His brother told him of his own journey with the others in the group, when they did not obey the prophet at any stage of the journey. At the end of the journey they were called out at the time of thunder and were asked what they wished for. They had replied that they wished for cows and goats. They were told to remove a branch and hundreds of hyenas came out. They were told to remove another branch and leopards came out, and when they removed a third branch they saw to their horror that they had released hundreds of lions, antelopes and zebras. They were told to take the animals away, but when they reached the bush some attacked them. Finally, all the animals ran away into the bush and the warriors were left alone.

SECTION FOUR

Meeting the Stranger

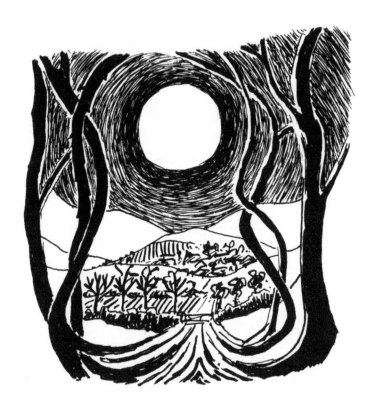

New Light
Jane Walton-Loxton

Introduction

Meeting strangers is at the heart of pilgrimage. The pilgrim leaves home, family and friends to go off through new places and to a new and uncertain destination and future. The exposure to strangers on journeys to new places leads to great uncertainty, vulnerability and even fear. Strangers may also be encountered at home, as visitors or newcomers. Sometimes they may be people who have been there for a long time, but have never been noticed.

Perhaps meeting the stranger is the most difficult challenge for the pilgrim because she or he is faced with the great risk that meeting may lead to humiliation, danger or even death, if trust is given and is misplaced. But it is often said that pilgrimage is about facing up to the difficult bits and not missing them out or going round them. The people along the way can never be missed out, or gone round. Meeting others is vital to pilgrimage, and if meeting is to take place, then the risks have to be taken. A new attitude can be worked for, which strips the pilgrim of prejudice and worry, of hostility and fear, and also of any feelings of superiority. Only then is it possible to accept the new person, as a guest or a host. Only then is it possible to learn to trust the other and to come to see the world in a new way, through the eyes of the person of another country, culture or faith.

The traveller to a new country, culture or faith can make encounter easier for herself or himself by living in the way of the 'strangers' along the way. There is little to learn and there are few people to meet in a tourist hotel or through the thick glass of a coach window. The pilgrim may arrange to live with people, in their families, and if that is for some reason impossible, to live in the accommodation the local people stay in, perhaps a local camp site or boarding house. There is no more valuable experience than staying with the 'stranger' and perhaps washing clothes and preparing food in the local conditions. The problems the people face throughout their lives are experienced, including local shortages of fuel, water and some types of food. The attractiveness of a new culture may be experienced rather than observed. The skills, recipes, customs, reflections and understandings of the new people may be shared and appreciated. Gradually, stories may be told and the enrichment of the new culture may become more obvious. Mutual kindness, generosity and understanding will be likely to grow, leading to enrichment and the appreciation of familiar places, even home, with new eyes and in a new way.

We have enjoyed many wonderful meals and hospitality, including the special sweets given out in a Calcutta slum, and a variety of tasty fish dishes in Sri Lanka and Japan. We travelled to visit a Muslim community in New Nubia, in Upper Egypt during the month of fasting, Ramadhan, with some trepidation, only to find a very warm welcome and a meal of scrambled egg, bread and jam. Nothing had ever tasted so delicious before. On one occasion, following a time of work in the desert area of north-western Kenya, we spent the whole day driving to a Maasai village. We knew the people were poor; we had taken sandwiches and water, and expected nothing. This was an injustice to our hosts, who produced the most delicious rice and barbecued goat we had ever tasted. On a visit to Christians in Tanzania we went to a remote village on the edge of Lake Langata to the east of Mount Kilimanjaro. The people were poor and ragged, and the village was covered in dust. There was a small primary school and a small stone church with wooden benches on the dusty floor of the bush. We were shown round the village and met many people. Finally, we were taken to a low stone-built room where the rough wooden tables were laid out with tin plates and mugs. We were all given delicious fried fish, from the lake, and chappatis made by some of the women that morning. It was easy to think of the time when Jesus was faced with the hungry people and was offered the loaves and fishes by the small boy.

The development of friendship can never be one-sided

but must be based on a recognition of equality, where all are givers and all are receivers. The stripping down of the pilgrim means the casting-off of the feeling that he or she represents something better. There are many sad stories of Western travellers going to developing situations and telling people how to run their lives. Sometimes people think that if they give money they have the right to give advice. This attitude gives far too much importance to money. The true pilgrim will be humble enough and open enough to discern the wealth of the 'stranger' who becomes the new friend, and to realise that this wealth may not be money at all, but a different way of living and working in the community. In Calcutta we were faced with people living in bustees or slums who had received Western visitors for years and had always felt that the visitors left them much worse than they found them because they 'told them what to do'. The Westerners knew best how to feed children and keep a home clean; they knew about education and development generally. The Calcutta bustee-dwellers were left feeling helpless and hopeless in the face of such expertise. No wonder the people wanted us to be patient, to listen and learn and share, so that when we went away the people would know they had enriched us and that we had shared together. They would also feel confidence because they had received and looked after visitors and had made new friends. We the pilgrims went away rejoicing in the new friendships, which have in fact lasted for many years now. We were blessed by seeing the world through the eyes of the residents of the Calcutta bustees.

Sometimes pilgrims go out to meet others with the belief that they have the only faith worth having, which they have to share with 'strangers' at all costs. This attitude makes it impossible for equal friendship and mutual learning to take place. It sometimes makes it impossible for any learning at all to take place by pilgrim or host.

Ronald Wynne is someone who is a good example of a man who was able to go to Africa as a pilgrim, recognising the value of the people he went to meet, including the value of their faith. Ronald worked with the Hambukushu people at Etsha by the Okavango River in Botswana. He lived with the people and learnt their language and culture, and gradually he became part of their community. He did not attempt to share his Christian faith during his first six years in Etsha, and when he did so he began with the Exodus story which the people themselves had endured in moving as refugees from Angola. After a few more years had passed Ronald shared the Christian Gospel with the people of Etsha, and what emerged was a new Church, of no Western denomination, but an African Church of the people, where offering to God was the offering of Africa and not a pale European imitation. Ronald said of his learning experiences in Etsha, 'One never goes to a place where God is absent.'

Ronald also said, 'Do not try to teach anyone anything until you have first learnt something from them.'*

Sometimes pilgrims are surprised by the richness of life and wisdom of the people and cultures they visit, and if they are honest they will admit this, and stop in their tracks, to listen and learn, as Ronald Wynne did, before they share anything. Many of our examples of people 'meeting the stranger' show them moving from trepidation to a guarded openness and on to joyful surprise as they learn just how much wisdom exists in people who are so different from themselves in culture, condition and even faith. The stories included in this section are mostly taken from Christians Aware visits and exchanges. Martin Dore's visit to East Timor was through Christian Solidarity Worldwide. The Halsons went to China with Friends of the Church in China. We include the story of the 'Silence' community, of disabled people with a 'real feeling of understanding and co-operation', and a visit to the Sri Ramakrishna ashram where wonderful work for the people is going on. We

---

* This saying by Ronald Wynne is used on Christians Aware literature, including the leaflets for international visits and exchanges.

include an interfaith young people's exchange when, although there were real cultural difficulties, the visitors were surprised by the level of education and the creativity of the young hosts, and the way religion is taken so seriously in India.

For the pilgrim to become part of the new place and community, no matter how fleetingly, it is very helpful if he or she is able to join in local community or work projects and to work alongside the people. Work provides a remarkable opportunity for human barriers to be broken down and for friendships to develop very quickly. We include some stories of work being done, in Kenya, Johannesburg and Tanzania. In Kenya the work we have previously been involved in has included the building of teachers' houses in the semi-desert area of Mukogodo, with Kenyan Christians and the local Maasai people, the building of a youth centre, a youth worker's house and an agricultural centre. Tree planting has been shared with local people in Kenya and in Tanzania. International work camps in Britain have included work with visitors to churches, a children's holiday camp in London, and farming, gardening and general help in a number of communities, including a village for disabled people.

Members of the major world faiths may cross continents to meet those of their own faith who actually may be strangers in every other way. This meeting may take place as members of a religion gather from all corners of the world at a particular holy site. We have seen that Muslims go to Mecca from every part of the Muslim world, and meet people from cultures and conditions they had only dreamed of, mostly to be inspired by sheer variety and numbers.

The Hindu gathering of the Kumbh Mela, which took place in January 2001, was said to be the biggest religious gathering in the history of humankind, with 25 million people attending on one day. The gathering takes place every 12 years where the three rivers – the Ganges, the Yamuna and the mythical Saraswati – converge in Allahabad. It is a purification ceremony, based on the story of Vishnu, who was carrying a pot of kumbh, or sacred nectar, when he got into a fight with the gods and four drops of nectar were spilled. There are melas every three years, at places where the drops of nectar were spilled, and the most important one is held at Allahabad every 12 years. Hindus go to Allahabad from India and from all over the world for the Kumbh Mela, including many from the UK who meet and bathe alongside holy men and hermits, often naked, who have come out from the caves and forests of India. The bathing is said to cleanse people of any wrongdoing.

Sometimes the faith which is shared may not easily be recognised in its strange clothes in a new country and culture. Sometimes the pilgrim in a world religion may travel to a new place to meet new friends of the same religion only to be faced with confusion and disorientation when he finds it difficult to recognise the faith he thought he had always known, because it is now clothed in a culture which is totally new and often unattractive to him. It is possible that an aspect of faith which the pilgrim had hardly considered, or which he thought had long fallen into disuse, is alive and very prominent in the new place with the new people. This encountering of the new, which is intrinsic to pilgrimage, is not necessarily an easy or pleasant experience.

However new the people met, of whatever faith or of none, there is always something to learn because we know that no person can be deemed outside God's love, grace and salvation, because all are created by God and have the spark of God in them. It is only by approaching others in the humble way of learning that meeting them at a deep level is possible. This meeting may lead not simply to personal enrichment and to a new awareness of other people, but also to a new awareness of God, and therefore to a new commitment to the development of all the people of God.

East Timor: Meeting Our Christian Brothers and Sisters

Martin Dore

East Timor does not feel dangerous. It feels a happy place. Smiles, waves, and 'Hello, Mister!' – wherever you go in East Timor there are scores of children, all friendly, all eager to greet you. It seems as if two-thirds of the population are under 25, though no one has any official statistics. There are children on the roadsides, children serving in the few restaurants, street children in gangs, and hundreds of children in church – they lead the beautiful singing, they are the servers and the sidesmen and women – they feel at home there. Every church service is full to overflowing. It is their church, which stood up for them in their darkest hour. Of course, some of them are tragically orphans, and the Roman Catholic sisters are doing a wonderful job looking after them. But also they are the hope for the future. Behind the smiles, of course, there is a hidden trauma: people have witnessed savage horrors which will haunt their dreams for years. Some wonderful trauma counselling is going on – we met Anna-Paula from Fokupers (supported by Oxfam) – but the hidden problem is far larger than their resources. I am hoping to enlist the aid of the Medical Foundation for Victims of Torture,* who can provide training. The people of Timor certainly need our prayers.

I was there with Christian Solidarity Worldwide† to find out how we could help. But the highlight of my visit was to meet the former 'prisoners of conscience' I had been writing to and supporting for years in their jail in Semarang (Java) –

* Medical Foundation for the Victims of Torture helps those who have suffered to recover their humanity.
† Christian Solidarity Worldwide is a campaigning organisation for those who suffer human rights abuses.

Gregorio da Cunha Saidanha, and my own great friend, Francisco Branco. I was able to bring them both hundreds of cards from supporters in the UK, and much needed financial aid (after-care) from the International Secretariat of Amnesty International.* At the end of each letter, Francisco always wrote, 'a big hug to you'. Can you imagine the great hug we gave each other when we finally met? But that was nothing to the joy of meeting his wife and seven children (aged 9 to 23), all of whom, wonderfully, escaped the violence, hiding in a convent and then in the hills above Dili. I was able to give them each a card (a dove of peace – each one different) and a personal present. Francisco's wife, Ermelinda, received a card with seven doves! We had them all back to our modest hotel for a special meal on the last day. It was then that the older boys mentioned some familiar names to me – David Beckham, Paul Scholes, Michael Owen! – and the girls mentioned names like Ricky Martin!

Of course, we could never forget the terrible destruction we saw in Dili (70 per cent of the houses burnt), and as yet nothing has been rebuilt. The promised money and materials are taking so long to get there; and over 80 per cent of the people are unemployed. But we did see a lot of re-roofing in the Liquica area. The UN and international agencies are all there in Dili with their huge four-wheel-drive vehicles, but it's clear that most of the Timorese NGOs have no transport – not even a car for the only East Timorese surgeon.

We were able to bring 400 kilos of aid (donated by generous Australians and flown in free of charge by Air North). We met some wonderful people like Sister Lourdes, working with 'village-motivators' and catechists (mostly young women) in primary health care and literacy, who fed 15,000 refugees for weeks in September. And we were privileged to be able to give some financial help to Father Raphael, the brave local

---

* Amnesty International campaigns for those who are wrongly imprisoned and who suffer other abuses.

priest in Liquica who told the world the truth of the April massacre of refugees camping by his church.

We found him organising a meeting of hundreds of local people to start a foundation for the East Timorese students whose higher education courses in Indonesia have been abruptly terminated. This is a major problem. Where are students like Francisco's two eldest sons to go to complete their studies? They speak Indonesian and Portuguese. Who will pay for their fees and provide them with a degree course? Surely we in the rest of the world must help? These courageous people are having to build their nation from scratch, with help from the UN. Ninety-five per cent of them are Christians. Of one thing I am utterly certain: they do not want to be forgotten again. They are so grateful to have a country which is now free after 25 years of terror. But they also deeply need our love, our prayers, and our help.

Silence

Silence is an organisation, based in Calcutta, which speaks
for some who, being deaf and mute, can neither speak nor
hear. It stands for others who, being physically handicapped,
can neither stand nor move freely. It therefore provides its
participants with a steady monthly income. We visited the
office, the factory and the outlet, which meant we got an
overall view, following in the footsteps of many Christians
Aware groups. Silence employs disabled people, especially
deaf people (90 per cent of the staff are profoundly deaf). I was
interested to find that there was no teaching of an accepted sign
language, but the workers evolved certain body language and
domestic signs to communicate with each other. The factory was
a three-storey building where hand-painted cards, perfumed
candles, incense sticks and jewellery were produced. The cards
were produced by screen printing and then hand-painted,
although some were freely painted. On the first floor candles
were produced with wax from a large cauldron which was
poured into various moulds. About a dozen men worked on
candle production but any employee could be used in any
department as occasion demanded. The lack of chat was
noticeable in the workshop. 'We are called Silence,' the guide
reminded us. We went upstairs again where women and men
were producing greetings cards, and to another room where
women assembled camel-bone necklaces. In yet another room
men were making the wooden boxes to hold candles. Silent it
was, but there was a real feeling of co-operation and understanding. So to the shop – an Aladdin's cave of jewellery,
candles, incense sticks and gifts of all shapes and sizes. Silence
ran the shop and all their products were on sale but they also
sold things from other similar sources, thus saving on rent as
well as showing solidarity with other ventures. Look for
Silence products on Oxfam or Traidcraft stalls! The Christians
Aware office has the hand-painted cards. Silence employs 72

artisans and after their training Silence encourages them to be placed in stable commercial houses so that new and untrained persons can be brought under its care and guidance.

Sri Ramakrishna Ashram

The furthest point from Calcutta that we visited was the Sri Ramakrishna Ashram, about three hours' journey from our guest house. We were met by the President, Sri Tulsidas Kanaria, and duly transferred to his well-appointed 'people carrier'. Having passed through the Indian countryside with many villages and paddy fields, we arrived and were first shown the mother and baby unit, being allowed to hold a newborn baby and shown the modern-looking operating theatre and two shiny ambulances to fetch pregnant women to the antenatal clinics or for the births. A visit to the ashram site and a talk by the principal told us of its beginnings in 1961 to devote itself to offering its services to the hapless and hopeless and to bring them to God. Beginning with poverty alleviation programmes, education became the priority, and there are now eleven educational institutes under ashram management with 500 girls and boys receiving elementary and vocational training, housed in hostels on site. We visited the community hall being built to provide a centre for cultural and (one assumes) political activities for the area. As well as schools and hostels, an important part of the whole was the agricultural production in the Eastern Delta region – for example, mushrooms grown for home consumption as part of an on-going nutrition programme, and the development of state-wide markets. The work is closely linked to the needs of local farmers. 'What do you want?' and 'Can we give it?' were the motives. New banana tissues were tested in the labs and the new little plants were hardened off before being put out in field experiments. Local shellfish were also part of the on-going programme, as well as the growing of lemon grass and experiments with green manure from the algae on the ponds (they are full of nitrogen). The hope was eventually to introduce appropriate flora and fauna on some of the islands in the Delta. The lasting impression of this vocational school was the high standard demanded. 'It must be professional experiment,' they insisted, and yet it was earthed to local needs, and local young people were given hands-on training. Apart from the excellent work going on, I was impressed by the venerated founder of the ashram and the love and respect for him. People were honoured to do the work he had started more than 20 years ago and determined that it would carry on. They shared their expertise with scientists from Germany and Israel.

Oil Painting of a South Indian Village
Jyoti Sahi

Visit to South India

Barbara Tyas

David, Jacqui and I embarked on this three-week visit to village, town and city in South India with Christians Aware. All our travel was by bus, train or auto rickshaw, and we tramped miles by foot, getting to know the towns and cities. The visit was very enriching and we were challenged to rethink any conceptions we may have held. We had opportunity to observe and to experience some aspects of the life of India. It is not possible to claim any real understanding of how it is for Indian people. The complexities of culture, language, social and economic make up, and religion present differences which we can only observe and attempt to understand. It would demean the life and struggles of the people to claim any inside understanding of what life is like for them.

From Mumbai (Bombay) we travelled south on the overnight train to Calicut, where we were met by Sri Radhakrishna Memon, taken by jeep to meet his family at Navodaya Danagram in Malappuram District, and welcomed as their guests for the following three days. Our time there was extremely interesting and an opportunity to see the development of a Gandhian project at first hand.

Radhakrishna Memon has spent almost 30 years in developing the Gandhian ideal of people empowerment; he had the vision of setting up a self-help project for Indian people who were homeless or limited in educational opportunities. During the Land Gift Programme, when the government encouraged landowners to gift virgin land for the development of self-sufficient living, Radhakrishna left his job as headteacher of a local school to become the leader of the project. Now there are approximately 65 families living in community-owned homes. Self-interest is the antipathy of community, and people are not encouraged to have this attitude. The only way for the community to survive is to be aware of the needs of the community, and to pull together for the benefit of. all.

This village is a member of the Kerala Grama Nirmane Samithy, a society registered in 1986. Its aim is 'the establishment of an egalitarian social order based on truth and non-violence, inspired by human and democratic values, free from exploitation, injustice and oppression, affording full opportunity for the development of human personality.' Such integrated development of individual and society becomes possible only in a decentralised system of politics and economics, comprising face-to-face self-sufficient co-operative village republics which Gandhi termed 'Grama Swaraj' – village self-rule.

The basic character of the Samithy is that of a sardovaya organisation dedicated to social change for justice through non-violence. The Gandhian four-fold programme of the movement has been set out as the basic guideline of their activities, as explained to us by Radhakrishna.

1. Idea/Vision – spread of ideas
2. Organisation – of appropriate organisations of people power
3. Construction (work) – in the social, political and economic areas of the citizen's life
4. Confrontation – looking at the result and confronting problems along the way

Self-help groups are thriving in Navodaya Danagram. A banking and loan system operates, both for adults and children; the village produces bananas, coconut, jack fruit, cashew nut (which generate a good income on the market), turmeric, pepper, mango, sweet potato. The coconut produces milk, and fibre for jute and rope making and baskets. There are also various local registered organisations engaged in integrated rural development activities. The small weaving shed produces and dyes cotton; makes soap, and sells honey. Granite is quarried for walls and wells. There is an adult education centre, teacher training school, nursery school and creche; to name some of the achievements and developments.

During our stay we were privileged to participate in Republic Day on 26 January. Village members congregated on the village compound, standing in open square formation, in preparation for the ceremony of raising the Indian flag, led by a young teacher, trained at the village college, and now teaching in a local school. All those assembled sang 'We shall overcome' which was very moving. The women sang in Malayalam, the local dialect, and prayers were said. It is traditional for a 'work hour' after the ceremony, and the aim this year was to work on the water development project, the government scheme for providing water to the village. The well area was approximately 60 feet square, 15 feet deep to clay level, and built by the villagers using granite blocks. The task was to deepen the well. The young men climbed into the bottom, filled up pan trays of clay, climbed up and passed them up to those of us standing at the top; a human chain system deposited the clay, and passed the trays back to the beginning. This was very efficient and very hard work. At the end of the hour we all shared a meal of curry served on a banana leaf.

Each evening we shared prayer time before the worship area in their home. On a small table were religious artefacts and symbols, including Buddha, Shiva, Ganesh, Jesus on the cross, and Hanuman. Songs shared were 'Lead, kindly light', 'Give me oil in my lamp', 'Be still and know', and we always ended this prayer time with 'Aum . . . shanti, shanti, shanti'. It was a very special and moving time together.

From here we were taken by jeep to another project in Wyaned inspired by Gandhi's philosophy. This provided a range of appropriate services and training needs for different groups of people, some of whom had learning difficulties.

We left here on an early morning bus for a six-hour journey to Bangalore, our base being the United Theological College.

This was an opportunity to experience a very noisy and crowded city, visit Hindu places of worship, see the religious and cultural artefacts in the museum, and learn about the history of the Sultan's Palace.

Our stay at the Vellore Christian Counselling Centre provided a wonderful opportunity to meet students on an eight-week course. They came from all over India, representing a wide range of professional environments, work with street children, drug dependants, youth and school groups, health projects, and families living in extreme poverty. We were very impressed with their professionalism, commitment and Christian witness. At the Christian Hospital and Christian Medical College in Vellore we were given a brief tour and an opportunity to meet with a chaplain to hear about his work in this busy modern hospital. It was an inspiration to see a hospital and medical college of international repute which had grown from one woman's Christian witness of 100 years ago, that of Doctor Ida Scudder. She responded to the call of God, not without resistance, to begin a ministry to the health needs of the people of India, particularly women and children, and CMC now offers 90 recognised training programmes in medical, nursing and allied health fields.

Three days in Chennai (Madras) were very positive, largely due to the coincidence of the consecration ceremony of Sri Ramakrishna Temple in Mylapore attended by over 30,000 devotees from all over India.

'Religious Harmony Day' representatives of the Neo-Vedantic, Jain, Buddhist, Sikh, Christian, Islamic and Hindu faiths gave a 15-minute presentation on their religious perspectives, and ways forward to a peaceful and tolerant multi-faith India. This made us think about our role as Christians, representing both Christians Aware and our home communities, in furthering this vision.

Each day of our three weeks was enriching, stimulating, humbling and challenging. We were so aware of our worship of consumerism in the West. We have so much to learn about human values, compassion, tolerance, helping those less fortunate than ourselves, self-sufficiency, and acceptance of our fellow beings.

From the Christian Medical College, I end with this quotation: 'If we would learn to fear the Lord, if we would strive to keep his word, our neighbour's good would always be of great concern to you and me.'

China Pilgrimage

Bryan and Bernice Halson

Our three-week visit to China was so full that all we can do is give you a few impressions. We went with a party of 17 with Friends of the Church in China. The purpose of the visit was to see some of the work of the Amity Foundation.* Our visit took us to central and southwest China.

It was a journey of contrasts. In the cities there seemed to be building going on everywhere, with wide main streets lined with modern shops, banks and offices, throngs of well-dressed people and bicycles in droves. The side streets were quite different – narrow, full of stalls selling everything imaginable from live chickens to second-hand doors and window-frames; people cooking and eating outside their shop fronts, women working sewing machines, men repairing bicycles or working (unprotected) with oxy-acetylene welders. Each journey to a mountain village was an adventure in itself, as we negotiated rough tracks, hairpin bends and streams. On one occasion two of our four-wheel-drive vehicles sank in mud up to the axles. All this went along with spectacular scenery of great beauty and wonderful glimpses of 'country life' – mile upon mile of terraced fields (rice arid maize), water buffalo pulling ploughs or wallowing in muddy pools, black pigs snoozing in the sun or running in a squealing herd ahead of our vehicles.

But the deepest and most lasting impressions came from the Chinese people we met. The projects which Amity funds are designed and proposed by the 'recipient' themselves and they are nearly always involved. This encourages an

* The only all-Chinese non-government organisation, begun by Christians in 1984. Its work is to plan, monitor and help fund projects in the fields of medical, educational, church social work and rural development projects.

independence of mind and self-confidence which is impressive. One mountain village had supplied the labour to bring electricity to their village over 22 kilometres of steep mountains and deep valleys. This village was inhabited by people of one of the (many) minority ethnic groups, noted for their colourful costume and magnificent choral singing. (Ten villages were electrified.)

We will not soon forget the welcome from the people. As we came into view of the villagers gathered on the mountainside (after four hours on very rough roads), we heard firecrackers bursting. When we alighted, musical instruments accompanied their singing as we made our way along the path leading to the largest building, the church. The folk had strewn pine needles (eight inches long) along the path and into the courtyard – their way of honouring guests. Some broke 'file' to give us a hug. Inside the church, the floor had also been strewn with the long fragrant pines and when we squatted at low tables for a meal the fresh needles served as tablecloth. The people had been preparing food for two days – unusual local fare. Greetings, speeches, singing and exchange of gifts were always part of every visit.

The Amity officials likewise made a deep impression on us – dedicated to their work whilst in receipt of salaries considerably below what they could command in business or professional fields. We had interesting meetings with local government officials too, from the Government Religious Affairs Bureau and the Foreign Affairs Bureau. We were surprised at their positive attitude to the churches and their co-operation (financial) with Amity projects. They now recognise that some rural development projects might serve as a model for the government's own work.

Another major experience was of lively and expanding churches. On several occasions we met congregations who had pulled down their old church building and were building bigger ones to accommodate larger numbers now flocking to services. Bryan preached to a congregation of 1000 at a service in which 100 adults were baptised. The service was held in a tent because there was no building big enough to hold all the people. It was inspiring to experience the union of all the old Protestant denominations into one church – the Three Self Patriotic Church (self-governing, self-propagating, self-supporting) – no longer a 'missionary' church but an indigenous Chinese Church from which we have much to learn. We learnt so much from the people on this visit. We feel very inspired.

Journey to the Philippines

Paul Weary

In April my family visited the Philippines – myself, my wife Mary Ann and our children Sophia and Nathaniel. It was ten years since I had travelled to the Philippines, although Mary Ann, who is a Filipina, had been home more recently. Our excuse for going was a cousin's wedding and we were looking forward to the family reunion which would inevitably follow. The wedding was to be held on 2 May. It transpired that this would be a busy weekend, for 1 May (a public holiday in the Philippines) was the anniversary of the Methodist Church in Mary Ann's home village of San Simon. Apparently I was to be the guest preacher for the occasion. This sowed the germ of an idea, that we might use the visit to explore the possibility of a 'twinning' arrangement with one of my churches in Croydon. What was supposed to be a vacation was rapidly turning into a busman's holiday.

One becomes aware of the realities of Philippine life even before reaching the country. Travelling via Dubai, the plane on the second leg of our journey was packed with overseas contract workers returning home from various parts of the Middle East. Many were carrying hi-fis, computer games, even televisions – the fruits of their labours in Saudi Arabia, the UAE and further afield. For all, this was a welcome return home to friends and family, though many must have been worried about their future prospects in a country where unemployment is high.

After spending a couple of days with an aunt in Manila, we set off for San Simon, a rural community on the bank of the Pampanga river, some 60 kilometres north of the capital. The river gives its name to the province, a mainly flat, rice-growing area. Crossed by the main road north out of Manila, Pampanga has attracted some industry, not always of benefit to local communities. As we sat in the back yard of an uncle's house overlooking the river, we were reminded that a generation ago it had been possible to swim across the river. Now nobody would bathe because of the pollution from factories upstream. For a community reliant on water for supplying fish farms and irrigating rice fields, this was a great concern, and twice after crops were poisoned by dirty water local farmers had taken matters in their own hands by attempting to burn down an offending brewery. But now it seemed that even local people had given up on the river, for the banks were strewn with household rubbish.

San Simon is typical of many small towns in the Philippines. Roads are in an appalling state, occasionally relieved by stretches of concrete which suddenly end, indicating that the money ran out or was purloined by some corrupt official. The area is prone to flooding, and traditionally houses are built on stilts. Old houses built of wood and thatched with palm leaves sit uncomfortably next to modern constructions of concrete and steel, often indicating a family that has members living or working overseas. Gardens and yards contain flowering shrubs familiar in Britain as houseplants, and all but the poorest families find room for a coconut, banana or mango tree.

Most of Mary Ann's family are members of the United Methodist Church. In 1898 the USA invaded the Philippines, putting an end to a short-lived revolutionary republic. With the Americans came Protestant missionaries. The church in San Simon was one of the earliest, and this year celebrated its 95th anniversary. When I had last visited, we worshipped in a tiny chapel, but the foundations of a larger building had been laid next door. Now this new church is largely complete but there is still much work to do internally. The old chapel is used for a kindergarten and Sunday school.

While still in Britain I had been given the text for the anniversary service – Nehemiah chapter 1, in which Nehemiah hears of the ruinous state of the walls of Jerusalem and determines to rebuild them. I decided to preach on the subject of 'walls'. Walls are important, for they offer strength and security and shelter, yet they can become a danger to the Christian community, for they can become a barrier, dividing the church from the world. I was gifted with a perfect illustration when I was shown around the church grounds, for behind the church (and overlooking the river) a large nipa hut has been built, of bamboo, wood and palm leaves. The walls are reduced to uprights supporting the roof. A pleasant breeze blew through the building. I was immediately reminded of the prayer that asks that we might be 'a church with open doors and large windows, a church which takes the world seriously'. What a beautiful model of the church! A place where people inside can look out and people outside can look in. A holy place, yet totally part of the world in which it is set.

In fact, Filipino Christianity is not as hidebound by a division between church/world, sacred/secular as we in the West. One Filipino pastor has written, 'In contrast to the Westerner who is conscious of, and often even obsessed with, boundaries, the Filipino is spaceless. His sense of space is not contained nor limited by artificial divisions. His diffused sense of space makes him extend his parties, stores, shops and he even wakes to the streets. He dries palay [rice grains] on roads and highways, chats, cooks, eats, even sleeps on streets and sidewalks. He practises his religion and he prays, repents, mourns and celebrates anywhere . . . What has the West done to Christianity? The West, with its obsession with taxonomy, classification and division, spatially divided the Church from the world and bound it within four walls. Like salt within the salt-shaker, the Church prayed, sang, taught, worshipped within four walls, and, in a sense, lost its power of saltiness. We should note that while the Catholic Church also put the church within walls, it nevertheless never lacked in street processions, outdoor extravaganzas and community-based celebrations and rituals.'*

On the day of the anniversary it was very hot, and to make

* Ed Lapiz, *Becoming a Filipino Christian*. Makati City: Kaloob, 1997.

matters worse, there was a power cut so the fans were not working. But the people would not let that spoil their day. The windows were thrown wide open, as were the doors, to welcome the inevitable latecomer. The service was occasionally interrupted by the sound of children playing outside, a cockerel crowing, or a motor-tricycle putt-putting along the bumpy street. It didn't really matter, because it also meant that those passing by were also aware of the celebration taking place within the church. After the service we shared lunch, sitting in the shade of the nipa hut.

A church with 'open doors and large windows'. This is a challenge for Christians in Britain, for we are so used to building up walls and sheltering behind them. We need to rediscover what it means to be truly hospitable; to be open to our world and to our neighbours. How can we develop this openness, so that even our minds have open doors and our hearts large windows? This is one of the reasons for setting up the twinning arrangement between Christ Church Methodist in Croydon and Covenant UMC in San Simon. We are seeking ways of involving all parts of our respective church communities, from the youngest to the oldest, and my prayer is that others might appreciate the rich resources of spirituality, faith and wisdom that I have discovered amongst Methodist Christians in the Philippines.

Work Camps in Kenya

Working with Children

We were five students who went to work with the Diocese of Mount Kenya South, with Timothy Ranji and Charles Muturi. We have known both Timothy and Charles for many years now.

When we stepped on to land in Kenya it was the beginning of many amazing experiences. Initially we went to work in nursery schools. We also got involved in many other aspects of Kenyan life. We worked in two different orphanages. There were 250 children, many with special needs. Our duties ranged from playing, teaching, feeding, changing nappies and, most importantly, loving these very special boys and girls.

We went to an orphanage for 63 youngsters who were HIV positive. Instantly we were almost overwhelmed by the cheerfulness and love the children showed, not only to us but also to each other. In fact, they were the happiest children we have ever encountered. Our teacher roles were carried out in nurseries and primary schools, and at one point we found ourselves teaching about AIDS prevention to 17- to 19-year-olds. The vast majority of schools were equipped at a very basic level, and yet the pupils' morale was high. The subjects we taught ranged from English to RE, Geography, PE, Drama and Music. It's amazing what can be produced when necessary. Having 50 pupils in a class became completely normal to us. Even the time factor became part of our daily routine. We started school at 8am and ended at 5pm. We learnt to teach without preparation.

Unknown to us, construction of toilets was the next thing on our agenda. This is one of the things that doesn't naturally equate with British women – but hey – why not! Hammers, chisels and saws were all at the ready, as were many young men! Some of us found that we were naturals, whilst others were better as an audience. This work gave us the thirst for more hands-on tasks. When the opportunity arose for transforming a rubbish tip into a flower garden, we jumped at the chance.

One event which will always stay in our minds is the party we organised for street children. At first we were all slightly apprehensive about mixing with those whom society has so sadly rejected. However, we soon warmed to the 15- and 16-year-old boys, and many games of frizbee and football followed. Afterwards out came the sodas, loaves of bread and sweets. The party atmosphere was enhanced by lots of balloons. When they were leaving the boys said, 'We feel this is as joyful as our wedding day.'

In many of the experiences we had, the communities became a unity. Now, back in Britain, we realise more than ever how vital it is to keep the link and enormous sense of love with our African brothers and sisters.

Water in Mount Kenya West

David Jones travelled with Rachel, Ian and Jessica to the Diocese of Mount Kenya West to work with very old friends in the diocese where Alfred Chipman is bishop and Godfrey Ngungire is development adviser. Simon Mugwimi is the youth organiser who coordinated the hosting arrangements and work camp. David has written about the experiences.

The camp was out in the semi-desert Mukogodo area of Kenya, in the North West, at the Oloborsoit Centre, where water has been very badly needed. The aim of the camp, which lasted for 10 days, was to put in pipes from the Kimanjo borehole to Oloborsoit and this was accomplished. Some extra work has had to be done, to strengthen the pipes.

After the work camp, the group went for family visits. David went to Karatina where he saw a new dispensary, large and lined with tinfoil, to protect the medicines.

The group travelled on safari together, with Kenyan friends. They visited Thompson Falls, Lake Nakuru National Park, the animal orphanage, the giraffe centre and 'bomas of Kenya'. They also hiked up Mount Longonot.

Nine Months in Johannesburg

Rachel Stephens

In 1999 I had a wonderful experience and opportunity in Johannesburg. It felt as if everything I had done before in my life was a preparation for these nine short months.

My mornings were spent on the sixteenth floor of the civic centre with a panoramic view of the city, as part of the Tourism and Marketing Department. I was trying to develop the priority projects for town twinning. One contribution was introducing people working in the same field to others they had never met. For example, there were people involved in designing and building low-cost, environmentally friendly housing.* There are about 10 different groups, including the design students, trying to find the cheapest acceptable building material. Some say mud brick is best but that is not acceptable to many people, while expanded polystyrene is not ecologically friendly. How does one get away from the expensive concrete blocks? Habitat self-build versus government mass build is another heated controversy.

From facilitating the visit of the chief librarian in May, linking the Wits University Schools Partnership with British Council staff and provincial education officers, to meeting the museum staff and environmental enthusiasts, there were so many new contacts.

Afternoons in the IMPACT (Community Volunteers Serving South Africa) office in downtown Marshall Street, brought me down to earth!† I met five young South Africans who had been volunteers in UK. Eva is training for occupational therapy, Anna is in charge of a women's refuge, Dliswa is

---

* Habitat for Humanity is a charity which enables the building of houses at low cost.

† IMPACT is an organisation that started in the Methodist Church.

159

a trainer for the correctional services, Faith is training for ministry, Zech runs a youth club. My task there, apart from helping generally to boost morale, was to find volunteer placements and to raise funds for the volunteers. There are now 60 volunteers in post.

I also helped to build a house in Soweto. I appeared on South African TV, arranged for 29 visitors to Johannesburg, was a marshall for a human rights day parade, had breakfast once a month with the bishops and was part of an ordinary Methodist congregation.

I returned to Johannesburg, after time in UK, in November 1999 for a further three months to develop the Birmingham/ Johannesburg City Link and to work with IMPACT.

Borders and Binoculars

Inderjit Bhogal

Binoculars to my eyes, from a hideout, I looked over the India-Pakistan border at Khem Karan in Punjab. I could see people, though I could not make out their features. An odd experience. Most of my neighbours in Pitsmoor, Sheffield, are of Pakistani origin.

At the Wagha border point near Amritsar, a spectacular Indian and Pakistani military performance shows how strongly borders are preserved and defended. Where there are gates, there are gatekeepers to hinder or allow a carefully observed and monitored crossing. Some of our group crossed the border and stepped into Pakistan briefly under the watchful eye of the gatekeepers.

The India-Pakistan border was drawn in just 36 days in August 1947 by Sir Cyril Radcliffe without travelling anywhere near the area.

The border area is very beautiful. It includes Kashmir, Punjab and Kutch, and remains a matter of dispute to this day. Hindus, Muslims, Sikhs and Christians live in uneasy tension. The testing of nuclear weapons recently by India and Pakistan has heightened tension.

A visit to India had been on our family agenda for 15 years. Kenneth Wilson heard me talking about this, and the result was that we and 26 others made the journey. It became an opportunity to join the President of the Methodist Conference on a Pilgrimage – 'A Christian Exploration of the Sikh Faith in India'.

Some members of the group had been to India or Pakistan before. For others it was a whole new experience. For all of us it was a unique experience in which we explored borders and boundaries, not least in terms of faith and spirituality.

India has a population of one billion, and offered us a

million images each day. The population increases by 18 million each year. It is not easy to get away from people and sound. Yet the gift of India is the art of solitude and deep inner stillness in the midst of crowds and noise.

We visited the Taj Mahal, a marble monument to love. Rabindranath Tagore defined it as 'a tear on the face of eternity' that echoes the cry 'I have not forgotten, I have not forgotten, O beloved' (The Flight of Swans). The Taj evokes love and romance. There is an interplay of the boundaries of dreams, fantasies, realities, pain and pleasure here.

We spent time in the bustling city of Delhi, but India lives in villages. There is breathing space in villages. The fields are green, water supply is plentiful. India is fed from the food grown by the villagers of Punjab. We glimpsed something of this when we visited the villages my mother and father hail from, Dhanowali and Kotli Than Singh. In Kotli we were welcomed and fed by some of my relatives. The village has grown considerably since I was last there; it is practically a small town. In another place I enjoyed milking the cows and buffaloes. We noted that animal feed is a fresh, green supply of fodder.

We travelled to Amritsar, the second largest town in Punjab, and the home of Harmandir Sahib, or the Golden Temple, the holiest Sikh shrine.

Thirteen members of the group visited the Golden Temple for prayer in the 'ambrosial hours' of the morning, between 3am and 6am. A procession brings the holy scriptures, the Guru Granth Sahib, into Harmandir Sabib which is surrounded by a large pool of holy water. A constant flow of pilgrims follows the route of the procession to pay homage, to worship, to make offerings and receive Kara Prashad (sacrament). It is an inspiration to observe people of all ages, including infants, make this prayer pilgrimage while it is yet dark. I reflected that the practice of prayer early in the morning is part of Methodist heritage.

In the daylight hours we visited Jalianwala Bagh, the site

of the most brutal massacre which took place under the command of General Dyer in 1919. This visit was a painful experience for our group, bringing most to tears.

The whole group spent time together at the Golden Temple, and accompanied me when I met the Supreme Sikh Leader, Mr Joginder Singh, known as 'the Jathedar'. He stated the core of Sikhism and the challenges facing Sikhism. I asked him to comment on Christian perspectives like Jesus is God Incarnate, Jesus is uniquely the Son of God, and the words attributed to Jesus in John: 'no one comes to the Father but by me.' He stated his view without in any way ridiculing or undermining the views of Christians. There were about 50 people, including the Bishop of Amritsar, the Rt Revd Samantaroy, in the room when this conversation took place. I felt exhilarated and exhausted after this engagement. The meeting had been organised by Daniel Das, a Church of North India layworker whom I met when he came to study at Kingsmead College in Birmingham in 1982.

The next day we went to Baring College, Batala, where Prof Clarence McMullen has developed a resource for Sikh-Christian dialogue. He and Daniel Das had organised a day conference for us on 'The Status of Women in Religion: Theory and Practice'. The conference began with prayers led by representatives of different faiths, including me. The speakers were three women and three men, including the vice-president. The conference provided a useful platform to share insights from different faiths. There was heated debate over the view that there is an in-built bias against women in all faiths. The final statement of the conference recognised that gender bias and oppression of women has been sanctioned by all religious traditions, and that there is a need to stand in solidarity with each other as women and men. All faiths, in theory, call for equality of women and men. It is in the practice that there is inequality.

In all these experiences, we stood on many frontiers with people from different backgrounds. The boundaries that we explored have, in many cases, been drawn by others, on our behalf from a distance. The India visit demonstrated the need for us to stop peering across divides through binoculars from distant spaces. We need to meet face to face, flesh to flesh. Such encounters can be costly, not least in terms of time and effort, but can be enriching.

Borders have a place. Where we have invitation and opportunity to cross them, we are beckoned to travel a little further on journeys of exploration. When we meet as good neighbours we do not need binoculars.

This article was first published by Penistone Publications in *Theology on the Hoof.*

An Interfaith Visit to India

Carrie Seaton

'This is India' became the catchphrase. It calmed away all the frustrations and complexities, as if it could make sense of a 'love with no illusions' relationship with a country. This was a pioneering venture with Christians Aware, to Rajkot in Gujarat, where Leicester had already been forging links, via education. We were a group of six, three of us Christian, including a young man who is culturally Jewish, and three young people of the Hindu faith.

We flew from Heathrow on 23 March, with an overnight stay in Bombay. India is always a culture shock after Western living, even for the three Gujarati team members who, having been born in Uganda, had never lived in their motherland. All its ambiguities and our expectations were jumbled up with the wonderful people, food and sights. The heat was hot! It reached 45 degrees some days, and meant we tired easily, needing to sleep most afternoons. This resulted in us having to be flexible with our itinerary, but flexibility is never a problem in India. Our hosts had devised a very ambitious schedule of visits, morning and afternoon, with a different host family to eat and stay with each night. After two days we had to ask for more space – not least to prepare for our evening youth programmes.

The hospitality we received was wonderful, and co-ordinated by Janardanbhai Pandya, project leader of the Balbhavan Youth Centre in Rajkot. We were accompanied by a team leader, and Kroopa, an amazing woman who had taken leave from her English teaching to ensure we got to the right place at the right time. She stayed with us every day and saw that we had all we needed. (This included medicines, and two unscheduled visits to the hospital.) The Balbhavan Centre is a project for young people to develop their skills through cultural, artistic and technological expression. We used youth work methods including ice breakers, brainstorming and small group work, which was new to them. The girls especially were strikingly self-confident, in a culture where women are expected to have a particular 'place'. Both the boys and girls portrayed a deep and faithful love of India, expounding values, hopes and dreams that would sit uneasily on the lips of many cynical British youngsters. Most were Hindus from various denominations, and others were of the Sikh, Muslim or Jain faiths.

At first there was plenty of anger expressed against anything British. It was evident that the legacy of colonialism had burned deeply. Two hundred and fifty years of outside rule cannot be erased in 50 years. However, a few others were saying, 'Wait a minute, there were some positive aspects – the British gave us the railways, sanitation.' I remembered with a chuckle the scene in the film *The Life of Brian* and the famous question: 'What have the Romans ever done for us?'

Religion is taken very seriously in India. The Indian young people were shocked to hear that Christians were a small minority in England. They had the understanding that all white people were Christians – presumably because the ones who visited previously were missionaries. There was an interesting session where we asked the groups to write down words to describe God. The results showed that the majority could be included in all the religions represented. One brave boy tentatively suggested 'mother', and the giggly and nervous reaction did not seem very far from a supposed response of a group of Christians at home. As we grew more familiar with each other's culture and religion, we discussed our differences with sensitivity. We rejoiced at our similarities and recognised the global need for peace and understanding through learning and by valuing and validating each other's faith journey.

For the rest of our time we were kept busy and in the spotlight, and often on the receiving end of a microphone or a camera. As 'relaxation' for the first two days we were taken to the zoo and to a village museum/rural heritage centre. We visited the Saurastm University where we had a meeting with the principal, and even the voluntary blood bank. We asked to spend an evening in the slums, which turned out to be a very noisy and crowded experience, where we were treated like royal guests, to our embarrassment.

The planned visits to two different schools impressed us greatly. As we arrived at the first, we were surprised to find a long line of uniformed children waiting outside. They were there to greet us, with some slightly older children in khaki, carrying sticks to 'discipline' the other pupils. Each tiny classroom had been cleared to display the children's work. The director had bought the building and devoted his life to the school with his wife, the headmistress. He charged low fees, and used integrated and practical teaching methods. The second school made even more of a fuss of us, and treated us to a cultural programme. In a hot, tiny room, almost the whole school began by singing, unaccompanied and with eyes shut, a Hindu song in praise of Krishna. The devotion on their faces was awesome, not one childish giggle or snigger. After the programme of Indian dance and music, Amit and I spoke of our hopes for the youth exchange. The pupils were then allowed to ask questions of the whole group, mainly about life in England and Christian festivals, particularly Easter. This school, taking children from all castes, and from the Dalit community, was cleaned from top to bottom for our benefit, and flower-petal pictures laid out painstakingly on the floor all done by the girls and boys themselves.

Numerous visits to places of worship and religious centres became highlights of our trip. We visited the Shree Rama Krishna Ashram and talked with the Swami, before seeing the gallery of paintings, and information on the denomination. That same afternoon we spent a long time in the Jain Girish Myni, listening to the guru and the saints. We even had a few strands of hair pulled out! (The women had this done by women saints, of course, sitting away from the men – it was unbelievably painless.) The day after, we went to the beautiful newly built Nariya Temple. There were mixed feelings within the group about this, as only the men were invited to meet with the swamis of this denomination. The women had to remain outside because the monks live secluded lives and are forbidden from seeing women, to retain their purity. (You may be able to imagine my thoughts on this!) The spectacular ceremony in the main part of the temple, after the deities were dressed, was vibrant in sight and sound. The men in our group had the honour of coming in with the swamis to the front; behind this section sat the male worshippers, and behind them the women. The females of our group felt more welcome at the Ashram Vidya Mandir in a beautiful spot outside Rajkot. Here, Swami Parmat Mandand Sarvati discussed with us the philosophy and practices of Hinduism.

One afternoon we had tea with the Roman Catholic Bishop of Rajkot. The Bishop's house incorporated a school, and was enclosed within a lovely garden. We had an interesting discussion about the incidents between Hindu extremists and Christians. It was acknowledged that it was a political issue, and most people were trying to play down the incidents, as sensationalist journalism only made matters worse and incited more suspicion and intolerance. In fact, most of the religious leaders we spoke to from all the faiths could not understand how the trouble had arisen, as each faith community in Rajkot had lived and worshipped in harmony and tolerance of each other.

As our exchange took place over Easter, we all went to the Palm Sunday service in the Church of North India, and then again on Good Friday. We also attended the Catholic Church for the midnight Mass preceding Easter Sunday. This began with a procession outside to light a fire to symbolise resurrection as new life. At both these churches we were all, of mixed faith and traditions, warmly welcomed as sisters and brothers. It brought to mind 'In Christ there is neither Jew nor Gentile'. We felt enriched to be in each other's places of worship, and also spent time at night, sharing prayers, hymns, songs and meditations and readings from the Bible and the Bhagavad-Gita. We discussed at length the relevance of Easter for Christians throughout Holy Week, and shared a footwashing ritual on Maundy Thursday.

Throughout the time we were in Rajkot we were given a high profile, and interviewed by three newspaper reporters, including an extensive coverage in the national paper, the *Times of India*. I personally felt it was a privilege to be given the opportunity to publicise our hopes for a better understanding between faiths, and to recognise the value and depth of the spirituality within the lives of young people from different and varied cultures.

The Road to Zanzibar

John Higginbotham

Following in the steps of Bing, Bob and Dorothy, my wife and I took a long weekend in Zanzibar in the midst of our action-packed work camp in Arusha, Tanzania. The old sultanate is no more, although many traces of it remain: since the end of the British protectorate, Zanzibar has been amalgamated with Tanganyika to become the Republic of Tanzania, although there are those who hanker after independence and some unrest therefore bubbles beneath the surface.

This was apparent during our visit as elections were pending, and riots, fortunately more raucous than lethal, were audible from our balcony overlooking the cathedral at St Monica's where we stayed, comfortably accommodated en suite, and well fed by Jean Howe who provides on a shoestring an excellent variety of local fare.

The contrast with Arusha was marked and this is what we came to see. Zanzibar is still predominantly Muslim, although both Anglicans and Roman Catholics signal their presence with cathedrals. Zanzibar Cathedral was founded by the Universities' Mission to Central Africa and still not only bears its Anglo-Catholic stamp but is also still known as the UMCA Cathedral.*

We were entertained to dinner by Bishop John Ramadhani, the doyen of the Tanzanian episcopate and formerly Archbishop of the province. He talked of the challenges and problems of being a Christian minority in a Muslim country. On the whole, thanks to his careful and wise diplomacy, relations are good, but there are stresses and strains whenever signs of Christian expansion are detected, as in the case of a recent proposal to build a new church.

* UMCA amalgamated with the SPG (Society for the Propagation of the Gospel) in 1965, forming the USPG.

The symbol of the two religions living side by side was audibly apparent. 5 am brought the cry of the muezzin calling the faithful to prayer, soon to be answered by the bells of the Angelus from Zanzibar Cathedral followed by the daily Mass celebrated by Fr Toto, the Dean of the Cathedral. This fine, though ageing church, built symbolically on the site of an old slave market and commemorated by a tableau of manacled slaves in the cathedral precinct, has a tall spire which one always looks for when disorientated by the maze of narrow streets which make up the bustling port.

It is a hive of activity, with fish of all kinds being constantly unloaded, vegetables sold in a huge open market, and the spices and seaweed for which the former Sultanate is famous much in evidence.

Church life, too, is flourishing. The cathedral is comfortably full on Sundays and there is always a devout quorum at the weekday masses as well. Country parishes, outside the main port, are smaller but no less vigorous. The Diocese of Zanzibar and Tanga has recently been split into two, Tanga (on the mainland) now having a separate bishop, recently consecrated, while Bishop Ramadhani continues to reign supreme on the island. He is a patriarchal figure of grand wisdom and energy for his years, who treads his delicate path with great diplomacy.

The folk of Zanzibar betray its mixed history of African, Arab and British influences. The old British Club is currently being refurbished as a luxury hotel. The house of wonders still stands, majestic in the evening sunlight, greenery adding an appropriate spice island touch. It is affected but not altogether spoilt by the curse of the age – mass tourism, evidenced by the many hotels and bureaux advertising everything from diving and fishing to 'spice island tours'. Packed open buses of a certain age run out to the beaches and country districts where not all tourists venture. We were warned of the dangers of the old town at night, but, on venturing forth in search of local cuisine, did not encounter any harrassment and very little of the pressure to buy local crafts evident in so many Arab lands.

Zanzibar is a many-faceted crucible of great vitality and colour. We were only there for a long weekend, but I would recommend a longer stay to immerse oneself in its rich and vibrant panorama.

SECTION FIVE

Journey for Justice and Peace

Jesus Walking Through the Cornfields on the Sabbath
Etching by Francis Hoyland

Introduction

Hopefully the pilgrimage for others is at the heart of all pilgrimage. Every true pilgrim begins the journey with love for the world and for the people he or she will meet along the way, or sometimes the inspiration for the venture may become clearer as the way unfolds, so that the pilgrimage is for life, never ending in this world and ever trustful of God.

The pilgrim's love of the people he or she meets along the way may change his or her life and future commitment, and it may also be a catalyst for change in the people and situations met. The pilgrim may prod people met from different backgrounds to begin to work together. The true pilgrim may have a vision of what is possible for people and for the world, and will go on and on in hope, trust and love for the people.

Alfred Willetts has worked all his life for peace between the peoples of the world. He was born during the First World War and when the Second World War broke out he offered to drive ambulances in Italy and North Africa rather than join the fighting forces. He decided to celebrate his 80th birthday in 1995 by walking to all the cathedrals in England, to meet people and hold vigils for peace and justice.

In the 'old days' of apartheid in South Africa we organised a pilgrimage through Christians Aware, which took British and South African people, Christians and Buddhists, from Henley-on-Thames to Trafalgar Square, stopping to sleep in church halls along the way and giving talks and entering discussions with members of the communities. There was an electrifying moment on one occasion when a meeting was held in a village hall. A video of life under apartheid had been followed by a brief talk by one of the South Africans, who had been a political prisoner in South Africa. The moment came when an elderly woman stood up and gave a speech, the first she had ever given, during which she told everyone that she had always thought that apartheid was sensible and that her son and his family lived in South Africa. 'I will write to them and tell them that apartheid is wrong, and that they should come home,' she said.

It was love of the people which led John Osmers, now the Anglican bishop in Eastern Zambia, to continue the struggle against apartheid after he and four others were badly injured by a bomb in Lesotho, which had been planted to kill them all. He wrote, 'My right hand and the front of my legs were blown away . . .' The group was defiant, and as a symbol of this they placed a placard above their hospital beds which displayed the words of Nelson Mandela: 'There is no easy walk to freedom.' He continued the struggle, and later said that he himself, like Archbishop Desmond Tutu, had been inspired to do so through the life and writings of Trevor Huddleston, whose own journey for justice with his beloved people of South Africa lasted for more than 50 years, from the time when he went as a priest to Sophiatown in Johannesburg until the ending of apartheid.*

Margaret Morris is a good example of someone who set off on the journey into a new vocation through love of people suffering from HIV/AIDS. She has written here about her journey and has reminded us that pilgrimage for others is never easy.

Bill Peters, who founded Jubilee 2000 for the cancellation of the debts of the poorest countries, is a good example of a modern pilgrim, who moved from his long career in the diplomatic service to a challenge which he will never put down until it is fulfilled. Bill has known Africa for many years now, and has worked for better agriculture, education and health for the people. When he went back to Malawi as British High Commissioner there, he had to ask himself why

* The story of the early struggle with apartheid can be read in *Naught for Your Comfort*, Trevor Huddleston, Collins, London, 1956. Also *Return to South Africa: The Ecstasy and the Agony*, Fount, 1991, and *Trevor Huddleston. A Life*, Robin Denniston, Macmillan, 1992.

so many people were visibly poorer in 1983 than they had been 15 or 20 years earlier. He realised that the debts which Malawi, and of course many other countries in the developing world, owed to the Western nations, the International Monetary Fund and World Bank, and to commercial banks, had made them prisoners to the repayment of the debts, much of their available national income going in this direction. He knew that the debts had been encouraged by Western nations and banks which had been overflowing with money in the late 1970s, due to the surplus deposits of the oil producers from rises in oil prices. The love of the people which had made Bill work for education and health was not part of the agenda for world governments and international financial institutions narrowly concerned with lending, and with recovering debts.

Bill made a decision to embark on a long campaign for a better future for the poorest countries and peoples of the world. With Martin Dent of Keele University, he set up Jubilee 2000 in 1993 and began the very hard work of persuading the governments of the richest nations of the world, known then as the G7 nations, and now the G8 because Russia has joined, to cancel the debts of the poorest countries to mark the Millennium. What was the vision of two people has grown into a worldwide movement with groups in most countries of the world and with a petition which has been signed by over 24 million people, more than ever before in history. There has been some success, with £150 billion worth of debts cancelled, but the Millennium has come and gone, and much more remains to be cancelled. The pilgrimage for justice goes on into the future and Bill will not put it down.

It was from love of materially poor people that John and Rita Bennett went to work in Bangladesh, one of the poorest countries in the world, in the Millennium year. Rita has written about her journey from security and the beautiful country-side of the Yorkshire Dales to the uncertainty and unknown country and people of Bangladesh.

John Spinks has described his hair-raising journey to Liuli

in the heart of rural Tanzania, a journey he took because he was committed to the work being done in the hospital there, and wanted to encourage people at home in London to do more.

Our examples here represent the many people who have travelled in this way, into the unknown out of love for the people they trust they will meet and work with for a just future.

Sometimes the journeys taken are symbolic of work with others for a better future. They are important because they may raise material support and they may also be the inspiration which moves other people to set off on the journey with no end.

We have included some short accounts of symbolic journeys. One is a journey in Ribblesdale, from Settle to Giggleswick, with reflections on local history and also on people and issues throughout the world. The second is of a sponsored walk held in Derbyshire for the street children of India. The people who undertook the walk learnt about the street children and also raised some money for them. They also grew to realise that this journey of partnership could not end when the walk was over, but would and must continue. We have also included a glimpse into the pilgrimage against poverty which took place in 1999 from Iona to London and Holywell or St David's to Cardiff, through Church Action on Poverty.

We have included a section on pilgrimage in the Middle East, perhaps the most famous place of pilgrimage for people of the Christian, Jewish or Muslim faiths. There are also Middle Eastern pilgrimages in 'Pilgrimage in the Faith Traditions'. Here we focus on those who have set out through love of the people, though no one can avoid that love coming to them when they visit the place with open eyes and ears. The title of the journey from Nazareth to Bethlehem speaks for itself as a 'pilgrimage for justice and peace', and it is very obvious that it must continue, as justice and peace seem so far away for all the people who live on this route.

Archbishop Rowan Williams went to the Middle East in 1995 for the BBC. He travelled as a modern magi, with two others, Paul Valleley of *The Independent*, and Heather Couper, an astronomer royal. The group visited three countries in six days and went from trauma to sadness to a kind of inspiration, as they travelled from Syria, which they found rather drab and bureaucratic, and into Jordan and then finally into Israel. Jordan was then, as it still is, suffering from its generosity to the refugees from Kuwait who arrived there during the Gulf War. It is also now suffering the effects of the sanctions on Iraq, including the loss of many of the middle classes. The group met a Roman Catholic priest who was working with refugees from Iraq, who also visited Iraq and its people which he described as 'hell on earth'. The group found Israel very tense, and it is of course much more so since then, with Christians especially leaving every day.

We include a section written by the Bishop of Jerusalem, Riah Abu El Assal. He is constantly pointing out that the Christians are leaving the Middle East so rapidly that soon there will be none left. Rowan Williams asked himself whether the old city of Jerusalem might become a museum in 20 years' time.

His reflection on his journey and experiences is germane for every pilgrim:

> There is the image that came to me as we reached the end of our journey in Bethlehem. Making your way down into the centre of the town, you have to push through crowded and dirty alleyways, through the visible signs of poverty and war, past the soldiers and the beggars, before you come out into Manger Square. Pushing through the tunnels – like being born. Somehow or other, now as then, to get to the place where Christ, and we ourselves, are born, there is no going round the dark and narrow places of human pain. It isn't a consoling thought, but the Middle East isn't a consoling place; crosses in Jerusalem or Tel Aviv; dying children in Bethlehem or Baghdad. At least the Holy Land pushes you towards a kind of truthfulness.

Reconciliation and Peace in Coventry Cathedral

Alfred Willetts

Alfred Willetts decided to celebrate his 80th birthday in 1995 by travelling to every Church of England cathedral to witness to his lifelong pilgrimage for peace with justice. Before he set off he wrote a letter to all the diocesan bishops and the deans of the cathedrals, explaining his intention:

> I have embarked on a peace pilgrimage. . . . I intend to hold a silent vigil outside each cathedral at the time of public worship, to be seen by the worshippers as they enter and leave. I will have local support and we will carry posters to explain our purpose which is to raise awareness of the necessity for individual and corporate action in accord with the 1978 Lambeth Conference Resolution 5: 'War as a method of settling international disputes is incompatible with the teaching and example of our Lord Jesus Christ . . .'

When Alfred went to Coventry Cathedral he was at home in a place which is known all over the world for its ministry for reconciliation and peace. This is what he wrote.

Every Friday at noon there is a Litany of Reconciliation followed by a celebration of the Eucharist in the ruins of the old cathedral which was destroyed by German bombs in World War Two. I walked about in the precincts. There were many Australians about and almost immediately one of them asked to take my photograph against the background of the sculpture of St Michael overpowering the devil. Another Australian group of two men and two women paused and one of the women began to talk to me, much to the annoyance of one of the men. She told me that she preferred to talk to me rather than go into the cathedral, and would still be talking with me when they came out, which in fact she was. I talked of conscientious objection in this country, of war experiences, of German Christian witness during the Nazi regime often at the cost of their lives, and of my wife's six-month prison sentence for sitting in the entrance to an atomic weapons research establishment. I told her how we had done a motor cycle trip through parts of Germany ten years after the end of the war and had come upon city after city that was just mile after mile of rubble. I told her how I had been able to travel to Germany, Italy, Romania, Hungary, the USSR (before its break-up) and the United States. Everywhere I went I made a point of talking with young people, teenagers and young married couples, and their message is the same in every country: 'Why should we continue the quarrels of our forefathers? Why should we think of people just like ourselves as enemies just because they live in another country?' The three companions came out of the cathedral and the conversation ended.

The numbers attending the noon Litany and Eucharist at the cathedral vary greatly with the tourist season. The liturgy is printed in twenty languages. There were about twenty communicants and I was glad of the opportunity to concelebrate. In 1986 I had told my bishop that I would no longer celebrate in an Anglican Church where women were not able to do so. The first ordinations of women had taken place in Bristol the day before I set out on my pilgrimage, so from then on I have been able to celebrate when invited.

I went with Paul Oestreicher to his study, and I remarked that I felt that Coventry had some strange advantage with a cathedral ruin hard by the new cathedral. He laughed and told me where to look in the new cathedral to see the inscription inlaid in the metal on the stone floor: 'This cathedral burned down to the glory of God . . .' Because of the immediate action of the Provost in making a cross from some of the

181

ancient nails from the rubble and putting up the words, 'Father, forgive', the events which have led to Coventry becoming a place of reconciliation were set in motion. I remember a very moving service for women's ordination which began in the ruins as a symbol of the past, and about halfway through moved into the new building to symbolise the change we were then looking forward to.

I spent the afternoon in the cathedral precincts. I met a South Korean student who was studying in Coventry. He told me there were no Christians at all in North Korea and was staggered when I told him of faithful Christians I had met in Moscow. I met a teacher with two sixth formers doing a video recording of sights and sounds of Coventry. They asked to include me.

Paul drew my attention to the absence of military flags and banners in the cathedral.

The next stop on my pilgrimage was Lichfield, and then on to Sheffield.

Some Buddhist Peace Walks

When we walk together our feet touch the same earth, we walk beneath the same sun and soak the same rain. As we journey together with a common purpose, we realise that joys and difficulties can arise, but difficulties need not stop us. In walking we begin to restore the spiritual strength to reverse the vicious repercussions of our history, and to move towards a genuinely peaceful society nourished by the innate generosity of human beings and the natural world.

The Nipponzan Myohoji Buddhist order is a branch of Japanese Nichiren Buddhism which was founded by Nichidatsu Fuji, a disciple of Gandhi. He devoted his life to peace work whilst living through World War Two, the Holocaust, and the bombing of Hiroshima and Nagasaki. He said:

Civilisation is not to have electricity, nor aeroplanes, nor to produce nuclear bombs. . . . Civilisation is to hold one another in mutual affection and respect.

His work for peace included his pilgrimage round the world, during which he built peace pagodas. His example has been maintained by members of the order today. They spend much of their time building peace pagodas and columns and walking for peace. There was an interfaith pilgrimage for peace and life in South Africa in 1994, just before the first democratic elections took place, and in the hope that the elections and the future would be peaceful. It was 80 years since Gandhi had walked with 2000 people on the same route from Durban to Johannesburg, in support of the Indian community's resistance to the anti-Indian ordinances passed by the South African government. Some of the laws were in fact repealed as the result of the walk.

From 1998 to 1999 the community led the great pilgrimage

which retraced the journey of slavery, walking through the USA, the Caribbean, Brazil, West Africa and South Africa.

In 1994 the order planned a pilgrimage of 10,000 miles, from Auschwitz to Hiroshima, two places of horror. Three thousand miles of the journey were on foot. The pilgrims were from all the faith traditions and from none. They travelled through countries which had suffered and were suffering.

Reverend Gyoshu Sasamori, who organised the pilgrimage, said:

> We started our journey at one of the most tragic places of the war, where there was a massive killing industry. We ended it at the place where the first atomic bomb was dropped on human beings, ushering in the possibility that all human kind and the Earth herself could be destroyed. This is why we walked on pilgrimage. We offered prayers for the victims of all wars. We heard the voices of the victims in our hearts: voices of survivors; voices from the war zones; voices from areas of conflict. All those voices, overcome with sorrow, seeking hope. I believe that if we face painful facts of history unflinchingly and convey the lessons drawn from them into future generations, we will be able to bring peace to the souls of those who died in anguish in time of war. From the loss of their precious lives, we can establish new values today and for the future.

The hope of the pilgrimage was that people would be reminded that in 1995 it was 50 years since the end of the Second World War and 20 years since the end of the Vietnam War. The hope was that it may be possible to stop the cycle of hatred.

Jim Levinson, an American of Polish-Jewish descent, told the story of how he met Helga, the German daughter of a Nazi SS officer. Helga had always thought that her father was a hero, but when she discovered the truth of his war story she became estranged from her family and began to have nightmares. She told Jim that her father had been the Nazi commandant responsible for the liquidation of the Jewish ghetto in the town of Lida in Little Russia. This was the home of Jim's family. He writes:

> My knees became very shaky and a knot formed in my stomach as I walked up to the front of the room after the session and proceeded to speak with her. As I made the connection, Helga became visibly pale and then nearly hysterical. . . . I was filled with dread as I wondered whether Helga would ask me for forgiveness that was not mine to give. . . . Helga and I talked and talked. What became clear from the hours we spent together is that we were both victims. The broken and tormented Helga was a victim just as clearly as any of us who had lost our families. . . . At Auschwitz something very rare happened: the opportunity for the children of the murderer and the murdered to grieve their terrible griefs together.

The pilgrims walked through snow, rain and fog, through Poland, the Czech Republic and Austria. Many people were injured in the walking and some had to stop. They covered between 12 and 20 miles every day, walking for seven days and then resting for one day. They were welcomed in many places with civic receptions, food and friendship. They travelled by train from Vienna to Zagreb, and then walked and saw old and new war devastation. They travelled on to Mostar, once the cultural capital of Southern Bosnia and now a ruin. They saw the devastation and also the courage of the people.

> We fasted for two days and prayed for a full day in each section of the town. In east Mostar the people gathered round us and watched in silence all day.

The pilgrims moved on to Budapest and then briefly into Serbia, but they were forced to leave and moved on to the

185

Middle East. In Israel they met Jewish and Palestinian people, all struggling. They spent two days in Gaza, went to Galilee, to Jewish settlements, places of reconciliation, and to the kibbutzim.

> Like those who settled in modern Israel, we arrived with some of the ash of Birkenau clinging to our boots. That ash still floats in the air of the Holy Land, creating a permanent haze through which everything is viewed.

The pilgrims went to Jordan, and on to Iraq where they shared the suffering of the people for ten days. One pilgrim wrote:

> In a Baghdad hospital I held the withered, cold hands of infants, their eyes wide and hearts beating out the minutes and hours towards a quiet death.

In India the pilgrims walked long distances, mostly through very poor villages, but arriving finally at Gandhi's memorial in New Delhi. One woman wrote:

> Each day I become more conscious of how we in the United States are consuming huge amounts of the planet's resources while most of the people in third world countries have almost none. . . .
> As we drum across the plains, water buffalo lift their massive heads, languidly curious at the passing tableau and go on chewing . . .

The pilgrimage went to Malaysia, Thailand, Cambodia, Vietnam and the Philippines, where 'The Japanese monks were very aware of the brutality of their soldiers during World War Two, and with us and other walkers they listened to the stories of suffering, atrocity and destruction . . .'

The pilgrimage ended in Japan itself, at Hiroshima and Nagasaki. A wreath of 1000 peace cranes was laid at the memorial for the children who had suffered. The pilgrims prayed at the peace pagoda and fasted at the Atomic Bomb Dome.

When the pilgrimage ended, the pilgrims went away, 'to continue the pilgrimage in our own ways in the different corners of the world in which we live'.

You don't say goodbye to the pilgrimage experience. It whispers a profound, new insight: you are a spiritual being on a human journey.

A Life Lived for Justice

A Buddhist Nun

I went to South Africa for the first time in December 1985. There is a long fast each year and I did it outside the cathedral in Johannesburg, and this gave me a taste of Africa. The cathedral is on the main route from the station to the centre of the city and people coming from Soweto all walk past the cathedral every morning, and they came and prayed with me. It was the first time in my life as a Buddhist nun – and I've prayed in many different countries – that people actually knelt down and prayed together with me, and they asked me to pray for them and they all donated money.

Every day I had a huge mountain of money in front of me from very poor people, which I was able to give back at the end of the fast to people in detention who could buy food in the prison shop, to unemployed people, and I also gave to Desmond Tutu for his work. I still had enough money to pay for a third-class ticket down to Port Elizabeth, and also to buy vegetables and fruit for when I had finished the fast.

I travelled third-class because no white people travel third-class, and I had a very interesting journey and people took great care of me. All the time the African people took great care of me. Then I walked from Port Elizabeth to Cape Town. I hoped that a lot of people would come back and walk with me the next year, but when it came down to it I got a letter from South Africa from a Catholic Women's group, saying, 'Don't come. The State of Emergency is so dreadful that if any people help you, they will be put in prison as soon as you leave the country.' I thought that without having asked people about this, I shouldn't go ahead and do it.

Between my two visits to South Africa I went to America, and in America I joined a fast by four veterans from the Vietnamese War. One of them was an ex-Roman Catholic

188

priest, who received the congregational Medal of Honour. There is a huge long wall in Washington – it's a long black marble wall and it's covered in names of the people who have died from alcohol, suicide and drugs, because their minds were so disturbed by what they had done and what they had seen in Vietnam that they couldn't lead a normal life afterwards. And these four veterans were also disturbed. One of them is an alcoholic – he's a really, really charming man, really lovely, but he's an alcoholic.

They managed to get themselves together enough to do a long fast. Charlie Likely, the priest, and George Mesow, the alcoholic, did 49 days' fasting and the other two did 36 days' fasting, and they came to our ceremony for the peace pagoda in Leveritt and spoke about what they were doing. They had also helped during the construction time, and three of us monks and nuns were moved enough to go and support them by fasting – one monk did three weeks' dry fast, only breaking on the seventh day every week, and two of us did ten days, and then because of veterans we stopped fasting. Their fast was an open-ended fast, which means that they said that they would go on fasting to death if the American government didn't show a significant change in its attitude towards the situation in Nicaragua, so the fast was against the American government funding for Contras in Nicaragua. It was a very similar situation, I suppose, to what was happening in Angola, and it was an amazing experience.

In America, because of the work of Dr Martin Luther King, it's possible to do a very strong action on the steps of the Capitol Building itself, and so every day we met on the steps of the Capitol and there were prayers from Christians, prayers from American leaders, the Foreign Minister of Nicaragua, and also a priest came and addressed the people, and we were invited to go together with the veterans to Nicaragua after the end of the fast. I couldn't personally go but two of the monks did, and now one is going to construct a peace pagoda there in Nicaragua. It showed me how strong an effect this action could have on all the people who witnessed it. People were coming from all over the States, and the American government was also affected by it.

People were coming out, senators were coming out and speaking to the people on the steps. Because I couldn't walk in South Africa I wanted to do something else, and Ellen had come and addressed our assembly at the peace pagoda last year in London, and she had spoken about the plight of the children in jail in South Africa. There were thousands of children in jail and they don't tell the parents where they have taken the children. There wasn't any provision for the children's education in the jail; they were just put with criminals and left there.

Some of them had been in for 10 or 11 months, and I wanted to do something about this situation. I can't do anything very much, but what I can do is pray, and what I can do is fast because I have been trained to do both these things. And so I thought, well, I'll go back and I'll fast now that I've seen the benefit of this long fasting. People hold vigils at the cathedral continuously. There were regularly prayer services for the people in detention. It really performed a kind of spiritual strengthener for the movement for liberation in South Africa. The Church and the movement were totally one. The Church seemed to have woken up to its position of leadership, and gave spiritual comfort and food to the people in their struggle.

I began to do my practice, which is sitting and beating the drum outside the cathedral, sleeping in the crypt, facing the government. It was quite frightening the first time as we were working always against the law in that country. If you obey God's law or Buddha's law, you are continuously having to break the law of the country, and this is quite a strain. All the time you are breaking the law. And my prayer was breaking the law. They said it was a riotous gathering. There were two others with me. One was an elderly woman Quaker from the United States called Liz Pearson, and the other one a young

Dutch woman, 23 years old, and the three of us were beating the drum and praying, and they said that was a riotous gathering and the police came to arrest us. The cathedral wrote a letter to the magistrate and asked permission for our fast to continue, and so we had the excuse we could wait until we got the reply to the letter. That was the first stage. We got permission for a week, and at the end of that week Botha was to open parliament and everybody thought they were going to arrest us. All the journalists came to take photographs of us being arrested and the place was full of police, absolutely full – I've never seen so many police gathered in one spot.

Then a woman turned up, a white woman about 70 years old, with very bright dyed orange hair. She came at me and she started shouting. She told me that I was an idolater, and that I should not be allowed in South Africa. Then she got hold of my small Buddha statue, which is a Japanese birth Buddha, with the baby Buddha – it's bronze and gold-leaf, and it's very, very pretty – and she took hold of this statue and she smashed it on the ground. I was really shocked but this had a miraculous effect because all the police who had previously been very hostile towards me came round, and they picked up the Buddha statue. They put it back, and they read the paper I had with the words of my teacher, which was all about law and evil, and when you have to obey evil law. It's much better to try to go the opposite way, and religious people in history had sacrificed their lives to the point of being crucified, and they are the free people. From then on everything changed. The journalists came and interviewed me about the woman. They put it in the paper and the police read it, and one of the top policemen came and interviewed me and asked what was I doing. I explained: 'Look, in this country the worst thing, the worst enemy of everybody here, is fear. Everyone is fearful and my mission, if you like, is to help people to get rid of their fear.' They understood, and I said, 'Don't throw me out. I really want to come back here and work and live in Alexandra and build a peace pagoda there. If you throw me out I will never be able to get back in again. He said they were behind me. I couldn't believe it. That was another miracle. The third miracle was that 250 children under the age of 15 were released. Now there were still more than 1000 children from 16 to 18 in prison, but the government didn't regard them as children.

I went on with the fast. Then the grind started day after day, day after day, day after day, and it never seemed to end. Then the weather was terrible – it was freezing and it was pouring with rain, and we put our feet in plastic bags – and then awful food fantasies started and all I could think about was planning a menu for when I stopped. And that, Gandhi said, is very bad. If you think about food and dream about food, you are not fasting properly. However, when I was confronted with the government building, I could focus my mind properly. I was very well supported by the Black Sash, which was an anti-apartheid organisation of white women. I respected them very much and they took me to their houses every three days for a bath, so I could stay clean and wash my clothes. There was another organisation called Free the Children Alliance, which is different groups who are working together for the particular purpose of freeing the children who are in prison now. I hoped that we might organise a walk.

I think two images of the children stay in my mind. One was when we were staying in Soweto and I'd been walking up the hill opposite to where we were staying; Desmond Tutu's house is down one side of the hill and I was staying on the opposite side. I came down the hill and there was a little kid making a kite – he'd found some plastic and some pieces of stick and he was concentrating very hard on making this kite. I was really pleased to see him and I said, 'Hello, that's a nice kite you are making.' And he looked at me; he was utterly terrified and he ran. He absolutely bolted away. I have never had that effect on a child before. It was such a shock because my face was white and he was totally unused to seeing any white faces in his place. In fact, we went to a supermarket there, the biggest supermarket in Soweto, and the manager came out to say, 'Oh, welcome, welcome to my supermarket. You're the first white people who have ever been in this supermarket. Please come and visit my house.' So that little child showed the reaction, and I was very, very worried by it.

The second image is of two little children playing in Alexandra. I went away and sat down at the edge of the township, and there were two little children beside me, two little boys, and they started playing. They picked up stones and made them into guns and they sat one behind the other, and they started driving and shooting at the other children. They were obviously playing at being one of the horrible machines that the soldiers and police use in the black towns.

They shoot the children and shoot the people from these machines. This really horrified me because it was the only time that I saw children playing violently; not to each other – they were doing it in fantasy, if you like, but they do it, because they turned round to look at me to see if I had understood. They couldn't speak English, but they showed me in a little play, in a drama. This really was a very upsetting lesson for me because I could see that the minds of the children were being turned, and unless we managed to get those troops out of the townships – get those police to start regarding people as human – the people would lose their humanity and it would take so long to get it back again.

My life goes on, and I rejoice that I can walk and fast for other people, especially the children.

An African Journey into the Unknown

John Spinks

Last year, I was fortunate in being able to take a three-month sabbatical to pursue some postgraduate studies into Afro-Caribbean culture. I visited South Africa, Mozambique, and Malawi and Tanzania. Africa has always held a boyhood fascination for me, including its inaccessibility and wildlife, and the friendliness of the people. Most people will know the beauty. Television gives attractive footage of the wonderful wildlife that exists and the attractions for tourists to visit on the continent. That was not the reason for my visit; indeed, I only visited one wildlife park, and that exclusively for elephants. I went to meet people and to learn about the work of a special hospital.

Tanzania is a vast and beautiful country, rich in its scenery and in its welcome. Financially its development is impeded by the burden of debt. I reached the small bay on the other side of Lake Nyasa from Mbamba Bay in Malawi via the ferry.

I was taken to a small hotel where Fr Sam Ndimbo, the medical director of St Anne's Hospital, with a team from Liuli, greeted me. After some refreshments we journeyed on to Liuli. It was the most traumatic journey in a motor car I've ever experienced, and I've been in a few! There are no made roads between Liuli and the lakeside, only tracks and ravines to be crossed; however, by the grace of God and a fantastic driver we arrived at Liuli. Liuli is in southern Tanzania on Lake Nyasa, with Mozambique to the south and Malawi to the west.

The main reason for visiting Liuli is that St John's in Harrow has supported St Anne's Hospital, which is run by the Anglican Diocese of Ruvuma. The area itself is mainly dependent on subsistence farming. People grow cassava and other crops, and fish in the lake. The hospital has about 100 beds serving

80,000 people living in a 100-mile radius. The main diseases affecting the area are malaria, stomach disorders and the increasing and ubiquitous diseases associated with AIDS. This continues to have a devastating affect as it does in so many African countries. St Anne's has a four-wheel-drive vehicle, donated by the Friends of St Anne's, which is used by the diocese and the hospital to visit sick patients in the villages, and if necessary bring them to the hospital. The hospital has no mains electricity, but survives on a generator for use in emergencies. Therefore, there is no television; the consequence of this is that some of the younger children have never seen a white face before. Travelling around Liuli and visiting the villages with the medical team was an enlightening experience, being greeted in such a warm and friendly way. The children were wonderful and uninhibited in their welcome, very tactile and unsure whether the white face was real or not! The production of a camera caused ecstatic excitement as they all wanted to be part of the picture.

Around Liuli there are several very large Roman Catholic churches, built in the nineteenth century with outbuildings, sadly falling into disrepair, but staffed often by a single priest and some sisters faithfully serving their communities. Again, the reception was warm and hospitable, and refreshments were provided. There was a visit to the church where prayers were said. Because of the remoteness of Ruvuma everybody is dependent on each other for survival – particularly Dr Sam who is a much loved and a respected priest and doctor. There seemed to be no demarcation lines between the two churches.

Apart from the work at the hospital, Liuli houses the cathedral for the diocese, and for a village of this size it is quite an imposing church, built in the colonial style. There are no windows, of course, and the temperature is constant. There were three choirs: the nursing staff, the children's choir, and an adult choir. They have no music but just sing as the spirit moves amongst the people, and what beautiful melodic sounds they made, enhancing the worship so beautifully. The cathedral was full and people were there because they wanted to be. At the end I was invited to bring the greetings of our diocese in London and our parish, and they were warmly received.

The schools in southern Tanzania contain the bare essentials, and education has to be paid for by parents. Surprisingly, school uniform is compulsory; education is a prized procession. It is so sad that many children have to live without it. The children will walk for miles to both school and hospital; there is no other way of reaching them. Sadly, if a person is so ill they cannot get to hospital, they die. Often nobody but the village knows this, as no proper records are kept in the way they are in the UK.

My long journey was hard, but nevertheless a wonderful experience. I left with the feeling of a caring Christian community struggling mightily to survive. If only people in the UK could witness the lifestyle and especially the children, and realise the value of their education and other services which we so take for granted.

Liuli was always a hard place to get to and to live in. In the early twentieth century all the transactions were by barter and people were often hungry. There were many leprosy patients, treated by the hospital and living in a separate colony. Some of them had had treatment for most of their lives.

Journey to the Margins:
A Ministry with HIV/AIDS Patients

Margaret Morris

It was 1987. My daughter and I were watching something on television about AIDS. 'There's nothing in school,' she remarked. 'No posters, information or anything.' There had been a flurry of activity a year or two earlier. Everyone had received a 'tombstone' leaflet through the door and I remembered going to school with other parents for a performance by a drama group addressing some of the key issues. But she was right; a silence now surrounded HIV and not only in school.

My knowledge was somewhat limited but I began to realise that our children were probably at their most vulnerable as far as their sexual health was concerned. Our son was already continuing his education away from home, and Jane was preparing for A-levels and planning to go to university. Both would soon be away from home, embarking on new relationships. I wanted to make sure they knew about AIDS and how to prevent infection. (In those days we used the term AIDS rather than HIV. Now it is more usual to use HIV or HIV/AIDS.)

First, I needed to inform myself. I cast around and discovered a course of ten evening seminars –'AIDS – A multidisciplinary approach' – and duly enrolled. Two weeks into this and I realised that not only was HIV a great challenge for society at large but it was also an even greater challenge for the Church. I soon saw that not only the Christian churches but also most mainstream religions would find it very difficult to respond adequately to this virus and the people affected by it. To speak of HIV, sooner or later one has to refer to sex and sexuality, gender, relationships, blood, birth, disease, dying, death. These define the taboo areas of any society and any religion. They are the places where societies and religions

197

exert the greatest controls, and HIV cuts across all of them exposing all their weaknesses – and strengths.

I resolved to stay with it. At this time I was training for ministry and my whole world was being transformed by the revelations of biblical criticism. I was excited and thrilled by the insights and connections which were unfolding through study and encounter. With faith both enhanced and shaken by these changes, I flourished as an individual. Venturing into the unknown at that time was more to do with the promise of the threshold than the fear of the abyss. It was exactly the right moment for me to begin an exploration into the theologies of HIV.

It was challenging stuff but I found I had good companions on the way. A small group of individuals concerned about HIV and the support needs of the people affected by it had formed a steering committee to set up a voluntary agency which could offer practical support, information and advocacy. An Anglican woman deacon was actively involved in this initiative. I joined the group with its first intake of volunteers, and she and I were the first to be invited to befriend a man with HIV on behalf of this fledgling organisation, Leicestershire AIDS Support Services, or LASS. LASS grew rapidly and is now a key partner in HIV service provision throughout Leicestershire and Rutland.

Ordination to the Diaconate followed for me in 1989 and I was elected chair of the LASS management committee the same year. I combined my voluntary HIV work with a non-stipendiary parish attachment. It was a heavy workload. Each area of ministry was to inform the other. And yet it was LASS that was more like church than church. In supporting people affected by HIV, we were committed to justice, to diversity, to standing with the marginalised and excluded. An essential compassion fostered an ethos of mutual understanding and respect. Outstanding individuals inspired me with their courage and their vision, their kingdom-of-God vision, though few if any would have described it in those terms. Some of us from those days continue to be fellow travellers but many, too many, have died. Warren, Martin, Pete, Tim. Tim's friend Millie wrote this poem some time after his death. It speaks to my soul too.

The Flowering
Something spawning
Barely breathing
Petals unfurling
Awakening time

Something precious
All accepting
Freedom granted
Feeling fine

No pretenders
Times remembered
Friendship tendered
Flowering time

Unconfining
Ever roaming
Unconditional
Friend of mine.

Over the years HIV has become the main focus of the ministry I exercise. As Bishop's Chaplain for People Affected by HIV in the Diocese of Leicester, I established 'Faith in People with HIV', a project offering pastoral and spiritual support to people with the virus, their partners, friends, relations and carers. The project is funded by the area Health Authority and local authority Social Services Departments. Apart from some start-up funding from the Central Church Fund and a little 'in kind' assistance, there has been no Diocesan money involved. We work very closely with LASS.

Championing the cause of the marginalised from a position

of marginality is not a comfortable enterprise. Then we are not promised comfort, and ultimately we have to learn that pilgrimage is people. Magnificent vulnerable people, hurting people, laughing, weeping people, gospel people, too often shunned and all but crushed by Church and society. Whatever befalls, my hope is that we shall continue to journey together. I treasure the company.

Pilgrimage and Partnership

Rita Bennett

Rita Bennett writes here about the journey she and her husband took from the beauty of the Yorkshire Dales to a strange, sometimes frightening, and certainly surprising life in Bangladesh, where she has discovered a new way of living and working with new friends; and where she has begun to make a contribution towards a more just meeting of human needs and a more just development of the gifts of all.

What am I doing here? Almost like someone waking up from sleepwalking, I gaze down from the concrete footbridge. It is before eight o'clock in the morning but already the sun is hot. Below me there are six lanes of cars, lorries, buses and baby taxis moving towards the Dhaka city centre or towards the airport. The pollution from ancient exhaust systems hovers over the city as far as the eye can see. Filth litters the pavements, and beggars are carefully positioned by their exploiters to extract 'taka' from those like myself, lucky enough to be on their way to their morning work. At that moment my overwhelming feeling is that I would much rather be somewhere else. I must be still asleep surely. I don't belong here. I just want to go home – now!

Still, the only way is forward. I complete the crossing of the bridge and work my way down the steps to the opposite side of the road. This is far from home in many ways. There is no social worker to whom I can take the eight-year-old girl who is sleeping on the pavement. The woman who drops a few small coins into the bowl of the cripple who is reading the Qu'ran out loud is performing a pious act. Unselfconsciously a man urinates into the open drain and the ticket seller neatly tears the ticket he has just sold me before dropping the pieces onto the ground. It's the system, and if I find it appalling, then, in all these crowds of people, I am the one out of step.

Still the morning is improving. I eventually manage to buy my ten 'taka' ticket and board the air-conditioned bus. The ticket sellers are used to me by now and know where I want to go, but they clearly think that I am eccentric. I am a foreigner, so I must have a car and a driver. Why am I boarding a bus? If I get one of the ordinary local buses (fare three taka) then I shall be asked, 'What is your country? What are you doing here? How many children have you? (What! No sons!) Do you like Bangladesh?' If I manage to understand and reply in my halting Bangla, this will be greeted by delighted smiles. I shall have made the morning of a busload of people more entertaining. The air-conditioned bus is a much quieter. I am not forced on to a dangerous and overcrowded women's seat, right by the driver's left elbow. Even amongst the more middle class passengers on this bus, many of the mostly male passengers clearly do not approve of women sitting next to men, so I try to sit next to one of the few women, who are on their way to banks and offices. Sometimes they ask the usual questions but in English. Often I have fifteen minutes of quiet, cool reflection on the question I asked myself on the bridge: 'What *am* I doing here?'

The obvious answer is the one I have been giving to my fellow passengers: 'Ammi Churche Bangladesh Kaj Kori. Englander ammi shikikar. Ammi Churche Bangladesh Education Adviser.' (I work for the Church of Bangladesh. In England I am a teacher. I am the Education Adviser for the Church of Bangladash.) This often does not satisfy them or myself. Bangladesh is hot and sticky. Dhaka's inhabitants know how polluted and crime ridden the city is and feel powerless to do anything about it. We do not even live and work in the better areas of Dhaka, where ex-pats are driven between their luxurious flats, restaurants and clubs. So why did John and I leave a beautiful area of England and our beloved daughters? Why did we leave the rural churches where we had been busy and happy and fulfilled?

An answer forms round the idea of 'Pilgrimage'. 'Pilgrimage,' I used to tell my pupils at school, 'is a journey to a place of special significance undertaken for a spiritual reason.' This is a good definition for middle school children because it enables teachers to introduce their pupils to colourful places, with lots of possibilities for map work and interesting displays of artefacts. The 'places' are much easier than the 'spiritual reason'. How does anything I ever learned or taught about 'pilgrimage' enable me to prepare for our experience of being mission partners in Bangladesh?

First of all, 'pilgrimage' is something deep in my background. As a child in the early 1950s, the headmaster at my primary school read to us in morning assembly from *Pilgrim's Progress*. The story with its challenge to the individual to think for oneself, to dare and to hope for a goal which can be attained by the grace of God, became part of my 'personal myth'. Its force intensified as I grew and understood more of the religious and political significance of the story. I was clear that I had begun a 'pilgrimage' with my life as surely as 'Christian' in the story sets his feet on the King's highway on the other side of the wicket gate. Later I understood that real 'pilgrims' pass not once but many times through the House of the Interpreter, the Palace Beautiful and the Valley of Humiliation. They fall carelessly asleep in By-ways Meadow and become imprisoned by Giant Despair. They return again to that low green hill, with its cross, and find that their burden slips from their back and is swallowed up in the tomb at its foot. But the journey is not circular. A serious pilgrim is called to *progress*.

There must be a time to say, 'Time to move on. Time to go somewhere else, do something different.' For many reasons, both of family and work, John and I felt that it was time to close a very happy chapter in our lives and to look for something new. Since childhood we had both had our imaginations captured by the work of Christians overseas. Since teenage years we had been involved in seeking a better, fairer life for people in the developing world. As our eight-year term in Settle, North Yorkshire, was coming to an end, and my school was about to be reorganised, it seemed like a good time to ask the Methodist Church if they would consider us to serve overseas.

So one cold November morning, when the frost made the green hills look blue and the little puddles crunched under our feet, we boarded the train to Leeds station and our connection for London Kings Cross. We held hands and talked quietly about what they might ask us in Church House about why we thought that we would like to be considered to work overseas. We wanted to be genuinely open to whatever was the right direction for us, so we made no stipulation about where we would like to serve. We only felt that it would be good to be in an ecumenical appointment. Many months later, while we were on holiday in warm and sunny France, we opened a letter from the World Church office, which said that there was this opening in the Church of Bangladesh. The Church of Bangladesh wanted John to be a pastor to an English-speaking congregation, lecture at the theological college for pastors in training, and co-ordinate a lay training programme. From myself, they wanted help in the Education Department and work with children.

We both felt that our previous experience had equipped us to begin on what we were being asked to do. It confirmed to us that this was the right next step. Of course you could always say that, having told them about our previous experi-ences, that was the sort of appointment towards which we *would be* directed, but I think that is only to say that one can trace the human mechanisms by which God acts.

Once having said that we were happy with the idea of going to this appointment in Bangladesh, the personal dis-coveries on this 'pilgrimage' began in earnest. Most obviously was the importance of 'home'. Our daughters needed a family base and we were very thankful that we were able to leave them one. I am enormously comforted by the thought of 'home' just being there. That's one difference between being a pilgrim and being a refugee. Home remains – even if you cannot be there.

Going back to college was another rather strange experience. We were sent to the United College of the Ascension at Selly Oak. This brought back memories of many years ago when we were both in training. Some things were amazingly the same. I had to accept that people had changed, not least myself. Mostly I found myself satisfied with the changes. Having time to read and reflect, I found that life had been kind to me, adding years of husband and children, friends and satisfying work and leisure to the student teacher I was then.

Pilgrimage is for discovery. The early Celtic Christians set out with the promise ringing in their ears that if they embarked on journeys for Christ's sake, they would 'discover wonder upon wonder and every wonder true'. Having read about the voyages of St Brendan, I could say that they consisted of a company of Christians, inexperienced outside their own territory, who set off ill-prepared, blundered about for a while in their coracle, read the miraculous into everyday occurrences, and returned home not quite sure where they had been. This may not be too far from our own experience.

We are in touch with most parts of the globe by telephone, news-media and e-mail, and yet life, out of our culture, is baffling to us. Preparation courses do their best but it is not the physical facts but the whole 'mind-set' of another culture which is different. I struggle to know what aspects of a culture can work for the development of a full life for people, and which aspects stifle life and are frankly against the gospel. Only by travelling through daily life here can we begin to discover this.

At the end of nine months, in some ways, the place I find myself is less known than at the beginning. I have discovered new questions to which before I assumed answers. For instance, in what sense are the poor blessed? If it means the legless beggar who crawls through the traffic and accosts me, how is he blessed? How does he find the courage to go on living? In his place, I think I might not. Is there something, beside fear of death, which keeps him going? Does he know in a deeper way than I do that 'life is more important than food and the body more than raiment' (Mathew 6:25)?

Long-held values about aid to the developing world, which John and I have steadily campaigned for since we were teenagers, are not easy to carry with us. The argument for supporting 'aid projects' can easily become an extension of the requests from the beggars on the streets. Put simply, it is 'You are rich, we are poor, so you ought to give us some of your money and we will spend it. Goodbye.' There has to be an understanding on both sides, which brings partners into a real relationship of respect and responsibility. Many aid organisations are moving into setting people up in their own small employment projects. The real situation is that people have got to earn their own living properly and justly. Encouraging signs are businesses where people expect to deliver quality service to others and a better future for themselves and their families.

Pilgrims do not go alone. They travel with company. I have had excellent company. First of all, John and I have each other. When we invited our friends to celebrate the beginning of this new stage of our lives before we set out from England, we had evening prayer together in the tiny Fountaines Chapel in our village. Our friend Wendy sang for us Richard Gillard's servant song.

> We are pilgrims on a journey,
> and companions on the road,
> we are here to help to help each other
> walk the mile and bear the load.

There are other friends, too, both other foreigners and nationals. Many 'Bedeshis' (foreigners) are here in very stressful jobs, working under difficult social and political conditions to complete intergovernment-funded civil engineering, which the country desperately needs. Others work for non-government organisations or for the diplomatic service. We never know who will turn up at our Friday worship service, or on the telephone, or at the BAHGA club where we might go for lunch afterwards. Unknown before, they may only be with us for a short time but we have a very real sense of journeying alongside them.

It is our privilege to be received by Bangladeshis in the Church of Bangladesh, other Christian communities and other faiths. We could not know before we set out if people really wanted us to share with them what we had to give. How would they look on new methods of teaching? Or on new ways of lecturing new subjects? This has not turned out to be a problem. Bangladeshis are truly welcoming. The unknown factor is how to *really* change the system and whether, or in what way, people want it to be changed.

I am glad that I did not know on that frosty November morning, when we set out for our first formal interview in London, what I know now. Honestly I don't think we would have come. That would have been a tremendous personal loss – we would never have seen the beautiful countryside of Bangladesh or the strength and skill of the people in the pavement shops practising a hundred different trades which in Europe are only done in factories. We have had to develop and adapt our own personal skills and experiences in order to be of any use here. If we had not set out, we would not have had so wide and so natural an opportunity to share the good news about the grace of God in Jesus, as we have had here.

A few months ago, with some colleagues, I crossed over in a flat-bottomed boat to a very poor area in the south-west. There two Hindu women run a two-shift Church of Bangladesh school for about 100 children in one small room. The doors and windows badly needed repair but the walls were bright with pictures. The children are neat and well taught by their dedicated teachers. The words of John Bunyan's hymn crossed my mind:

Who would true valour see, let him come hither!

It is not our own 'valour' but theirs which leaves me humble and hopeful as I keep travelling onward.

Photograph: Barbara Butler

Pilgrims at Giggleswick Church

Walking Locally and Thinking Globally in Ribblesdale

A weekend conference on issues of world poverty and debt was held in the Yorkshire Craven Dales, and as part of the conference the participants walked around Settle and to the domed chapel at Giggleswick School. They listened to short talks on local history given by Bill Mitchell, interspersed with meditations on people who struggle around the world today.

An outline of this pilgrimage is included here as an example of what can be done in any local setting. The walk planned may be long or, as this one was, short. The opportunities for reflection and the encouragement to action for justice may be tremendous.

This journey began at Settle Parish Church, founded in 1836. Pilgrims were reminded of the men who worked on the building of the Settle to Carlisle Railway, which passes on a high embankment close to the church. Prayers were held for those who had died, and for those who have died in building railways all over the world. The plaque in the church remembers the men who died. There is also a gravestone for the Welsh workman who died when he was hit by the boom of a crane in Langcliffe cutting.

Meditation – for all those who have died at hard, difficult and dangerous work, all over the world.

Special thought and prayer may be offered for those who died in building the Burma railway during World War Two.

There is a memorial to them in St Martin-in-the-Fields Church in Trafalgar Square. Special thought and prayer is offered for those who do dangerous work today, for those at sea, for those in mining work everywhere.

The walk took the pilgrims on to the market place where, in

209

1652, William Dewsbury stood by the market cross and proclaimed 'the terrible day of the Lord which is hastening and coming upon the ungodly and the workers of iniquity'. He was beaten and abused by the townsfolk. In due course a meeting took place at the home of the widow Alice Armistead, and the Quaker faith was established in Settle. In 1777 John Wesley preached from the old mounting stone at the head of Kirkgate and all but two or three gentlefolk were seriously attentive.

Meditation – for all those who put their faith first all over the world today, and especially for those who are persecuted for their faith.

Special thought and prayer may be offered for Christians who live in the northern states of Nigeria, who are facing the withdrawal of many of their rights.

The walk continued to the Zion Chapel built up on the hillside and opened in 1817. The chapel had a famous member in Benjamin Waugh, the founder of the NSPCC.

Meditation – for children who face cruelty, in our own society and around the world.

Special thought and prayer may be offered for children who spend their short lives as soldiers in terrible situations.

Special thought and prayer may be offered for the street children of the world and for those who seek to work with them, for shelter, food and training towards a better future.

(There are over 65,000 street children in Bangalore, in India, alone.)

The walkers descended the hill and went into Chapel Street and on into Kirkgate to visit the peaceful Friends Meeting House with its beautiful garden.

Meditation – for the peace and for the peacemakers of the world.

Special thought and prayer is offered for the people who risk their lives in reconciliation and peace-making.

The path was followed to Giggleswick Parish Church dedicated to St Alkelda. The church includes a memorial to George Birkbeck, who founded the Mechanics Institute Movement. This was the beginnings of adult education for the men of Glasgow, which spread very widely.

Meditation – for those around the world who are illiterate, and for more effort by governments and voluntary agencies to bring literacy.
Special thought and prayer may be offered for the people who are brave enough to join literacy classes to improve their usefulness to their families and communities.

The long hill took walkers up to Giggleswick School Chapel which is set on a gritstone knoll above the village. The chapel is a Gothic building with a large and Oriental dome which is lined inside with beautiful mosaics. The chapel was built by Walter Morrison to mark the Diamond Jubilee of Queen Victoria.

Meditation – for all those who work for human rights around the world in spite of the danger to themselves.
Special thought and prayer may be offered for the work for democracy and human rights in Burma.

The walkers moved towards the end of the journey by crossing the bridge over the River Ribble and walking to the Methodist Chapel back in Settle.

Meditation – for all the pilgrims who now return home, though not to stay there. Whilst we live, the journey is never complete.

Photograph: Katy Haddelsey

Sponsored Walk

Sponsored Walk

Christine Allen

This sponsored walk and meditational pilgrimage in Derbyshire was to raise money for street children in and around Bangalore in South India. It is given as an example of what may be done by any pilgrim who wishes to share the journey *with* others and to make the journey *for* others.

For those of us not able to commit ourselves to a pilgrimage which may take place over many days, a sponsored walk is a valuable substitute. This may take the form of a mini-pilgrimage. What turns a sponsored walk into a mini-pilgrimage is having meditational stops, or some input which links the environment and the people who are walking to the concerns and the environment of those to whom the money raised is to be sent.

A good large-scale map of the route is a must, and it is helpful if the walk is mainly off-road with wide paths. The route needs to be fairly accessible to the leader in order for him or her to become familiar with it. Getting lost tries everyone's patience.

Toilet stops at strategic places, and sufficient eating/drinking stops, especially if the weather is hot, need to be considered for the overall timing of the walk. A good average length for the walk is around eight miles. A longer walk may discourage some people from signing up.

My preference for the walk is that it should be circular. Over the last ten years my own thinking has been transformed by an awareness that a cyclical, rather than linear, perception of life may be more helpful. Thus, hopefully, a circular walk brings us back to our starting place a little changed – to begin again from a slightly different perspective. This may be a sort of death and resurrection.

The motivations to participate may be on several levels. First of all there is the desire to raise money for a specific cause. There is a desire to deepen commitment, and an enjoyment of walking. For me, in particular, the walk is a means of bringing understanding and transforming of differences, whatever those differences may be. Walking also allows us to see and familiarise ourselves with people and their lives, in a way passing through a district in a car does not allow.

Perhaps I can illustrate what I mean. Whilst walking the route in order to familiarise myself with it ready for the 'real' walk, which was on 23 September 2000, I found part of the route crossed a field, which was fenced off, with RJB Mining notices displayed. The positioning of the stiles had changed from those marked on my map, and I could not find the stile which seemed to be in the yard of a farm attached to the land. I knocked at the farmhouse door and asked if their land had been sold to RJB Mining. I was not given the answer to this question, but the next time I walked the route, the land had been reinstated. No one would have known RJB Mining had taken out coal from this open-cast site. Farming is struggling to survive. Farms are having to diversify.

Further on I lost my way, and came across a tumbledown farm, absolutely deserted, with a little bit of everything – free-range hens scratching in the dirt, a tethered goat on the farmhouse lawn. The house door was open wide – reminiscent of a bygone age in the UK and much like Indian villages today.

Further on still, farms had been converted into riding schools, and there were a number of expensive-looking houses. I had seen a cross-section of society in an eight-mile square.

Were the rich aware of the struggles of the poor? Are we? Am I?

This last thought gives me an opportunity to introduce the idea of a sponsored walk being an opportunity to transform our thinking.

Because I am Christian, I use a Christian symbol to illustrate my thoughts. Perhaps other symbols may be used when people of all faiths are participating.

Over a period of time, thinking about the Christians Aware

logo, I have come to see Christ's Incarnation as the on-going struggle to bridge differences between cultures, between different perspectives, anywhere where differences occur.

There is a space, which lies between the differences, that can be bridged providing – as feminists Luce Irigaray and Julia Kristeva suggest – we lose our subjectivity. In acceptance, in openness and emptying of self, the way is there for true listening communication and a more compassionate world.

In this I am reminded of the dying of the grain of wheat that Jesus speaks of in St John's Gospel. 'I am telling you the truth: a grain of wheat remains no more than a single grain unless it is dropped into the ground and dies. If it does die, it produces many grains.'* I believe symbols are very important as catalysts in the process of transformation.

We began our walk standing by the remains of the nave arch of Dale Abbey. Once, this was home to a small community of Praemonstratensian Canons, who sought to combine worship with practical service and hard work, and to bring an awareness of a transcendent God who informs our daily living. The Abbey was dedicated to St Mary on 15 August 1204. We stood and thought about the homeless in Derbyshire, trying also to link our thoughts to the street children in India, who were going to be the recipients of our sponsorship.

One homeless person had died lying on a mattress in the Hermit's Cave, which looks out on to the Abbey Arch. What were his thoughts, and what are the thoughts of many whose bed is the earth or a pavement?

In order for transformation in our thinking to occur, the question needing to be asked was 'What does this arch say to you with respect to homelessness?' It is perhaps only when we all place our thoughts into this space that energy is created for change.

Our next stopping place for meditation was a small lake. I had chosen this place to stop for a short while, because the

* John 12:24.

lake had been cleaned out and re-established as part of a community Millennium project. Once a private boating lake for nearby Smalley Hall, it was now a place for everyone to enjoy. The small lake reminded me of the myriad of pools in India where communal washing of all descriptions takes place.

So, our second symbol was water. This time everyone made a contribution.

Clarissa, who had returned from a Christians Aware visit to Tanzania the previous day, told us of her part in helping to dig a well, without any assistance from mechanical equipment. Just the co-operation of many human hands.

Barbara reminded us how vital clean water is for all the people in the world. World Health Organisation statistics are as follows:

- Every eight seconds one child dies of a water-related illness.
- Around one billion people in the world still lack safe water.
- Adequate access to water is defined as 20-40 litres per person per day located within a reasonable distance from the household.

There was then some discussion about a programme on organic farming that had been shown on television the previous week. It said that there was no significant difference between food grown organically and non-organically.

It was suggested that though this may perhaps be the case, the problem was the build-up of pesticides and fertilisers in the water table if farming is non-organic. It was also suggested that our tap water has become too pure, leaving us vulnerable to impurities.

Returning to the lake recently, I found the site access barred, due to the foot and mouth epidemic, another reminder of the vulnerability of our farms.

At our final stopping place, in the garden of Morley Retreat Centre, David Hart, from the Multifaith Project of the University of Derby, showed us photographs of the project for which we were raising money. David had visited the project on several occasions.

We were each given an opportunity to choose one of the photographs and look at it, as David spoke to us about Samuel Issmer and his work with the street children through South Asia Children in Crisis run from Bangalore. In a sense, we chose our own symbol on which to meditate.

In March, Samuel came to stay with David, and a visit to a Christians Aware India Group meeting was arranged. As a result, Christians Aware is supporting an orphanage in South India.

Transform our individual lives, Lord,
so that as we walk through life,
we shall so identify with our fellow pilgrims
that we become inspired by a common vision
in order to bring fullness of life to all.

Pilgrimage Against Poverty

The pilgrimage was organised from August to October 1999, from Iona to London, from Holywell to Cardiff, and from St David's to Cardiff. It arose from the vision of Church Action on Poverty and was a tremendous effort, by organisers and walkers. The struggle of the walkers was symbolic of the on-going struggle of those who are materially poor in the UK, and it was a commitment to bring change for them and their futures. The aim of the pilgrims is to work for the eradication of poverty in the UK by 2020. The 'Agenda for Change' sets out the key priorities for action, including the provision of 'enough good work for all'.

The journey began with a service in Iona Abbey when the pilgrims were given a Celtic cross and a blessing:

God be with you now
as you start your journey of faith.
May your long walk
be a sign in our land
of the unending walk
of those who are poor,
and the agenda for change they present.
May the companionship
that you find on the way
herald new solidarity for the
marginalised ones,
and may Christ, who befriended them,
and who said, 'Follow me',
befriend them now.
The Spirit of justice and joy empower you.*

* From the Church Action on Poverty Report on the walk – available from Church Action on Poverty, Central Buildings, Oldham Street, Manchester, M1 1JT. Telephone 0161 236 9321.

Seven people set off from Iona, including an unemployed man, and thousands joined in along the way, making this perhaps the biggest anti-poverty demonstration since the Jarrow march of 1936. The pilgrims were met by bands, meetings and speeches along the route. Issues of poverty, some of them hidden from ordinary visitors, were raised in the places they stopped in and passed through. They camped, stayed in church halls and even churches. 'We went through Dumbarton to Clydebank . . . our hosts were the Baptists in their church and hall, opposite what had been John Brown's shipyard. Nothing was too much trouble. Even the cushions came off the church benches to provide extra padding for floored hipbones!'

Many school children met the pilgrims along the way. One girl wrote, 'It was a special day today because we did a play for the pilgrims. . . . After the play we watched a video on poverty, it was really interesting . . .'

After 700 miles the pilgrimage ended in Trafalgar Square and with a service in St Martin-in-the-Fields Church. Fifteen pilgrims met the Chancellor, Gordon Brown, to ask for the Government to act against poverty. The Chancellor gave his commitment to full employment.

A Pilgrim People

Riah Abu al-Assal, Anglican Bishop in Jerusalem

Bishop Riah lives in one of the most famous places of pilgrimage in the world, Jerusalem. He is someone who has long appealed to people of faith around the world to go to the land which is holy for Christians, Muslims and Jewish people, not just to visit the holy places but to meet the people and to work with them for justice and a peaceful future. He has also organised a scheme which helps visitors to meet the local people, to visit their homes and share the issues they face. He says, '. . . come and visit us in this land that we long to make holy – we will give you a wonderful welcome . . . but do not come and pass us by. We need your visits, your support, your fellowship and your prayers.'*

Bishop Riah feels strongly that many of the people who have left the Middle East to live all over the world should return, to help to bring peace. He has especially appealed to Palestinian Christians to return to their homeland to work for justice: 'Christians, not only in Israel but in the whole of the Middle East, are rapidly becoming an insignificant factor, in terms of both numbers and influence. . . . More and more Christians, especially the young, are leaving for other countries. Whereas in 1967 there were 28,000 Christian Arab Palestinians in Jerusalem, today there are closer to 7,000 . . .'†

He has written here about pilgrimage to the Middle East in the context of his Christian faith and as an unfinished journey for justice.

* From the preface to *A Candle of Hope* by Garth Hewitt, published by the Bible Reading Fellowship in 1999.
† *Caught in Between* by Riah abu El-Assal is published by SPCK, 1999. It is Riah's story and also the story of his people, the Arab/Palestinian Christians.

Introduction

Normally one thinks of pilgrimage as a journey made by pilgrims to a sacred place, as an act of religious devotion. But pilgrimage could also refer to life as a whole. In traditional religious terms, life is a journey towards a future state of rest and blessedness. In recent times, pilgrimage has been used to indicate any journey made for respectful, nostalgic or sentimental reasons, to come and stay with the strangers, people we never met. So pilgrimage does not mean only to visit sites in this sense, but it is also to encounter people. Thus it could mean enhancing peace and justice between strangers and enemies as they seek to meet and journey together.

Pilgrimage therefore has a message. And that message has a very long history and its central focus remains common to an enormous variety of different traditions. Pilgrimage is not restricted to the Judeo-Christian tradition only. The shrines of ancient Greece are part of that history too. The pagan deities had their own cultic centres. The most famous of them is that of Apollo at Delphi. Pilgrims would come to visit Delphi on particular days to celebrate a specific festival. Similarly, pilgrimage in Islam, to the cities of Mecca and Medina, is one of the most central pillars of religion. There has always appeared a human instinct, which combines religious sensitivity with travelling out from one's home. Travelling ensues from being willing to achieve that which cannot be had except through the grace and gift of God himself. Prayer thus becomes a major part of the journey.

The Biblical Tradition

In the biblical tradition, the roots of pilgrimage go back to the story of Abraham in the Old Testament. Abraham sets out with his family into a strange land, following the call of God.* Abraham responds to God's promise that his people will be taken into a new land where they will both be blessed

* Genesis 12:1.

221

and be a blessing unto many. This becomes the firm biblical tradition for the early Christian Church: wandering for God, and moving always onward.

Christians across the centuries have considered Christian life itself, for individuals and groups, as a pilgrimage. Apart from being a discipline within Christian spirituality, pilgrimage becomes an image for the Christian life. In Hebrews 11:13, in some translations of the Greek the image of the pilgrimage is used to describe the Christian life itself: 'These all died in faith, not having received the promises, but having seen them afar off, and were persuaded of them, and embraced them, and confessed that they were strangers and pilgrims on the earth.' Some translations use other words like 'exiles' or 'sojourners'. But the meaning is still there. We are aliens in a strange land, hoping and preparing for our arrival to the presence of God, who is Eternal Truth.

A more central theological Christian tradition is the Passion narratives in the gospels. Scholars believe that the Passion narratives are the most ancient continuous narrative elements within the gospels. However, many scholars also believe that the Passion narratives reached their present form as a result of being at the centre of pilgrimage liturgies. The story of Jesus' death was acted out in procession moving between the holy places within Jerusalem, ending in Calvary and the empty tomb.

These prayers, these celebrations should not be held together for our benefit only, however important they are for themselves, and however beautiful they are to remember and enact. They are there to uphold others as well. As we pray and celebrate Jesus' life, we think of Jesus and worshippers massacred in Hebron. We think of Jesus and of children killed for no blame of their own. We think of Jesus and the dead, or mentally handicapped. Here appears the power of pilgrim prayers. Our prayer becomes a sharing in Christ's costly struggle to hold God and the world together. It reflects the full implications of faith in Christ crucified.

Pilgrims and Local Christians

Pilgrimages, in this case, were to join the worship of the Church in its birthplace, recalling and celebrating the death of Christ, proclaiming the gospel as it is rooted in self-giving love, culminating in the Cross and Resurrection, reconciling humanity and divinity together. This, of course, becomes the ministry of all Christians and faithful pilgrims. As St Paul reminds us in his second epistle to the people of Corinth, 'God was in Christ reconciling the world unto himself not imputing their trespasses unto them; and hath committed unto us the word of reconciliation'.* Being pilgrims also means being entrusted with God's mission of reconciliation.

In fact, in the early Irish Christian tradition, there appears a connection between pilgrimage and martyrdom. Pilgrimage becomes a particular form of martyrdom. The individual's own will was resigned to the will of God. The self-giving love of Christ is reflected in the self-denial in the search for God on this earth, praying for the fulfilment of God's promise to all humanity.

One may conclude from this that pilgrimage is associated with a life of self-denial, solitude and contemplation, but, most importantly, is combined with missionary vocation. And here the understanding of the nature of mission may vary from time to time and from place to place. When it comes to the Land of the Holy One, our mission and the mission of the Church comes out strikingly to emphasise the importance of peace, based on justice, truth and reconciliation as our ministry is that of reconciliation. This is the mission of the Pilgrim Church in Palestine and all those who come to visit the land.

Historical Sketch

Historically, pilgrimage to the Holy Land has been a long-standing tradition. From virtually the earliest days of Christianity,

* 2 Corinthians 5:19.

individual Christians visited the Holy Land. The earliest known Christian pilgrim, Melito of Sardis, visited in 160 AD, in order to establish accurately the books of the Old Testament. But the interest intensified when Emperor Constantine became a Christian. A number of the accounts of those early pilgrims are preserved.

The pilgrimage of Egeria, a Spanish Abbess, to Jerusalem at the end of the fourth century is a sharp example of this ancient Christian tradition. Egeria wrote down what she witnessed during her time in Jerusalem. Her pilgrimage was punctuated by worship. She relates the patterns of daily prayer of the Church, and the celebration of the death and the resurrection of Jesus. The major concern at the time was to visit the biblical sites, especially those associated with the ministry of Jesus.

However, the Holy Land did not seem to attract many pilgrims and was not known to the west. The perceptions of the place were influenced by the imagined world of the biblical texts, with its green lawns, olive trees, a kind of William Blake's Jerusalem, and Nazareth's angelic scenes. The pictures have been westernised in the religious imagination, aided by European-like landscapes with no reflection on the real thing. Western pilgrims avoided contact with 'the natives', were disdainful of their customs and pious practices. This is probably unlike the early pilgrims who came to visit, and who had no other choice than to stay with local families. Remember, there were no hotels or other public houses providing accommodation for staying overnight, except for the local people who would offer other hospitality. The twentieth century provided further air travel facilitation.

The Land and the People

The twentieth century, however, brought about another distinctive phenomenon: the transformation of the demography of Palestine as a result of the fulfilment of the goal of political Zionism. Hundreds of thousands of Palestinians were expelled in 1948, and over 400 villages were destroyed to ensure they could not return. In 1967, more left their homes from the Occupied Territories in the wake of Israel's occupation in June of that year. The Church was lost in the middle of all this, and Christians left the country, with their fellow Christians from the west unaware of their history and tradition.

Many of those who visited the land after 1948 wished to walk in the footsteps of Jesus, to confirm their biblical pieties. They were more interested in searching out their religious roots than investigating the condition of those who live in the land. Mostly they shared a sympathy for Jews, and were in admiration of their achievements in establishing a state. But, of course, the Arab victims of the occupation included fellow-Christians, the 'living stones' who proudly trace their Christian identity to the first Pentecost.

In addition, pilgrimage to Palestine across the decades has become a very popular and almost commonplace in contemporary Christianity. Bogus forms of romantic idealism easily hijack pilgrimage, which is taken over by the commercialism of a materialistic age. Jerusalem T-shirts and bottles of Holy Land Water and soil (they have not produced Holy Land air yet) lure people to empty their wallets into the coffers of the cunningly designed souvenir centres and gift shops.

Pilgrims and Tourists

This may make some people draw a distinction between 'a tourist' and 'a pilgrim'. Others may say there is no such distinction, for there is no material distinction between God and the world anyway. True, but the pilgrim who comes to the country comes not only to visit and enjoy, but also has in mind a different target for his journey. Those who claim to come with a religious aim say that they seek to grow further into the mystery of Christ, and learn more about his faith and the aim of his mission in life.

It cannot be better. However, one cannot do that only through one's own efforts. If we want to learn more about

Christ, we do so with the people we meet, the activities we seek to attend and by the willingness to listen to those around us who seek to challenge our preconceived or already-decided ideas of the strangers we meet and of God. When meeting the people, one's discoveries integrate one's earlier perceptions, and in some cases the person is led to a life-changing conversion. This cannot be done without meeting the people of the land and the vigour with which the 'living stones' witness to their faith in trying circumstances. Encountering such people is a sacred experience. Eventually religious disposition and a determination to work for justice and a sense of walking with the suffering Christ rise to the surface when meeting the 'living stones', and going beyond the perfunctory visit to the holy sites.

Holy Stones and Living Stones

This in fact leads to another question, mainly the goal of visiting 'sacred space' and the whole understanding of sacred ground. It is not about an enactment of a religious impulse to reunite with sacred space and in so doing to separate oneself from the ordinary mundane or profane world. Here the distinction between 'holy' and 'secular' is an illusion. The whole faith and celebration of Christ's life in the Church and in the Sacraments is about the value of the material life we live, as it is a sharing in God's own life. The holiness of Jerusalem is not something to be found locked in a shrine. It is there because it reminds us that God's gift of himself is there even in the middle of chaos, disaster and suffering as revealed in the resurrection of Jesus. Truly God's presence is experienced in liturgies and churches, but it is also found in the trivialities of life, and when one walks down the 'suq' in the old city of Jerusalem.

Thomas Idinopulos writes in his article, 'Sacred Space and Profane Power' that the pilgrimage to the sacred sites of the Holy Land and Jerusalem provides little evidence of a neat set of dichotomies called 'sacred' and 'secular'. For in

Holy Land pilgrimage, ancient and modern, the pilgrim was also confirmed in political, ethno-national, and cultural identity.*

The implication of this evidence is important in our thinking about 'sacred space'. It means that either the dichotomies of 'sacred' and 'profane' are too narrowly conceived, or that some other concept must be found to clarify the mixture of ideal and material, religious and political-cultural motives that entered into pilgrimage to the 'sacred space' of the Holy Land. Theologically, there seems to be difficulty to make a clear material distinction between all these labels. The pertinence between the realm of politics and religious faith can be found in the acknowledgement of the need for a general repentance by all. Or the simple faith conclusion: 'All is in God and all belongs to him.'

Unfortunately we have witnessed recently a decline of numbers of pilgrims due to the political situation. Pilgrimages, as said earlier, were meant to make the pilgrims come and meet with local Christians, and support them in their distress and difficult times. However, many people continue to think that pilgrims were meant to visit holy sites. And since it is 'dangerous' to be in those places, with those people who have been witness to Christ since the first Pentecost, they decide to cancel their trips. The 'alternative pilgrimages', however, call upon us to journey towards the unknown, and meet the people who are different and strange to our culture and tradition. They call upon us to come and listen to humanity, hungry and eager for peace and justice. Not only do we need to hear them, but also understand them, accept them, and know them as they are, and as Christ knew them and us, forgave us and understood us. This is where our pilgrimage comes to fulfilment, when we seek to enhance the welfare of human beings created in the image of God, give heed to the value of human lives, and enhance the cause of peace based on the foundation of justice, truth and righteousness which is the cause of Christ himself.

The article appears in *Pilgrims and Travellers to the Holy Land*, edited by Bryan Le Beau, 1996.

Conclusion

To conclude here is a paragraph from William Sloan Coffin called 'The Task'.

> We are pilgrim people, a people who have decided never to arrive, a people who live by hope, energised not by what we already possess but by that which is promised: 'Behold I create a new heaven and new earth.'
>
> Sure, it's tiring and it's tough. Imagination comes harder than memory and faithfulness is more demanding than success. But see what if we fail? Remember, we are not required to finish the task – any more than we are allowed to put it aside.
>
> May our task and the task of our pilgrimage be that which is for the peace and stability of all, acknowledging that we exist by gift and gift alone bestowed freely upon us from God.

The Nativity Trail
A Walk from Nazareth to Bethlehem

Andrew Ashdown

In April 2000, in a scene reminiscent of biblical times, a Bedouin shepherd boy was playing a haunting tune on his pipe as he watched his goats on a hillside east of Bethlehem. An eagle soared overhead. In the fertile valley below, close to an ancient threshing-floor, was a cistern, which had fed the valley with water for many hundreds of years. Ancient channels dug in the surrounding hillsides led the rainwater to the cistern, and from there to the valley floor. But like so many cisterns we had encountered on our 100-mile walk from the northernmost reaches of Palestine, along the eastern hills of the West Bank, this one was sealed with concrete. 'Oh no,' groaned Mark, the Palestinian organiser of the walk. 'This cistern was open when I passed it two weeks ago.' Kefar, one of our fellow-walkers, a Muslim from Ramallah, sat down, his head in his hands. A sombre, depressed silence descended upon us. As we approached Bethlehem, another shepherd lamented that soon, without access to water, he would be forced to move elsewhere. The valley would become parched, enabling the Israelis to plant another settlement on supposedly unused land. The beauty of the valley, rich in biblical history, nurtured by generations of Palestinians, belied the tragedy which was facing it, and which faced so many of the valleys through which we had walked.

This scene encapsulated so much of the profound experience of joining a group of Palestinians on a newly developed ten-day 100-mile trail from Nazareth to Bethlehem. We were a small group. I had travelled to the Holy Land with Susan, a writer of children's liturgical resources and prayers. Our only European companions were Tony, a walker and climber, who had been invited by Mark to research a book on walks in Palestine, and

Drawing by Jane Walton-Loxton

his partner, Di. Together we were the first Europeans to walk the trail. Our companions were trainee guides. Eli was the group leader – a Syrian Orthodox Palestinian Christian with a deep love of his country, a bubbly sense of humour, and an amiable tendency to burst into Arabic love-songs! George, another Palestinian Christian, with a friendly and encouraging personality, was our driver, who transported our baggage and food supplies to our destination each evening. Sami, an earnest young man with a commanding knowledge of Palestinian history, amused us with his regular bursts of information. His parents still possessed the key to the family home and factory in Israel, which they had been forced to leave without compensation and with three hours' notice in 1948. Ramzi was training to be a guide, but had still not been given the necessary permission to spend any nights outside the Bethlehem area. His presence with us was, in effect, illegal. And finally there was Kefar, the only Muslim in the group. At first, he appeared withdrawn and regularly walked apart from the group, but as the days wore on we discovered how friendly he was. Kefar had been imprisoned as a teenager for throwing stones during the first intifada, and had spent several years in Israeli prisons. The experience had clearly been a brutal one and he was deeply emotionally scarred by it. He claimed to be an atheist, but had a deep love, and understanding, of Sufi spirituality. All our Palestinian companions, young men that they were, showed a passionate love and enthusiasm for their country and their people, and a profound frustration and sadness at the injustices and humiliation which they experience in their daily lives, simply because they are Palestinian.

For Susan and me, our pilgrimage had begun at St George's Cathedral, with an early morning Eucharist in the company of Bishop Riah, the Anglican Bishop of Jerusalem, who himself has an inspiring story to tell.* In all of Jerusalem, the Palestinian

---

*Bishop Riah's story can be read in his autobiography: Riah Abu El-Assal, *Caught in Between: The Extraordinary Story of an Arab Palestinian Christian Israeli.* SPCK, 1999.

231

territories, and Israel, there are about 165,000 indigenous Christians, but fewer than 3000 Palestinian Anglican or Lutheran Christians remain. They are served by 25 Anglican clergy. Nevertheless, Christians contribute far more to the national community, particularly in the work of education and health, than their numbers might suggest, and their senior figures have been instrumental in working for justice and peace in the Holy Land. (Of the 714,000 Palestinians who became refugees as a result of the creation of the State of Israel in 1948, over 50,000 were Christians – 35 per cent of all Palestinian Christians. Since then, many thousands more have emigrated because of the harsh conditions and limited opportunities for Palestinians in their land.)*

For two days prior to meeting our walking companions, Susan and I had wandered the streets of the Old City, pondered and prayed at the holy sites, walked over the Mount of Olives to Bethany, and reflected at the Dome of the Rock – the centre of so much controversy and a site sacred to Muslims, Jews and Christians. And yet, as we read the scriptures there, I was reminded of the Covenant made with Abraham. Wasn't the Covenant, the promise of the Land, made for all Abraham's offspring? Are not Jew, Muslim and Christian all children of Abraham? Moreover, the promise was made on the basis that, first and foremost, the land belonged to God, that his people were to be stewards of that land and that they were to 'let justice roll down like the waters, and righteousness like an ever-flowing stream'† – then there would be peace in the land that the Lord God gave his people.

In a Palestinian Christian shop on the Via Dolorosa, we visited Farida, who for 37 years has worked in the same shop, and has made most of the vestments used at St George's Anglican Cathedral. Throughout those years, Farida has trained

* The figures are from *Christians in the Holy Land,* edited by Michael Prior and William Taylor, World of Islam Festival Trust, 1994.
† Amos 5:24.

hundreds of young women in the skill of Palestinian embroidery, and had received an award from King Hussein of Jordan for her service. A very friendly old lady, she spoke lovingly of her work, and then in a sad voice urged us to pray for her people, as life for Palestinians in Jerusalem was getting more and more difficult. Later, in West Jerusalem, we watched in disbelief as teenage Israeli soldiers aggressively demanded of any Palestinian, whatever their age, their identity cards. Invariably, we noticed that even young Palestinian men responded with dignity and even politeness.

It was with some trepidation at the effort before us that we were met by our fellow walkers and driven through the desert into the Jordan Valley, past the refugee camps, the Israeli army camps, and alongside the triple-fenced border with Jordan towards Nazareth. Days of rain in the previous weeks had left a multi-coloured carpet of flowers along the valley floor – a rare array of colour in this, one of the hottest valleys on earth. Once again, the beauty of the scene belied the tension and the injustices which are always present, and which we were to encounter so powerfully during the next ten days. In one sense the pilgrimage had already begun, but in another it was yet to begin with the walking itself. For the moment we were getting a glimpse of the reality of life for the people of the land. But soon we were to encounter the people themselves, to 'feel' the land under our feet, to hear the people's story, and to witness for ourselves something of the reasons behind the years of conflict. This was more than just an ordinary pilgrimage – and I had been on several of those before. This was indeed to be a pilgrimage for justice and peace.

The Nativity Trail begins in Nazareth. Once a sleepy little town, Nazareth is now a 'city' of over 60,000 people. Once predominantly Christian, the Christian/Muslim population is now about 50,150. The large new Jewish town of Nazaret Illit dominates the hills above the old city, and is rapidly changing the demography of the area. In the Old City, we reflected on the beginnings of the Christian story at the Basilica of the

Annunciation, and sipped the cold, sparkling water of 'Mary's well' – where in all probability the women of Nazareth had gathered for centuries. From there we proceeded to Mount Tabor, rising 588 metres above the plain of Jezreel. Previously, and like most pilgrims, I had ascended the mountain by Mercedes taxi. This time, we climbed up the steep mountain amidst the pine trees, through the abundance of flowers, with magnificent views of the Jezreel Valley below us and the Sea of Galilee in the distance. One of the widest and most fertile valleys in the Near East, the Jezreel Valley formed a natural route on the 'Via Maris' from the Mediterranean to the East. Babylonians, Assyrians, Egyptians, Romans all marched through this valley in their quest for empire. Mount Tabor holds a commanding position in the valley only seven miles from Nazareth. A tradition holds that this is the mount where Jesus was transfigured before his disciples, and there is a beautiful basilica at the summit, but whether or not this tradition is true (Mount Hermon is the more likely location for this event) Jesus would almost certainly have come to this place with his disciples. The remains of a 3000-year-old Canaanite altar in the floor of the Basilica attest to the fact that this has been a holy site since ancient times.

With so much of the Jezreel Valley covered by pathless fields and busy towns and villages, we proceeded by vehicle to the village of Faqu'a in the Gilboa mountains, just inside the northernmost border of the West Bank. A beautiful route through low-lying hills, topped everywhere by Israeli watch-towers, led us past an abundance of Israeli army vehicles and checkpoints to this remote Palestinian village. Warmly welcomed by the villagers, we were accommodated in the Village Council Chamber and treated to an Arab dinner of chicken, rice and salad. Members of the Village Council and a teacher from the local school ate with us, and spoke of the many Israeli settlements that are being built in the surrounding hills (contrary to the agreements of the Oslo Peace Accord). Arab land is acquisitioned without compensation, and any

Arab building built within 75 metres of any of the many new roads to the settlements is immediately demolished for 'security' reasons. But the local people, with few resources, continue to lead a normal life in the simplicity of their homes and farming the fertile fields. A hearty meal was enjoyed in good company and with plenty of laughter, before a fitful sleep prepared us for the next nine days of walking.

We had an early breakfast of hummus, locally produced yoghurt, unleavened bread and mint tea, and the rising sun, streaming through the haze of a cool dawn, revealed the fertile, low-lying hills of the northern 'West Bank'. The village was already alive as we walked along a track heading south. Lines of cacti plants bordered fields – a traditional and very natural boundary in Arab villages. Throughout Israel and the West Bank, where one sees cacti in abundance in valley floors or hillsides, or even at Israeli settlements, it is probable that there was once an Arab village there – perhaps one of the 374 long-established Arab villages demolished by the new State of Israel in 1948. On the side of the track, Palestinians awaited transport to be taken to their work on nearby Israeli-held land.

Following tracks and footpaths, we passed through numerous olive groves and orchards. There were wild flowers in abundance, as well as herbs and carob trees. We were struck by the fertility of the land, and the fact that every foot of it, even in the remotest valleys, seemed to be cultivated in some way or another – smallholdings ploughed with a traditional donkey-drawn wooden plough. We passed through the ancient Canaanite villages of Jalboun and Mughayir, flourishing and sizeable Arab communities. Our Palestinian guides were essential since few Arab villages, no matter what their size, are marked on Israeli maps, although the smallest Israeli settlement is sure to be identified. Passing over two passes we watched as shepherds overlooked their flocks, calling each sheep by a different high pitched whistle or cry, and, walking along valley floors, we passed men, women and children at work in the fields.

Photographs: Andrew Ashdown

Pilgrims on the Nativity Trail

By mid-afternoon we reached the large Palestinian village of Zababdeh, one of the last predominantly Christian villages in the West Bank. It is situated on one of the old Roman roads between Nazareth and Jerusalem, and in another wide and fertile valley often used as a transit route from the Mediterranean to the Jordan Valley. (The neighbouring valley of Dothan is where Joseph was sold into slavery.) We were now in biblical Samaria, and with its numerous archaeological and early Christian remains, Zababdeh was very likely to be one of the Samaritan towns and villages visited by Jesus. Fr Louis Hazboun, the local Roman Catholic priest, enthusiastically and proudly showed the group around the village and his multi-faith, mixed-sex school. Drinking black coffee in a traditional stone house, we listened to Fr Louis speaking of village life, whilst in the distance gunshots sounded from a nearby Israeli military camp.

The following day, we walked through the highlands of the West Bank, through pine forests and olive groves, along tracks surrounded by flowers. Even our Palestinian companions had not seen such an abundance of flora – the extensive rains of a few weeks previously had been a blessing. As we progressed, the soil remained fertile, but gradually the ground was becoming more rocky and the scenery more dramatic. The stillness of the landscape was only marred by the regular roar of Israeli military jets which are constantly surveying the West Bank, watching for any 'unusual' activity, or checking for any unauthorised new buildings. One cannot but feel that one is being watched, and such constant and intrusive surveillance only creates resentment amongst the local people.

At midday we descended from the hills into the broad sweep of the Wadi Far'a. At its head lies the Spring of Ain Far'a. Here lie the ruins of Tirza. Originally a Canaanite town, Tirzah was adopted as the first capital of the Northern Kingdom, before it was transferred to Samaria by King Omri. However, there are few remains, and today a sleepy Arab village surrounds the spring. We joined some children for a swim in the cool waters before enjoying a 'hagila' – the 'hubbly-bubbly' pipe. The walk continued through the Wadi Far'a. This was in all probability the valley up which Abraham walked on his way from Harran to Shechem (Nablus). The valley is extremely fertile, and it was in a village house several miles down the valley, with peaks of 800 metres either side, that we spent the night. Seated on the floor in Arab style, with a feast before us, we talked with our hosts long into the evening.

At dawn, our first climb of over 700 metres began. Bedouin shepherds were camped high on the hill. One of the shepherds came over on his donkey. 'There is an Israeli settler with a machine gun living on top of the hill,' he said. 'When our children went there, he hit them. How can we have peace?' Avoiding the summit, we followed a track over a pass, and down into the village of Beit Dajan. We picnicked on a small hill in the middle of nowhere. But there was no peace there. Diggers were clearing the neighbouring hill. A new settlement was being established. And the extensive olive groves at the foot of the hill, farmed for generations by local Palestinians, would be confiscated. Ehud Barak had only declared two weeks previously that all new settlement building had ceased. In the next few days we were to be confronted again and again with the reality of the situation.

After a further steep climb of 866 metres, we discovered a barbed-wire fence and another new Israeli settlement. The olive groves surrounding the summit and the terraces were lying abandoned. The Arab farmers could no longer reach them without being forced away at gunpoint. From there we could see what was happening all around us. On every strategic highpoint on the surrounding hills, the ugly scar of Israeli settlements, watchtowers and 'security lights' could be seen. 'Look how beautiful they are,' cried Ramzi sarcastically, 'how they fit into the local environment and the landscape!' 'This is what the delays in fulfilling the Oslo Accords is about,' our friends told us. 'They are building on all the commanding summits, ringing our villages, separating one from the other.

Every settlement and "by-pass" road has a cleared zone on either side. If you happen to live in those areas, you are evicted from your home which is destroyed with no compensation.'

Avoiding the settlement we picked up the track on the other side of the hill, and amidst a carpet of flowers, passed through the ruins of a Palestinian village, perhaps hundreds of years old. Perhaps this was one of the villages destroyed in 1948. It was extensive – the pattern of streets and houses could easily be made out. Ancient cisterns and wells were visible. There was a tragic atmosphere. In the stillness, I sensed, in a very profound way, the stones bearing the memory of suffering and crying out for justice. Further down the valley we reached our destination for that day – the hamlet of Yanoun. We spent the night in the Ottoman compound of Abu Yassin. It was a beautiful starlit sky, but the bright orange lights of Israeli watchtowers dominated the valley. On a neighbouring hilltop was the tomb of Nun, father of Joshua.

The following day was an easy stroll along hillside tracks, past small villages and terraced hillsides to the village of Duma. Arriving early, we were taken on an excursion to Nablus, the ancient city of Shechem, originally a Canaanite town. There, in the middle of the souk, we relaxed in a Turkish bath built in 1480, before visiting the site of 'Jacob's Well' and the ruins of biblical Shechem. Everywhere the local Palestinians warmly welcomed us. However, the unkempt streets of the extensive refugee camp contrasted starkly with the 'orderliness' of the ominous Israeli settlements overlooking the town.

From Duma, the trail crosses deep valleys and ascends to high ridges with panoramic views across the desert to the hills of Jordan, and across to Jerusalem, and then proceeds down into deep gorges riddled with caves. All along the route we came across wells and cisterns that had been sealed with concrete by Israeli soldiers in an attempt to force people off the land. We descended the dramatic Wadi Auja into the Jordan Valley. Just before the wadi opens out into the Jordan Valley, some 300 metres below sea-level, a fast-flowing spring plunges out of the rock. It is a beautiful sight, and the cool, crystal water is deeply refreshing in the desert heat. Ain al-Auja is the largest spring in the West Bank. Yet, the Palestinian people could not claim even this. Two hundred metres downstream, the water disappears into Israeli pipes for Israeli settlements and Israeli farms. A small percentage of the water is sold back to the Palestinians at extortionate cost. But the people are not allowed to dig their own wells – the digging of new wells by the Arab people has been banned since 1967.

We spent that night in a Bedouin camp on the fringe of the Jordan Valley. Enjoying a barbecue and the sweet smell of the 'nargile' pipe, we heard about the life of the Bedouin. Traditionally nomadic, the Bedouin have no documents of title to the land. They are therefore considered to have no rights. Travellers to the Holy Land are probably often disappointed when they see the impoverished sight of permanent Bedouin camps along the main road from Jerusalem to Jericho, and up the Jordan Valley. This is because the Bedouin in that region have been forced off nearly all the land that they traditionally roam. Both Bedouin and Palestinian are now denied permission to put down dwellings in huge areas of the desert between Jerusalem and the Dead Sea and along the Jordan Valley. They are confined to small areas, mostly where they can be watched, and if they move out of those areas, then any dwellings are destroyed, and they lose all rights to settle there again. By contrast, any Jew of any nationality is given permission and encouraged to settle anywhere they wish in the land. Next day, walking south across the stony desert towards Jericho, we passed the barbed-wire fences of an Israeli army base, before passing another Bedouin camp and a temporary school – a tin shack with a few desks and chairs. The teacher, discovering we were English, said, whilst offering us tea, 'You gave our homeland to the Israelis, but you are welcome.'

By now we had reached the outskirts of Jericho, and we climbed the Mount of Temptation. We wandered through the Monastery visiting the cave 'where Jesus was tempted', and climbed up to the summit of the mountain. It is an awesome sight – the desert and the hills behind; the summit of the Mount of Olives appearing in the distance; and before us the whole of the Jordan Valley, the Dead Sea and the Mountains of Moab in Jordan. Our friends treated us to a swim in the Dead Sea and we were taken to a small Israeli resort by the lakeside. The entrance fee for Israelis and foreigners was 55 shekels; the Palestinians had to pay 105 shekels to get in. Returning to the camp that evening after a meal in a restaurant in Jericho, Israeli soldiers detained us on the way, whilst a military exercise passed by.

The Wadi Kelt extends from Jericho to Jerusalem and is a spectacular gorge. It is the route of the ancient road from Jerusalem to Jericho. Rock hyrax scurry amongst the cliffs, and in the cliff walls are numerous caves used in Byzantine times by Christian hermits. Further up the wadi is the fifth-century Monastery of St George of Koziba, a site linked to Elijah, and St Joachin, father of Mary. Welcomed into the monastery, we drank mint tea, and, visiting the chapel, were surrounded by icons and the bones of monks martyred by the Persians. It is a peaceful and beautiful place. Climbing out of the Wadi Kelt, we crossed the high places of the Judean Desert, but immediately one could see Israeli settlements on many summits. The most dominant one is Maale Adummim. Once a tiny village, this is now a constantly expanding Jewish settlement of over 10,000 people. But more disturbing is the fact that the municipal limits of this settlement have been set at an area larger than the city of Tel Aviv, and extend from the outskirts of Jerusalem all the way to the Jordan Valley. This means that no Arab settlement or dwelling is allowed within these limits – so a huge area has been denied both to the Bedouin and the Palestinian people of the land. Continuing south across the dry desert hills, we reached the shrine, mosque and caravanserai of Nebi Musa (the Prophet Moses) with its origins in the thirteenth century. This is where we spent the night.

The following morning we had hoped to walk to the Monastery of Mar Saba. Unfortunately, after five kilometres along a deserted road, we came across an extensive Israeli army camp. Ventilation shafts all across the desert floor testified to the presence of some substantial underground facility. No sooner had we appeared than a jeep full of armed soldiers rushed to question us. 'Where are you going? What are you doing here?' they asked abruptly. 'This area is closed for exercises.' 'Please could you drive us through . . . we've walked all the way from Nazareth,' we pleaded. Permission was refused. We had no choice but to resort to the mobile phone, to ring George to take us back by road round to Mar Saba – a distance of 30 miles. And so we missed 10 kilometres of the walk. As we waited for George in the shade of a desert cliff, the familiar sound of gunfire and explosions echoed through the hills. It transpired that the military exercises in this area take place five days a week. Clinging to the cliff-face of the Kidron Valley, Mar Saba Monastery is in a spectacular setting. Built in 478 by St Sabas, one of the leaders of desert monasticism, it is still a flourishing community. Sadly, the monks there are not known for their hospitality, and, true to form, we were prohibited from entering by a grey-bearded monk informing us that prayers were in progress. As it was mid-morning, we had no choice but to continue walking, from there to Bethlehem, a steep eight-mile climb through the desert hills. The views were outstanding. Kestrels and buzzards glided on the gentle breeze, and flute-playing shepherds watched their flocks in the quiet valleys. How long they will remain quiet and untouched is anyone's guess, as we realised sitting around the sealed well just outside Bethlehem. That night, from our guesthouse in Beit Sahour, just near the 'Shepherds' Fields', we looked across at the settlement of Har Homa. Only a few years ago this was a forested hill between Jerusalem and Bethlehem. Now, it is a growing town, with an anticipated population of 25,000.

Our pilgrimage ended the following morning at the Cave

of the Nativity in Bethlehem. Afterwards we took a taxi to Hebron, a town of 150,000 Palestinians, watched over by 1500 Israeli soldiers who are 'protecting' just 200 Jewish settlers in the centre of town. And later that evening, after negotiating numerous checkpoints, we joined our companions for a restaurant meal in the town of Ramallah. Ramallah possessed a real atmosphere of vibrancy and proud Palestinian identity. Little did we realise the tragedy that would strike the town just a few months later. Throughout our pilgrimage, we had witnessed signs of hope in the warmth and generosity of the people, the courageous struggles of the Palestinians to live in dignity, and their true desire for peace. But we had also witnessed their frustration, their despair, and their increasing anger at the theft and destruction of their land and their water supplies, and at the humiliation that they experience daily when they try to move within their own country. We had seen the effect of Israeli settlements and 'bypasses' on the land and the people, and witnessed how the so-called 'peace process' had yielded few or no results for the Palestinian people. It was not difficult to predict that violence was bound to erupt again, nor difficult to predict that violence would always be likely until the Palestinian people are given freedom and integrity in the land in which they have lived for thousands of years.

I feel that it is highly questionable to claim that any land can belong exclusively to any religious group, and it is a travesty of justice that people from any corner of the world should claim rights to own or live in a place simply because of their faith. I would say that no one should claim that right over and above those who have lived in the land for thousands of years. One may perhaps be charged with anti-Semitism when one criticises Israeli policies and actions. This is ridiculous. In fact, our Palestinian friends reminded us that they themselves are probably more ethnically Semitic than the vast majority of Israel's Jewish population today!

And so this was a pilgrimage with a difference. We were

not visiting places or sites simply because of religious associations. Of those there were many, and the biblical patriarchs
and Jesus himself must certainly have followed some of the
route we had walked. That in itself was an inspiring thought.
But this was a pilgrimage in which we also encountered the
people themselves, sharing their lives for a brief time and
learning from them. True pilgrimage, I believe, is one that
touches the reality of God's presence in both the past and the
present. In this encounter, God's will for justice and peace in the
world becomes ours. It is therefore a life-changing experience,
and one that moves us forward with new commitment to our
daily lives where we are, and in our relationship with and
responsibility towards the world around us.

SECTION SIX

Following in the Footsteps

Photograph: Jo White

Introduction

Following in the footsteps of someone else sounds an easy option, and for many people not a very attractive one. Surely the true pilgrim, called by God, ventures out into unknown ways and towards unknown challenges and destinations. She or he does not walk in the footsteps of others who have gone before; there can be no pioneering pilgrim spirit in that path. The true pilgrim knows, however, that he is never alone, for God is ever with him, along the way and at the end of the journey, leading, encouraging and sustaining.

The pilgrim is nevertheless a pioneer. The idea of following in the footsteps of anyone, even of Jesus, has great limitations if it is taken literally. There are Christians who try to do this, who try to emulate the life of Jesus in every respect, but this is impossible and is not the challenge of the gospels. The gospels are the key to understanding what 'following in the footsteps' really means for the true pilgrim, who would venture out into new and unknown ways and work. Jesus set a great example which was an inspiration to his followers, an inspiration which changed their lives and enabled them not simply to follow in his footsteps, but to carry on where he left off, and, with God, to build the Church of the future in new ways and by new paths.

The pilgrim, then, who goes out on a journey in the footsteps of a great person, perhaps a great saint, does so to listen and learn, and above all to be inspired by all that was noble and brave in the other. There would inevitably have been many aspects of the lives of the noblest saints which were not repeatable, because they took place at a special time in history, or in a particular country. There would always be some aspects of the lives of even the noblest saints which were not worthy of emulation. When he wrote about St Columba, for instance, Ian Bradley pointed out that 'He was no plaster saint'. He went on, however, to describe Columba as a real person, with good and bad points. It is because Columba was real that he is interesting today and that many people wish to learn about him. People also do become inspired by his life and achievements.

The pilgrim who follows in the footsteps of another often does so to gain confidence and encouragement, for not all aspiring pilgrims are independent, brave and strong. Most of us will be encouraged by learning about the lives of other people, through reading, praying and also going on journeys. Any traveller to a new place is grateful for maps, compasses and signposts. Sometimes there are paths which may be followed for part of the way. Walkers on the Pennine Way have trudged across unmarked and boggy moorland for many years. They are grateful for the huge stone slabs, taken from the Lancashire cotton mills which have closed down, and which, for some of the way, save them from thinking and from sinking, and give them extra encouragement and energy for the misty and unpredictable places they are moving towards.

The pilgrim expects to be changed by the experience of closeness, listening to and learning from the life of the other person, to a new life of energy and commitment, most probably then moving off into a new direction altogether. Those of us who are inspired by the life of Aidan, for example, may follow him into teaching as the most valuable way we have of influencing and changing the world, but we may equally choose to be strategic and loving in another direction entirely. We will nevertheless still be pilgrims of Aidan, inspired, influenced and encouraged by his example.

In this section we have included walks and other journeys in the footsteps of others, including St James of Compostela, Augustine of Hippo, Gandhi and the Buddha. We have also outlined briefly the lives of a small number of others, including Sts Aidan, Columba and Augustine of Canterbury.

Li Tim Oi was a twentieth-century woman who was a pioneer Anglican woman priest. She represents many pioneers who have led the way along a particular path and made it easier for others to follow. She is a great encouragement to those who are called to pioneer a new way and at first lack the spirit to begin.

St Teresa reminds us that:

> Christ has no body now on earth but ours,
> no hands, but ours,
> no feet but ours.

The pilgrim is a pilgrim because she or he is called by God, follows maps, signposts, religious leaders, saints and others, is sensible enough to use paths when they exist, and brave enough to carry on where there is no path or other companion, except God. The pilgrim does not lose sight of the vision and at the same time works steadily to bring it about.

In the Footsteps of St Augustine of Hippo

Katy Hounsell-Robert

The stone steps of the Roman amphitheatre in Carthage are not the most comfortable seats to sit on after an hour, even on a starlit balmy evening in August. The concert was supposed to begin at 9 o'clock and, like most things in Tunisia, it is running late. Everyone is in good humour from the jasmine and nut sellers wandering up and down the steps to the enormous crowds still ambling in unhurriedly. As the music strikes up, groups of aristocratic-looking gentlemen arrive, wearing the traditional long tunics which have remained in fashion here for at least 2000 years, and as the whole intoxicating entertainment begins with full audience participation, I feel this may well have been what Carthage was like over 1500 years ago as a lively Roman provincial city.

This interests me for I am trying to recapture something of the atmosphere in which St Augustine of Hippo studied, lived, loved and later inspired his students as a charismatic teacher and then preacher in this idyllic place on the Mediterranean sea.

In the light of day Carthage is beautiful but with many reminders of its violent, prosperous and tragic past. On the green Byrsa hill overlooking the sea there is nothing left of Dido's proud city or even the Roman villas built on those Carthaginian ruins where Augustine used to walk up to visit the Proconsul. Now on the summit of the hill is the nineteenth-century Cathedral of St Louis which has mosaics depicting St Augustine's life, and behind it the National Museum of Carthage which houses the works of Augustine. Nearer the sea are the ruins of Roman baths, temples and walls, the arena where St Perpetua and St Felicity, early Tunisian saints, were torn to pieces by the lions before Christianity became the state religion, and the site where St Augustine presided over many of the endless Councils of Carthage to settle religious disputes. Not far away is the original amphitheatre regularly frequented by Augustine, a great theatre enthusiast.

The next day I sat in the sun overlooking the sea in one of the popular restaurants specialising in delicious fresh fish. As I sipped the fine Tunisian rosé (forbidden, of course, in Islam but plentiful in Augustine's time and for tourists now) I noticed small tourist-laden cruisers tying up in the harbour – but when Augustine sailed for Rome in 383 CE, he left from the Punic port which once held 200 vessels. This lies a little farther along the coast and is now silted up and deserted.

Augustine spent four successful years in Italy as a professional rhetorician, first in Rome and then Milan where Ambrose was Bishop at that time. A zealous Manichean Christian, Augustine became influenced by Ambrose and, after much soul searching, decided that his vocation lay in returning to his homeland and founding a monastery in the Christian Roman tradition.

The route across the north of Tunisia to the mountainous area in Algeria, where Augustine was born on 13 November 354 and later founded his monastery, is rather different. Luckily the head of Tunisian Health Spas offered to go with me as a guide and his driver took us past green hills with sheep and cattle (one rarely sees a cow south of Tunis), up steeper hills cutting through woods of cork oak and pine where there were signs up to say you could hunt wild boar. (In Augustine's time there were also lions.) We passed a number of small spas visited by the Romans and then drove down towards the sea into Korbous which has a great variety of healing springs where people come for treatments ranging from rheumatism to infertility. The Beys (royal family) once had a summer palace here. We then went up into the hills, into peaceful Hammam Bourguiba, well known for its healing spring for respiratory ailments and its surprising Swiss-style hotel clinic. The spring was used in Roman times and it is possible Augustine may have visited here, for under stress he suffered breathing problems. In the hotel the tables, as in Augustine's time, were laden with an amazing variety of Mediterranean fruits and vegetables like figs, almonds, oranges, olives, to name a few, because everything likes to grow here.

Showing my passport and visa we passed through the frontier into Algeria which was one with Tunisia until the French occupation. We drove through more oak forest, streams and springs, so untouched and fairytale-like I felt that one could spend hours or days here just thinking and meditating. When we stopped, my companion cupped his hands and drank from a clear spring pouring out from under a rock, saying what a wonderful fresh flavour it had, and I could imagine Augustine doing much the same on the long trek by horse or foot to Annaba on the North coast (then called Hippo Regius) where he became a bishop. However, he always felt very much at home in Carthage, and as it was the diocesan capital he made the journey 33 times in 30 years, staying as long as he could and preaching as much as possible. You would think that since Carthage and Annaba are harbours on the same coastline and not far from one another, Augustine might have preferred sailing there on a fine day but the coast-line, then known as the Barbary Coast, is rugged and dangerous, and the sea was rife with pirates. In any case, Augustine was not a keen sailor.

Up in the mountains, some miles from Annaba, is the birthplace of Augustine, a small place called Souk Ahras (then Thagaste). His parents Patricius and Monica were Berber farmers who scrimped and saved so that Augustine could be educated in Latin and the classics like any noble Roman. His relationship with his mother was always very close.

In Annaba I saw the floodlit basilica dedicated to St Augustine, and his statue overlooking the harbour. Annaba is now a pretty French colonial town with mosques – in Augustine's time it was a Roman colonial town – wealthy because of its fertile lands. Not far out of town there are still abundant olive groves that meant Augustine had no shortage of oil lamps when writing or studying into the night, and he certainly missed this luxury when he was away.

The light is very special in North Africa, bright – almost ethereal – making colours clear and beautiful. Light was very important to Augustine, and although he was not a great 'nature' writer, he wrote of the sun rising in the valley. Perhaps this special sunlight was partly responsible for his passionate enthusiasm and energy which stayed with him throughout his long life. He died in Annaba in August 430 CE, just as the Vandals were entering the city.

In Annaba my companion pointed out enclosed gardens with small fountains and bougainvillea, rosemary, lavender, jasmine and pots of mint. Arabs and Romans before them always loved such secluded gardens where they could walk or sit in the scented shade. Augustine, too, in later life wanted a garden like this for his monastery, but where vegetables and fruit could also be grown for he made it a rule that a vegetarian diet was followed.

St Augustine is greatly revered among modern Islamic Algerians and Tunisians. After all, he is one of their famous sons, sharing many of their customs and aspects of their character – passionate, health-conscious, sociable and always eager to talk about God. I feel that as a very ordinary 'un-theological' person I have got to know a little better this great, very complicated and fascinating Christian saint.*

* Katy's account of her pilgrimage was first published in a slightly shortened version on 12 January 2001 in the *Church Times.*
Katy in Tunisia by Katy Hounsell-Robert, published by Nigel Day, 1991.

'Give Me My Scallop Shell of Quiet'
A Journey to Santiago de Compostela

Katy Hounsell-Robert

The great Cathedral of Santiago de Compostela is packed with worshippers for Sunday Mass – locals, tourists and pilgrims. People kneel on the hard stone floor, as there is a shortage of pews. When communion is offered, there is almost a stampede.

Before the high altar, glittering and gloriously ornate in the manner of Spanish cathedrals, the benediction is given in Spanish, English, French and German. Then eight well-built men in dark-red gowns heave in a huge censer and swing it, burning, high over the heads of the congregation.

After weeks in the open air, walking through remote countryside to reach this ancient shrine of St James the Apostle, it can be rather overpowering.

St James' body was supposedly brought by boat to Galicia after his martyrdom in the Holy Land, and his neglected tomb was rediscovered there 900 years later. From then on devout pilgrims in their thousands, including St Francis, journeyed to the tomb to do penance and to seek spiritual comfort.

Now as then, pilgrimage can be a cleansing process. Walking through open countryside to a place dedicated to higher things, and meeting and talking to thinking people, focuses one's mind on spiritual values.

In earlier times, all you needed was a staff (to help you to walk), a hat, a scrip or wallet, open to give and receive alms, and, to show your destination was Santiago, a scallop shell symbol of the saint. These days you need to add to your ruck-sack toiletries, a small first aid kit, a few clothes, a light sleeping bag, a passport and some money.

In the Middle Ages travelling by land was dangerous; and safe pilgrim routes were established leading from different directions. The most popular was the French route which runs from the Pyrenees across northern Spain. The Benedictines of Cluny built welcoming refuges along the road, and issued the first pilgrim guidebook, *Codex Callixtinus*. It is still relevant and available in translation.

Rather than walking the hazardous roads across France to Spain, English pilgrims often chose to sail to Corunna (fortified with malmsey to prevent sea-sickness) and I followed them taking the ferry to Bilbao, a little further east. I then joined the French route at Pamplona in Navarra, and made my way, alone, to Santiago using some trains and buses, as well as walking.

I stayed mostly at small, cheap pensiones where you share a lavatory and eat out. In the refuges, which are spaced out sensibly along the route, you share a unisex bathroom and dormitories with bunk beds, and usually you prepare your own food.

Some pilgrims camp out; others spend nights in paradors which are hotels converted from historic buildings. The important thing is that all make their own way to Santiago for their own good reasons.

The French route is marked spasmodically with yellow arrows. It avoids main roads and cities as much as possible, and often takes rough tracks.

In northern Spain the light is bright but soft and the air pure because of the influence of the sea and mountains. The route takes you by pine and oak forests, streams and rivers and rocky land, with meadows and farmland growing maize and barley. Vine-covered slopes and small homesteads with geraniums and washing hanging out are visible.

All the way along there are reminders – some in ruins – of medieval buildings that once helped pilgrims. An eleventh-century Spanish queen had a beautiful bridge built, the Puenta de la Reina, and pilgrims still use it.

St Dominic of the Causeway, having been turned down by the Monastery of Santiago, devoted his life instead to building roads and refuges for pilgrims. His cathedral always has two chickens in a glass-fronted run, because of a legend about him, which concerns a boy hanged unjustly for rape. His parents, having prayed to the saint for help, begged the judge to release the boy, but the judge joked that the boy was already as dead as the chickens on his plate, whereupon the chickens sprang up and cackled.

The cities along the route to Santiago all have their interest. Burgos was the birthplace of El Cid; Pamplona has its famous Bull Week in July; Logrono is the centre of the La Rioja wine industry, which is at least as old as the pilgrimage; in Leon the eleventh-century cathedral has a beautiful rose window; in Astorga the Bishop's Palace is built by Gaudy in his inimitable style.

I met many Spaniards doing the pilgrimage in their own way, in dribs and drabs. Many of them cycled in tight black suits, which slightly destroys the traditional feel. I drank coffee in an outdoor café with three sisters on a week's holiday and high on romantic religious fervour. A jolly Dutch lady, with whom I shared chocolate and chores for breakfast, was on her third pilgrimage, and this time had taken nearly a year over it.

A Buddhist who was a teacher in Scotland spent a lot of time sitting in the sun meditating. He was planning to go on to Finisterre, where traditionally people take off their clothes and wash away past sins in the sea.

You catch your first sight of the cathedral spires from Monte de Gozo (Mount of Joy), a peaceful hill just outside the city. From there it is still quite a walk and many people take the bus. New halls of residence of the university built up here include pilgrim accommodation. Close to, the cathedral is awesome. It is a baroque granite building set in stark granite plazas, where the only colour and warmth is provided by cathedral guides in their gorgeous velvet apparel.

Going through the Door of Glory, as so many pilgrims have done before you, is an emotional moment. You touch the Tree of Jesse just inside, and then embrace and say a prayer at the silver statue of St James behind the high altar. At 12 noon there is a daily Mass for the pilgrims.

Round the corner is an austere reception office. Here you report your arrival, and if you have walked more than 100 miles, or cycled or ridden on horseback for more than 200, you can receive a compostela (certificate).

In the Middle Ages people who were too old or sick or busy to make the journey themselves paid someone else to do it and received the compostela. Nowadays such people can come by coach or plane – the effort on their part is as great as that made by healthy young people walking for miles and sleeping rough.

Santiago is a medieval stone city, which is packed with churches, and the university colleges echo to the sound of their bells.

The shops sell souvenirs, including staffs, scallop shells and replicas of the saint's statue, an amazing amount of jewellery, plastic macs, and a delicious almond cake decorated with a cross and called 'tarta de Santiago'.

Most of the old shrines have lost their appeal and their pilgrims, but Santiago de Compostela is an exception. The reason may be partly geographical – northern Spain is still largely unspoiled and has a pleasant climate. It might also be because the Spanish love walking – they stroll for hours in the evenings and at weekends, and in Holy Week they spend about six hours in processions.

But perhaps also it is because the cult of St James took root in an ancient and holy Celtic region, and still has a healing power that is timeless.*

---

* Katy's account of her pilgrimage was published in the *Church Times* on 24 July 1998. To plan a pilgrimage contact the Confraternity of St James, Talbot Yard, Borough High Street, London SE1 1YP. Telephone 020 714034500. They produce a guidebook and have a library.

In the Footsteps of
Mahatma Gandhi

A group of eight people travelled across India by plane and train, to visit places where Mahatma Gandhi had lived and worked. They spent three days in Gandhi's ashram, visited people's homes, exhibitions and museums, and gathered each evening to eat and pray together.*

Hugh Maddox, a member of the group, wrote:

> Within two hours of arriving in Bombay, I had seen people, well dressed in white, walking purposefully along the beach, families cooking, and washing their hair on the street in buckets. I had breakfast in a very posh hotel, walked through streets of indescribable squalor, and visited a Krishna temple, where I began to respect and absorb Hindu worship – the one Lord with many manifestations.
>
> At Porbander I knelt at the swastika marking the place of Gandhi's birth. The crowds on the streets were full of colour, variety and dignity. . . . Gandhi's ashram and museum at Ahmedabad brought us close to him – his simple home, his vows of detachment, his pursuit of truth, his courage and his political leadership – all of a piece, integrated, each aspect depending upon and flowing into the other.

Paul Kelly wrote of a visit to the holy city of Gwarka:

> Gill, Kenneth and I visited this holy city of Lord Krishna. . . . We visited two temples, the main one dating from the sixteenth century, very elaborate with layers of balconies and pinnacles pointing upwards, representing the Himalayas, the high places of the gods There was continuous chanting . . .

* The pilgrimage was arranged by 'Soul of India' and Christians Aware.

Norman Toogood has written about the time he spent in Gandhi's Sevagram Ashram:

I made up my mind to enter into the spirit of ashram life. I knew that ashrams are akin to monasteries in that long-term devotees have taken vows including those of celibacy and poverty. . . . From a previous trip I had bought an Indian outfit of the white cotton trousers and cotton tunic which reached almost to my knees, so I decided to wear those. Also I decided that I would try washing my clothes with Indian soap in cold water.

In the event, there was rather more to it than I had thought. The beds had a single hard mattress and a couple of blankets, which reminded me very much of my national service. Fortunately, my body remembered it well. I was wide awake and ready for morning prayers at 4.45am. The real problems came with eating. Indians sit on the ground in the lotus position. I could not get anywhere near that posture.

Janet Stephens also wrote about Sevagram:

The focal point of the ashram is Gandhi's hut, surrounded by a bamboo fence, and now kept as a shrine. . . . It is a solid building constructed on a bamboo frame covered first with cow dung and then mud, fringed by an open veranda. The interior is simple and neat with folk art symbols moulded in relief upon the walls. The main room displays a few personal items and utensils used by Gandhi, simple palm tree mats spread on the floor, and a low wooden bench with a lantern on it. Here, at 4.45am every morning, we joined the resident ashramites at morning prayer. In the peaceful setting of the ashram I began to piece together a picture of all that Gandhi stood for. I learnt all about Gandhi's belief in cottage industry and the need he saw for villages to be self-reliant. The compact little spinning wheel, which opened and closed like a box, had become something of a symbol for manual labour, a means by which the very poor could earn their own bread and thereby regain dignity and self-respect. Spinning takes place for half an hour each day at Sevagram which was a model of what a village could be.

While at Sevagram we travelled some 16 miles to Paunar on the river Dham, where some of Gandhi's ashes were scattered. Our first visit was actually the anniversary of this event, and Indians arrived in their hundreds to pay homage to the 'Father of the Nation'. In scorching sun we made our way down a concrete ramp to where brightly coloured awnings supported by bamboo poles covered a sacred dais, in the centre of which was a pedestal surmounted by a sacrificial urn. . . . We climbed the hill to visit the Brahmavidya Mandir, a women's ashram founded by Gandhi's disciple, Vinoba Bhave.

Paul Kelly remembered:

Two places stick in my mind: the Delhi Brotherhood and the Golden Temple in Amritsar. It was a joy to take part in the Brotherhood's simple Eucharist and to hear afterwards of their splendid work with the street children. The golden temple of the Sikhs was a revelation, as a beautiful building and as a shrine. I was glad that we were able to go back in the evening to see the book being 'put to bed' with much religious fervour and the blowing of rams' horns. It was like the Ark of the Covenant – very Old Testament. Earlier we really did have a 'free lunch' along with hundreds of others.

Norman Toogood described the Golden Temple:

In Amritsar the Golden Temple is a most satisfying architectural composition with white buildings forming a very large square, and a wide marble promenade surrounding a large lake with the golden temple seeming to float on the lake. The whole place was thronged with thousands of Sikhs.

Hugh Maddox wrote of another aspect of the visit to Amritsar:

> We walked down the narrow alleyway that prevented General Dyer from bringing his armoured cars with their machine guns into the square. We saw the pillars built on the spot where the soldiers fired, the museum with the description of a widow's night with the dead bodies, and General Dyer's factual account of deliberate killing, and the great sandstone memorial to the freedom of the human spirit. Here I led prayers of repentance, sorrow and forgiveness; we could not separate ourselves from the general . . .

Norman and another member of the group, Ronald Watts, went shopping:

> In Amritsar I wanted to complete my Indian wardrobe with a turban, so with Ron Watts we hired a cycle rickshaw and went to a shop. . . . I bought a turban length of red cloth. . . . The rickshaw driver made the turban. . . . A length of about half a metre was held by the left ear and the rest wound round and round, narrower at the back and wider at the front, to produce a higher peak at the front, the piece at the side being tucked over the folds to lock them in place. It looked most effective, but will I ever be able to make it into a turban again?

Chris Morley wrote about Gandhi's ashram at Sabarmati:

> Trees gave shelter from the sun and this was most notable at the prayer ground which overlooked the river and which it was not difficult to imagine being the place where Gandhi gained much of the spiritual strength he needed for his campaigns. . . . It was from here in 1930 that Gandhi set off on the great Salt March, and the plaque told us that he vowed not to return to Sabarmati until India was free. . . . I feel challenged as I return to London to ask myself whether my actions and lifestyle are at one with my words when I speak about a commitment to the poor.

In the Footsteps of the Buddha

*Kenneth Wilson**

Dialogue between Christians and Buddhists has been growing in recent years. Perhaps more than with the other great faiths of the world, there is a profound dialogue to be had between us, based on our understanding of our founders. The life and teaching of the Buddha and of the Christ can be compared, and often illuminate each other.

There is another level, too, at which Christians can begin to understand the meanings of Buddhism, and that is through pilgrimage. The Christian pilgrimage to Bethlehem and Jerusalem is mirrored by the Buddhist pilgrimage to Bodhgaya, Sarnath and Kushinagar. We can begin our dialogue by travelling 'in the footsteps of the Buddha'. The Buddha attained enlightenment sitting under the Bodhi tree in what is now the town of Bodhgaya, in the State of Bihar in India. This tree is now pressed sideways by the Mahabodhi temple which has been built hard up against it. Its great branches are filled deafeningly with starlings, drowning out the chants of Tibetan nuns, circumambulating tree and temple together.

The wheel of the dharma began to turn at the deer park at Sarnath, when the enlightened Buddha preached his first sermon. Sarnath is now a suburb of Varanasi. Here there is a magnificent stupa more than 100 feet high, as well as the ruins of monasteries and temples. The remains of a pillar erected by the Buddhist pilgrim King Ashoka are nearby, and in the small museum is its capitol. This is one of India's famous images, its four lions facing north, south, east and west; adopted as the symbol of modern India. This great dome which once held relics of his earthly life, is supposed to mark the exact spot of that first sermon, in which the Buddha enunciated the

* Kenneth Wilson is Director of 'Soul of India'. See page 498.

new teaching, the dharma, which has shaped a quarter of the world in the last two and a half millennia.

There is one more place to visit, the place of departure, of the Buddha's *mahaparinirvana*. At Kushinagar, another of India's thousands of otherwise nowhere towns, the Buddha contracted food poisoning and died at the age of 80. The town had long forgotten its Buddhist history when nineteenth-century archaeologists, guided by the writings of a seventh-century Chinese pilgrim, began to uncover it. Now we can join a trickle of pilgrims coming to touch the gilded feet of a fabulous reclining Buddha statue. Even for non-Buddhists, it is a moment of unexpected reverence.

In the early evening, the sun illuminates the serene face of the Buddha's image. We walk a mile down the country road, to the mysterious Ramabhar Stupa, the site of Buddha's cremation, and perform the appropriate circumambulation. As the light fades, the silence of this inscrutable moment and the uncon-cerned grazing of a nearby elephant may still be the most fitting commentary on the life of the Buddha, in whose footsteps we have come.

Learning from St Columba

Ian Bradley

Columba had two very different sides to his personality. He belonged to the Irish warrior aristocracy – if he had not become a monk he would have almost certainly become king of his tribe, and quite possibly the High King of Ireland. He never lost the attributes of this upbringing and retained to the end of his life an autocratic imperiousness, a hasty temper, a fierce pride and a lingering attachment to the 'fascinating rattle of a complicated battle'. Yet he could also be gentle, humble and overflowing with Christian charity. This juxtaposition is perhaps the basis for the tradition, which appears in some later sources, that he had two names: first, Crimthann (the fox), and later, Columcille (the dove of the Church). It is just conceivable that the earlier name may reflect pagan origins, and that he acquired the second on being baptised as a Christian, but this must be conjecture. The characteristics of both the fox and the dove continued to manifest themselves throughout his life.

Ambiguity

If we are to encounter the true Columba, we need to acknowledge this ambiguity and to come face to face with Crimthann as well as Columcille. He was no plaster saint, but an intensively human figure with faults and weakness as well as extraordinary depths of gentleness and humility. Alongside the excesses of the Celtic psyche, we can perhaps point to another aspect of what might seem a double life. This was an understanding of the rhythm of Christian life, and the need to balance activity in the world with withdrawal from it.

The idea of pilgrimage, or peregrinatio, which was central to Irish monks and to Columba, involved a permanent sense of exile, renunciation and searching for one's own place of resurrection – one's desert. Except for those few called permanently to the solitary eremitical life of the anchorite, however, it did not mean a complete withdrawal from the world and its affairs. The monastic life was far from being one of retreat and escape. Indeed, monasteries were almost certainly the busiest institutions in Celtic society, constantly teeming with people and fulfilling the roles of school, library, hospital guest house, and arts centre and mission station. Most of the great Celtic saints alternated periods of intense activity and involvement in administrative affairs with lengthy spells of quiet reflection and months spent alone in a cell on a remote island or rocky promontory. In this, they were following the example of Jesus; one moment surrounded by crowds and engaged in preaching, teaching and healing, and the next walking alone by the lakeside or engaged in quiet prayer in the mountains.

Columba's life exemplified this balanced rhythm of engagement and withdrawal in the world. At times, he was busily engaged in founding monasteries, treating with kings, attending councils, going on missionary journeys and ruling his ever-expanding monastic familia. Yet his biographers also portray him spending long periods praying or copying the scriptures in his cell, and he frequently took himself to the lonely and unidentified island of Hinba for solitary retreats.

To a considerable extent these two sides of Columba's character were the product of his noble birth and monastic training. He mixed as easily with warlords and princes as with monks and scholars. Through his veins coursed the blood of a long line of fierce pagan warriors. It would hardly be surprising if this element in his make-up sometimes came to the surface and caused him to do things which he may have later regretted. It may, indeed, be, as some sources suggest, that it was to atone for the blood that was on his hands as the result of this involvement in a dynastic battle that he left his beloved Ireland at the age of 42 in the year 563, on the journey that was to take him to Iona.

Early Life

His upbringing, despite his noble birth, was entirely monastic. Born in Donegal in 521, he seems to have been marked down by his parents from a very early age for the Church, and he spent his boyhood and teenage years being tutored by priests in monastic foundations. This, in itself, was not particularly unusual. The children of the Irish warrior aristocracy were generally fostered out to tutors for their education, and 60 years or so before Columba's birth, Patrick had noted in his Confessions that 'Sons and daughters of Scottic chieftains are seen to become monks and virgins for Christ'.

Apart from this, we know tantalisingly little about the 40 years that Columba spent in Ireland. He seems to have belonged to several monastic communities in both the north and the south, and possibly to have founded some small houses himself. Medieval sources claim that he set up some 300 monasteries in Ireland before his departure for Iona, but this is generally dismissed by historians as without any historical basis. The truth is that we do not know where Columba was based, or what he was doing before he made his fateful journey from Donegal in 563. Nor do we know why he made that journey, although many possibilities have been speculated upon.

What we do know is that Columba was by no means unusual as an Ulsterman in making the somewhat perilous crossing to the Scottish Highlands and islands in the mid-sixth century. We do not know whether Columba set out to travel to Iona. Some historians argue that Columba did not actually move to Iona until 574, more than ten years after his departure from Ireland, possibly because until then the island was still in the hands of the native Picts and not safe for occupation. The picture is very unclear, and certainly more complex than the romantic story which has Columba sailing across in his coracle, landing first at Colonsay but finding that he could still see Ireland from there, and establishing his base at Iona only after climbing its highest hill and satisfying himself that he could no longer gaze back at his beloved homeland.

Missionary and Evangelist

The question has been asked as to how far Columba was a missionary and an evangelist. In my book, I argue – and I think the evidence for this is really irrefutable – that he was certainly not what he is sometimes portrayed as: the evangelist of Scotland who converted the native Picts occupying most of the northern, eastern and central mainland. Once on Iona, he actually spent most of the rest of his life there, occasionally retreating to Hinba, occasionally going back to Ireland on political or ecclesiastical business, sometimes venturing up to Skye, and perhaps just once, perhaps on a number of occasions, crossing the Highlands, going up the Great Glen to Inverness. Significantly, this journey was to meet with the Pictish King Brude. His biographies do not write of him converting great numbers of people across Scotland; rather, the picture is of someone who exercises a largely pastoral ministry on Iona, perhaps being involved in the conversion of one or two Scots (and remember, they were the Irish) but who is basically involved with founding monasteries and directing them from his base on Iona.

Columba's Ministry

There are many stories told of Columba's abilities to reconcile people both to themselves and to others from whom they have become distant or estranged. This pastoral gift is often portrayed as being exercised through the medium of penance. Many of those who visited Iona came as penitents, seeking to atone for some crime or to come to terms with feelings of guilt or remorse.

Columba was active as a teacher and scholar as well as a priest and pastor. He spent much time working in his cell on copying, annotating and interpreting the Scriptures. It is also quite possible that Columba wrote poems and hymns – there are four that can perhaps be attributed to him more certainly than others. Alongside priestly, pastoral and scholarly tasks, there was always the recurring manual work of the community – building, fishing, farming, distributing food to the poor.

In his last hours on earth, Columba is portrayed as engaging in many of the activities that have characterised his life-long ministry. He goes round the island in a cart, visiting the brothers at work in the fields and telling them of his forth-coming death. He attends Sunday Mass and had a vision of 'an Angel of the Lord flying above actually inside the house of prayer'. He blesses the heaps of grain stored in the barn ready for the community's use through the winter. Then, after his poignant encounter with the old horse which used to carry the milk pails, and which now puts its head against his bosom and weeps, he climbs the little hill overlooking the monastery and blesses the island, prophesying that it will come to be reverenced by Christians and non-Christians far round the world.

Death

Returning to his hut, he sits copying out the Psalms, stopping when he reaches the tenth verse of Psalm 34: 'Those that seek the Lord shall not want for anything that is good.' He then goes to Vespers and returns to sleep on the bare rock floor of his hut, with a stone for his pillow. After briefly resting, he summons the brethren, telling them to 'love one another unfeignedly' and commending them to God's infinite mercy. As the bell rings out for the midnight office, he runs ahead of them into church and kneels alone in prayer before the altar. The whole church is filled with angelic light around the saint. Helped by his faithful servant Diarmait, he raises his right arm to bless the choir of monks, and, at that moment, the venerable abbot gives up the ghost, his face transfixed with a wonderful joy and gladness for he could see the angels coming to meet him.

Columba's passing from the world, like his arrival into it, was accompanied by signs and wonders, miracles and angelic apparitions. In death, his powers of prophecy, pastoral aid and protection were to be undiminished. Indeed, his stature as a saint grew steadily as the cult of Columba spread far beyond the bounds of the tiny island on which he had chosen to spend the last 35 years of his life.

Columba's Legacy

There is much that we could say about the way that the church Columba founded and centred on Iona grew and developed in the centuries after his death – notably how it played a key role in the evangelisation of Northern England through the daughter house of Lindisfarne. There is, too, the whole question of Columba's legacy and what he has to say to us today.

How should we remember and celebrate Columba, 1400 years after his death? How should we follow in his footsteps? It is as a pilgrim people, walking, talking, praying and sharing together, that we most clearly carry the legacy of the Columban past into our own Christian futures. Pilgrimage was central to the Christian life and experience of Columba and his Christian contemporaries. Pilgrimage involves journeying back as well as forwards. Back, not just into the recesses of our own individual souls with their rich store of memories and experiences, and their untidy bits of unresolved and unfinished business, but also into our collective roots and traditions. One of our great modern malaises is that so many people have lost touch with their roots. Through exploring and celebrating the life and thought of Columba and his near-contemporaries in Ireland, Scotland, Wales and England, we are able to connect with a common tradition that has nurtured and influenced nearly all who live in these lands today, and which has, to some extent, made us what we are. We can connect too in a mysterious and meaningful way with the communion of saints, that great and silent company who have gone before us in the faith, and with whom we are bound in the one body of the Church, militant on earth and triumphant in heaven.*

* Ian presented this paper at a Christians Aware conference on Lindisfarne. His book is *Columba: Pilgrim and Penitent*, published by the Iona Community, 1996.

Drawing by Jane Walton-Loxton

Learning from St Augustine of Canterbury

A Benedictine monk of Ampleforth Abbey*

It is clear that Augustine was not the only missioner to Britain, *and* that the Christian faith already existed here before his arrival. There *were* British Christians – found mainly in the West, pushed there by the invading Saxons – and bishops too, the whole having a Celtic flavour. There is no reason to suppose that this was an impoverished faith for its having been isolated from the continental Church.

At Bangor there was a monastery with some 2000 monks, another monastery at Galloway (founded by St Ninian in 397 CE), and the famous monastery of Columba at Iona, from whence came the missionary thrust which led to the conversion of the peoples of the north of England – independent of Augustine's missionary effort, and some little time after it.

However, the Saxons, to whom Augustine came, were the most powerful force in the land, and a pagan one at that, and that influence could, it is supposed, have led to the weakening, or even the ultimate extinction of Christianity here. So Augustine's work had a twofold purpose – to win the Saxons for Christ, and to save British Christianity from becoming an endangered faith.

Bede was a monk of Jarrow, born in 673 CE, some 70 years after the death of Augustine, and it is his work, the *Ecclesiastical History of the English People*† which is our primary source. He completed this work in 731 CE, a work which sweeps eight

---

* This paper is taken from a talk given at Ampleforth Abbey during the Christians Aware walking pilgrimage from Easingwold near York to Whitby in 1997, the 'Year of Pilgrimage'.
† Bede's *Ecclesiastical History of the English People* is published by Penguin Books.

centuries of Christian history in England. And, as far as Augustine's story is concerned, we could not even begin to talk about it but for the fifteen chapters which Bede has in his history.

Gregory came across the blond, blue-eyed boys – slaves – in the market place in Rome and, having never encountered the like before, asked who they were, and where they were from. The popular version of the story says that he received the answer 'Angles' (that is, from Anglia) to which he replied, 'No, not Angles, but Angels.' Well, that's not quite the story as Bede tells it, but close enough for our purposes. We can fill in the gaps from the story as it was originally told by Bede and by an anonymous monk of Whitby in the early part of the eighth century in his *Life of Pope Gregory*.

Gregory wasn't Pope at the time, as many imagine he was. Rather, we are asked to picture the young priest Gregory coming across the Anglo-Saxon slaves in the market place, the encounter prompting him to rush to the then Pope, Benedict, requesting to be sent himself as a missionary to England. This means that Augustine was known by Gregory both as monk and superior, so Gregory was sure in his choice of leader for this missionary expedition – and we know that Augustine then became Abbot of the group of 40, and then he became their bishop.

Bede gives us no more information than that. But he was writing over 100 years after Augustine's arrival, and his historical sources were minimal – he had copies of some of Pope Gregory's letters, but very little else – so we ought to excuse him for not providing us with an exact portrait of Augustine. We can also excuse Bede for getting some of the details of Augustine's mission wrong, which he does, and which we know now through the coming to light of documents to which Bede had no access.

But perhaps Bede deliberately holds back on giving us details about Augustine! Perhaps Bede refrains from telling us too much, so that the man Augustine doesn't get in the way and block Bede's purpose, which is to use Augustine as a device, a missionary type, in order to present his readers of the eighth century (and why not us?) with a mission and a challenge equal to Augustine's own. We may thus be challenged by Augustine's mission to mission in our own times.

It is clear that Gregory wanted to ensure the utmost help for Augustine and his companions. We have some 14 letters of introduction from Gregory to various bishops en route, asking them to assist Augustine in every way possible (some of the letters can be read in Bede's work). The route they probably took was by a boat from Rome to the south-east coast of France, to the monastery of Lerins, then on to Marseilles, Aix, Arles, Vienne, Lyons, Autun, and on to the north – Gregory's letters give us no details after this, but Bede tells us that the group crossed the Channel and landed on the Isle of Thanet.

The journey must have been long and gruelling, and the prospect of going to a 'barbarous, fierce and pagan nation' not very inviting – so much so that they hadn't gone very far when the group of missionaries sent Augustine back to ask Pope Gregory to reconsider. The Pope, it seems, would not entertain the idea, urged them on, and sent Augustine back to them no longer praepositus but as abbot. As for Augustine being a bishop, that he was one we can be sure, but about when he became one we are uncertain. Gregory's letters, standing alone, imply that Augustine was ordained bishop during the journey to England, by bishops living in German lands. Bede, however, tells us that Augustine travelled to Arles once the mission was established in Kent, and was ordained bishop by Etherius, the Archbishop of Arles. We simply cannot reconcile the two accounts.

Perhaps the original route for the journey was north from Rome, over the Alps, and towards France, and the letters were sent by Gregory to the bishops of German lands, but the episcopal ordination didn't take place because there was a change of plan about the best route to take. Or perhaps something along the journey's way prevented the ordination as planned by Gregory, with the result that the ordination had to take place at Arles at a later date – and it was this information which came into Bede's hands.

Back to our question: how much credence should we give to this story of the Anglo-Saxon slaves? If we were to take Bede's own use of the story, we might be forgiven for seeing it only as a quaint tradition and refusing to accept any of it as historically accurate – and that's because Bede includes the story in his narrative only as an aside, and not even where it ought to be, chronologically speaking, before Augustine's departure for England; instead, it comes in a chapter after the mission is established, in a chapter in which Bede details the qualities and attributes of Gregory.

But we should not be too quick to reject the story. In one of Gregory's other letters which have come our way, there is evidence to suggest that there was a connection between Gregory and Anglo-Saxon youths. In one of his letters to the priest Candidus in southern Gaul, dated September 595 (the year before Augustine's departure), discussing the matter of the use of money raised from papal lands there, Gregory advises that the money be used to purchase Anglo-Saxon boys, aged from 17 to 18 years old, who should then be sent to monasteries to be given to God. Was it intended that perhaps later they might be sent to evangelise their own land? Also, does Augustine's mission then represent a change of plan? Who knows!

Bede knew nothing of these particular letters (because they were in Gaul!), but they show us that there was a link between Gregory and Anglo-Saxon boys, who were possibly sent to Gregory's own monasteries in Rome, a link which at least puts a frame around the encounter with slaves. But there may have been another reason behind the mission. In a couple of places Gregory's letters imply that he possibly understood the mission in different terms. Twice he refers to the desire of Englishmen to come to know the faith, and comments that 'the priests who are in the area do not have care for them'. Who were these Englishmen? What priests? Which area? We lack any kind of evidence. Nevertheless, it might be that these chance references in his letters point to another reason for the mission, namely, to provide clergy for the already existing Christian Church in England, and Augustine's brief certainly included the job of recruiting Frankish clergy to the mission as he journeyed through Gaul.

For a figure so central to the story of Christianity in this land, we know remarkably little about Augustine. The truth is there isn't very much to say about Augustine himself. One can tell the story, but about the man Augustine there is very little to say. We know that he was a monk, 'brought up by a rule in a monastery' (says Gregory), and that he was 'the praepositus of my monastery', that is, he was the prior, or second in command between the Church at Arles and the English Church – for there is some evidence that an English bishop attended the Council of Arles in 214 CE.

But one way or another – bishop or not – Augustine and his companions arrived in Thanet. England was not a united land at the time, but consisted of several kingdoms. By good fortune Augustine landed in the territory of the most powerful king, Ethelbert, whose extensive territories stretched from Kent right up to the Humber (that is, the eastern side of England, at least). To all intents and purposes the missionaries had landed in the territory not of a king, but of *the* King. They perhaps knew that if they converted him and his people, and the largest part of the country was thereby won over, the rest would follow. Ethelbert was in close contact with the Frankish Merovingian court, so he may have heard that the missionaries were on their way. Augustine had recruited Frankish clergy and interpreters. Their language and customs would have been already familiar to Ethelbert. Christianity was not unknown at the royal court – Ethelbert's Queen, Bertha, daughter of the King of Paris, was Christian and had a bishop-chaplain, one Liudhard. All these factors would have helped smooth the way.

The king came to meet the missionaries in Thanet and was fundamentally open to their message, but was not one to rush in. Bede records Ethelbert's response to Augustine's first sermon as this: 'Your words and promises are fair indeed but they are new and uncertain, and I cannot accept them and abandon the age-old beliefs that I have held together with the whole English nation.' So not a complete rejection, at least! His openness is perhaps better illustrated by his invitation to live at Canterbury, his seat of power – it was to be there that the conversion of the Anglo-Saxons was to take place.

Bede tells us that at Canterbury Augustine and his company 'began to emulate the life of the apostles and the primitive Church'. They were constantly at prayer, they fasted and kept vigils, they preached the word of life to whomsoever they could. Later Bede says that converts marvelled at 'their simple and innocent way of life and the sweetness of their heavenly promises'.

Anthony Marett-Crosby (monk of Ampleforth) says that this chapter is 'in some senses . . . an anticlimax. There is no great oration from Augustine, no knock-down arguments which force the truths of Christianity upon those who heard. It is not a second Pentecost. This sense of anticlimax is so clear that it must be deliberate.' For Bede, what converts is a combination of both preaching and the apostolic way of life, so that it was the witness of the lives of the missionaries as much as what they said that was significant. Their faithfulness and sincerity proved to be the vital witness that brought about the conversion of the king and his subjects.

The success achieved on the Canterbury mission was mentioned by Gregory in a letter to the Patriarch of Alexandria: 'On Christmas Day ten thousand Anglians were baptised.' The figure may be a slight exaggeration but does indicate that something great had clearly taken place.

Receiving converts was not enough; there was also the need for some permanent structure to hold the growing Church together, which was made more difficult by the existence of the native British Church – Augustine could not ignore its presence. Two meetings ended in a stalemate. Augustine requested uniformity of practice regarding the keeping of Easter (according to the Roman calendar) and the performance of baptism (according to the Roman rite), and that the British Church joined Augustine and the Roman missionaries in preaching the word. The British refused. Bede leaves the story of the reconciliation, which did ultimately take place, for the tales of another century.

Then we see Augustine (with Gregory) working through all the problems of a fledgling Church. Augustine writes to Gregory for instructions on the following:

- the life of a bishop with his clergy

- liturgical questions

- degrees of marriage

- the possibility of the ordination of a bishop without other bishops being present

- Augustine's authority over or relationship with the Gaulish bishops (Augustine *had* no such authority; England and Gaul were to remain distinct from one another).

Slowly, year by year, the mission made steady progress. In a letter of 601 Gregory established two provinces centred on London and York. Gregory clearly envisaged that the archiepiscopal seat would be in London, but Gregory's knowledge of the British Isles must have been limited indeed (he probably knew that London had been big in its day – its Roman day!). Augustine knew the political realities of seventh-century Kent better than Gregory, *and* Canterbury was more important by far, of course. Canterbury has remained the primal see of England and a place of pilgrimage to this day.*

* Canterbury is also now the centre for the worldwide Anglican Communion.

Gregory then sent a second wave of missionaries from Rome to assist Augustine. Mellitus became bishop of London, Justus became bishop of Rochester in 604 CE. Bede gives us no more information about Augustine after the ordinations of Mellitus and Justus except to say that Augustine died on 26 May – he omits which year but it was between 604 and 609 CE.

Augustine was buried by his monks outside the church of the monastery of St Peter and St Paul at Canterbury. Augustine was responsible for its building – the church was still under construction when he died, and when it was completed his body was moved inside. The ruins of that monastery, which was later rededicated as St Augustine's, still exist. According to Bede, Augustine was buried in the north chapel.

Learning from St Aidan

St Aidan was an Irishman, already a monk when he came to Holy Island in or around 635 CE. By that time the Anglo-Saxons had been coming in across the North Sea for well over a century, and Anglo-Saxon kingdoms had been established. This was part of the Kingdom of Northumbria, which in those days stretched from Edinburgh to the Humber. It was one of the biggest of the Anglo-Saxon kingdoms. Aidan was not the first Christian missionary to this area; he was the third. The first Christian missionary was Paulinus from Kent, who had been converted by St Augustine of Canterbury. King Edwin of Northumbria wanted to marry the Kentish Princess. The marriage deal was that she, already a Christian, should be allowed to keep her religion. She should also be allowed to bring her own chaplain, the chaplain should be allowed to spread the faith, and King Edwin himself would very seriously consider becoming a Christian. So she came, and with her came Paulinus. After a while King Edwin did become a Christian, the first Christian king of Northumbria. After that, conversions were very rapid.

All went well until King Edwin was killed in battle. Edwin had been a very powerful king, so when he was killed the kingdom fell into confusion. Paulinus thought it was his duty to escort the widowed young queen back to Kent and the only person who was certainly left behind was James the Deacon. He was still around, a very old man, when the historian Bede, as a little boy, went into the monastery at Jarrow. Edwin himself had driven into exile the family of the previous king of Northumbria, and that family had fled to Scotland. There were in that family at least three boys and one girl. Somehow, we don't know how, these children in exile in Scotland came into contact with the monks of the big Irish monastery of Iona, the monastery which St Columba founded. The children were converted to the Christian faith during their youth. The

279

Photograph: Barbara Butler

Statue of Aidan on Lindisfarne

second boy in the family, whose name was Oswald, decided to fight to regain the throne of Northumbria. The tradition is that he came with a small band of men to a place just outside the town of Hexham, where there is still a large wooden cross and a little chapel in the middle of a field. There, on the battlefield, King Oswald set up a wooden cross. He called his soldiers round it and told them that he fought as a Christian king. If he won the battle and became king of Northumbria, he would give his people the chance to hear the Christian faith. Oswald did win the battle. He became king of Northumbria.

Oswald had been converted by the monks of Iona to the Irish Christianity. So naturally, when he became king, he did not think in terms of the Christian kingdom of Kent, or the mission from Kent. He thought in terms of Iona. He sent a messenger over to Iona asking them to send him a Christian missionary, a missionary bishop. The monks of Iona were delighted because they were missionary-minded, and here was a mission field opening up for them. But for some reason they chose the wrong man, Colman. He came from Iona, and after a few months he went back to Iona. When he arrived back he said to the meeting of the monks: 'You cannot convert Northumbrians. Northumbrians are stupid and obstinate. They do not understand a word I say, they will not listen. You cannot convert them.' There was consternation among the monks of Iona. What were they to do? They could not merely acquiesce in the closing down of such an opportunity. While they were meeting and talking about it, one man raised his voice and said to Colman, 'My brother, do you not think that maybe you were too hard on these people? Do you not feel that if you had gone a little more gently you might have had more success?' The man who spoke was Aidan and he then went to Northumbria. Of course, he did not go alone. The Irish monasteries, when they sent out a mission, always liked to send a leader and twelve followers. They did this because they were very biblically minded, and Christ and the twelve apostles was their model. So Aidan would have come with twelve Irish monks.

King Oswald was very pleased to see him. Aidan must have felt rather scared. It is always harder to come in the wake of another man's failure than it is to break new ground for the first time. When he arrived, Oswald said to him, 'Take anywhere that you like in my kingdom for the site of your monastery.' Aidan chose Lindisfarne, an excellent choice. It was a far better centre for a missionary monastery than Iona. The tides behaved in that age much as they do today. By setting his monastery here he had a very nice alternation of periods of seclusion and periods of access. The tides created a rhythm. The monastery needed both seclusion and easy access to the field of mission. Another reason why it is such a good choice is because it is so close to Bamburgh, the original centre for the Anglo-Saxon kings of Northumbria. It was the first place where they set up their centre. It remained an important centre although the kings travelled round to many other centres of government as well. In Aidan's day it was possible to walk direct to Bamburgh, and Aidan could walk across to contact the King if he needed to do so. Alternatively, the King could ride across to the monastery. We cannot over-estimate the importance of the friendship between King Oswald and Aidan. In the whole of Anglo-Saxon England, there is no instance where a missionary ever succeeded against the wishes of the ruling king. Aidan was an Irishman; the people were English. Aidan spoke Old Irish; the people spoke Old English. As far as we know, just one man was bilingual – the king himself. He would have learnt Irish in his boyhood, and spoke English as his native tongue. So, in the early days of the mission, the king actually went round with Aidan and translated his sermons from Irish into English. It is hard to imagine what the people would have thought of this, but at the very least they would have known how much their king cared about the success of the mission. Had there been any opposition or hostility to the monastery, the king's support would not have been completely behind it. The king's forces were never too far away, in case of attack on the monastery.

So, having chosen his island well, Aidan could begin. The first thing he would have done on arrival would have been to plant a great cross. We cannot tell for certain exactly where his monastery was. The ruins that can be seen today are the ruins of the later, Benedictine, post-Norman Conquest priory. However, religious people tend to be conservative, thus it is likely that the priory was built on the site of the first monastery, because once a place has been made holy, it tends to remain holy. Secondly, this was the most sensible place to build a monastery. The whole of the village is crowded in this corner. Nobody lives on the rest of the island. So, down in the field under the hill across the south part of the island is the most sensible place for Aidan to have chosen. Perhaps part of the monastery was up on the hill. Later, the Benedictines had a chapel on top of the hill which served as a lighthouse as well as a chapel. Since Aidan's monastery was only a collection of small wooden huts with thatched roofs, and the churches were the same, nothing at all has survived, not even the knowledge of exactly where it was. The one well-known object which has survived from Aidan's monastery, although it is a little later than Aidan's day, is the illuminated book called *The Lindisfarne Gospels*. This is in the British Library. It was written here in about 700 CE. Also there are one or two carved stones in the little museum at the entrance to the priory which date from the Anglo-Saxon, Irish monastery. Aidan was an Irish monk. We can assume that what he built looked like the typical Irish monastery. Having planted his cross, he would have made a circular embankment, just a rough bank of stones and earth. This was not to keep anyone out, just to mark the perimeter of the monastery. Then, within that the monks would have their individual little wooden huts. The normal practice, at any rate for senior monks, was a hut for each monk. Sometimes two monks shared a hut, possibly sometimes a senior and a junior shared. Thus the junior could learn from the older monk. But there was nothing like the communal buildings which we associate with later monasticism, of the Benedictine tradition. They did not know how to build large buildings, nor did they want them. If wood was available, they never built of stone. They wanted perishable buildings because they wanted the physical side of their life to be as stark and meagre as possible. They did not want their minds, their hearts and their souls to be tied down to physical things. So they made do with these huts and lived in them.

In diet the monks were largely vegetarian. They lived on cereals, fruit, vegetables and the occasional fish. We know that the monks of Iona occasionally ate seal. They were not wholly against non-vegetarian foods, but they were largely vegetarian and would probably have had only water to drink. As for clothing, they would not have had the ample, warm, all-enveloping habits of later monasticism, but just a rough, woollen or leather tunic reaching to the knees, a cloak, and shoes made wholly of leather. These clothes were hardwearing, but not particularly comfortable. It was an exceedingly rough life. They did not have a long monastic rule, like St Benedict's rule, but they had principles. Among these were: 'Don't eat unless you absolutely have to eat. Don't drink unless you must drink in order to quench your thirst. Don't sleep until you fall asleep on your feet as you walk towards your hut.' This was indeed a very tough life. However, we understand that the climate was a little different in those days. The average temperature over the whole year would have been about one degree higher. This was made up of summers which were quite a lot hotter, but winters which were colder. The only detail we know about the personal appearance of the monks concerns the monastic tonsure, the way they wore their hair, although this is not absolutely certain. However, afterwards it appears to have become a source of controversy. The continental tonsure, which prevailed after the controversy had been resolved, was different from the Irish style. It is simply the little fringe of hair all the way round, with the top of the head showing. The Irish tonsure was either the whole of the front of the head shaved, and the hair growing as long as it will down the back, or a little fringe at the front, the whole of the top of the head shaved ear to ear, and the hair growing as long as it will down the back.

On the island, the most important thing that Aidan did was to start a school. He did this because he was a supremely sensible man. He recognised that Iona could not forever go on sending more and more Irish monks, that his generation would die and that the sooner there was a native priesthood, the better. So Aidan set up the first known school in Northumbria, for Anglo-Saxon boys. It was a tiny school at first. There were just twelve little boys. Although we don't know where they all came from, some were boys ransomed from slavery. At that time, slavery was still part of society. Aidan thought that if anyone gave money to the monastery, there was no better way in which he could spend it than to buy a child out of a life of slavery. If the boys proved to be suitable when they had been taught, then they became missionary priests and bishops.

The whole importance of Lindisfarne depended upon the existence of that school. Aidan himself evangelised the area. But the reason why Aidan's mission, Aidan's work, or the work which stems from him includes the greater part of England, lies in the fact that of the boys in this school a large number became very effective missionaries. The most memorable thing which has been said about Aidan, and it was a Bishop of Durham who said it, is that Augustine was the Apostle of Kent, but Aidan was the Apostle of England. More of England was converted as a result of his work than as a result of the work of anyone else. The bulk of the country, north of the Thames area, was converted by boys from Lindisfarne. So Lindisfarne was important for the whole of England because the school was started and the boys were trained there. The main subject which the boys would have had to learn was

Latin because the Bible and the Church's prayers were entirely in Latin. One wonders what difficulties the Irish monks would have had in teaching Latin to Anglo-Saxon boys. The practical things – such as how to pray and worship, how to be a missionary – presumably were learnt by living at close quarters with the older monks.

This monastery was for men only, and the school was for boys only. Aidan did, however, believe very strongly that the religious life should be open to women also. He did something in a practical way about this. What he did was to persuade Hilda, an Anglo-Saxon noblewoman, a niece of King Edwin, to stay in Northumbria and found religious houses. She had already decided to become a nun, but it was her intention to go to France where there already were religious houses. Aidan was responsible for making her change her mind. Hilda's most famous foundation, the last one of her life, was at Whitby in Yorkshire. Thus it was that the religious life was available to men and to women. This meant that Anglo-Saxon women did have a certain amount of choice in life. Women were quite highly regarded in Anglo-Saxon society, but this does not mean that there was a great deal of choice open to them. A woman would usually have married the man her father chose for her. The more high-born she was, the more she became a pawn in a marriage alliance. Because so many men were killed on the battlefield when they were comparatively young, there were a large number of widows. So there was a need to provide a religious life for both single women and for widows. Monasteries began to grow. They were usually double houses, for men and for women. St Hilda's great foundation at Whitby was certainly a double house. It is an interesting feature that in Anglo-Saxon England, whenever we hear of a double house, the head of the house is invariably an abbess and never an abbot. The organisation of the double houses seems to have varied. Some kept the two halves strictly apart, and although they used the same chapel or church, they built a wall down the middle, down the centre aisle. Other double houses seem to have allowed much more contact between monks and nuns. We only know of scandal at one monastery. That was at Coldingham, just north of the border, where Bede tells us there was much lax living after the death of the first abbess who was a sister of Oswald. As a result, the monastery was closed down. At the monastery at Whitby, Hilda was the director of studies for the men as well as for the women. At least five future bishops were trained by Hilda at Whitby. It is Aidan who was responsible for fostering the religious life for women in Northumbria.

As a missionary, Aidan had a very simple, direct method. He walked round the Northumbrian lanes, and he spoke to every single person he met. He said to them, 'Are you a Christian?' If they answered, 'Yes', he said, 'Find me a better one.' If they answered, 'No', he said, 'May I tell you about it?' That was the way the mission spread, on a one-to-one, person-to-person basis. The king thought it was dreadful that the bishop should walk, because noblemen usually rode and other classes walked. There is one delightful story of what happened when the king gave Aidan a horse. 'Thank you very much,' said Aidan and went out of the king's presence. Outside he met a beggar. 'Please give me something,' said the beggar. Aidan said that he had nothing to give. Then he remembered the horse. 'Here you are,' he said, giving it to the beggar. When the king heard of this he was rather angry. 'My Lord Bishop,' he said, 'if you must give horses to beggars, let me know in advance. There are plenty of poorish horses in the royal stables. That was a horse which I had specially chosen for you.' 'My Lord King,' said Aidan, 'are you really telling me that that son of a mare is more important to you than that son of God?' This story, if it is true, gives a clue to Aidan's attitude to people. If he could really look at a beggar and see him as a son of God, it is no wonder that Aidan was popular and that the mission succeeded. This is what he taught his disciples. And of all the disciples, the one most like him was probably Chad who later went down to Lichfield. We have a delightful picture of Chad wanting to walk everywhere, just like Aidan. But Archbishop Theodore of Canterbury said that it was not right. He himself heaved the reluctant Chad on to the back of a horse, and made him ride. As for money, the monastery had none. If money was given, they gave it away. They kept none. They maintained a very simple manner of life. They refused to accept money even for the founding of other monasteries. Bede tells us that wherever the monks of Lindisfarne went on the mainland, they were welcomed with open arms by the peasants. They were trusted by them. So the mission spread.

It is through things like this that we get a glimpse of the personality of Aidan. Bede admired him immensely. He would not have known him personally – he came a little too late for that – but he would have known many people who had known him. Although Bede had almost nothing good to say about certain types of Celtic Christians – for example, the Welsh – he had a great deal of good to say about the Irish, despite the fact that he disagreed with them about calculating the date of Easter. Here Bede supported the continentals. Despite this, it is moving to see how generous he was to Aidan. He wrote he was an entirely genuine and sincere man. He lived exactly as he taught others to live. He was a man of great discretion, strength and gentleness. This is the picture we have of Aidan. There are no other reports of him. If it were not for Bede, we would not have known about Aidan. We would have known that there must have been a mission leader of the first monastery on Lindisfarne, but we would not have known a single thing about what kind of a person he was. Bede gave a full picture of him. He was not a man who did miracles. This is interesting because this was an age when almost anyone who was anyone did miracles. There are a few, but very few, attributed to Aidan.

Aidan was bishop for 17 years. We don't know how old he was when he came, we don't know how old he was when he died. He died at Bamburgh and in the church there is a little shrine set in the wall which is supposed to mark the spot where he died. According to the story, Aidan died with his hand resting against the wall of the wooden church which was there at that time. Afterwards that church was burnt down, but this particular block of wood refused to burn, so it was built into the next wooden church. This church was also burnt down and the block of wood refused to burn, so it was built into the next wooden church, and so on. Whatever we may think of these stories in themselves, they show us something of what the people thought about the saint. Aidan did not live to see the success of his mission; he did not know what a vast success it was going to be. It is possible that he died almost broken-hearted because at the time when he died Northumberland was divided into two minor kingdoms and the king of one of these, who was a Christian and a friend of Aidan, had been responsible for knifing and killing the other king, who was also a Christian and a friend of Aidan. Aidan could have been forgiven if he wondered whether this was all they had learnt after he had been with them for 17 years. It is possible that he died with this tragedy in mind, that one Christian leader had murdered another Christian leader.

Aidan was important as the founder not only of the Lindisfarne monastery, but of the school and the mission which succeeded in converting most of England.*

---

* This account of the life and work of Aidan was written from a talk given by Kate Tristram for a Christians Aware group at Marygate House, Lindisfarne.

Learning from Li Tim Oi

Li Tim Oi was the first woman to become a priest in the Anglican Communion. She was authorised to do her pastoral work in 1941 and ordained priest in 1944 in the Diocese of Hong Kong. She was someone who set a great example of love and service which has been an inspiration to many women who have been ordained as priests in more recent years.

Li Tim Oi was born in 1907 in the fishing village of Aberdeen in Hong Kong. She grew up in Kowloon, where her father was a Christian headmaster, and where she escaped restrictions like foot-binding which were still being imposed on many women in China. She moved freely between Kowloon and Canton. She left school at 14, but then went back to full-time education when she was 21, and she became a teacher. She entered theological college in the 1930s. When the Sino-Japanese War began she led the first aid team and worked with refugees. She found it hard to come to terms with the cruelty she witnessed around her. She was sent to the Portuguese territory of Macao, which was then surrounded by the Japanese, but not occupied. It was there that she became a deaconess.

On Christmas Day 1941 Hong Kong fell to the Japanese, and many hundreds of refugees fled to Macao, which was cut off from Hong Kong. It was at this time that Li Tim Oi was given permission to perform the duties of a priest. She was very happy and worked very hard for the refugees in very bad conditions. As she walked to church each morning, she often followed the cart that picked up the bodies of those who had died of hunger. She herself was penniless but she ate the horse food offered to the girls at the local school.

The bishop was Ronald Hall who worked 400 miles away, also with refugees. He wrote to Li Tim Oi, 'If you dare to come and meet me, it is good that you be ordained priest and given a proper right to do your work.' She made the very dangerous journey by night through the Japanese-held territory, by boat and bicycle, and by crossing two mountains. She was ordained priest in 1944 when women were not accepted as priests in the Anglican Church. William Temple, the Archbishop of Canterbury at the beginning of the Second World War, said that he could not find one theological reason against women being ordained to the *priesthood*, but that he would have preferred Li Tim Oi to remain as a deaconess. Many people were outraged by his statement that women priests were a possibility. When she was interviewed in old age Li Tim Oi remembered one thing the bishop had said to her at her quiet and simple ordination service at the Lake of the Seven Stars. It was that the priesthood is a vocation for life.

When the Second World War was over, the new Archbishop of Canterbury, Geoffrey Fisher, put pressure on Bishop Hall and the other Chinese bishops to stop Li Tim Oi's priestly ministry, and for a while she went to work as a deaconess in Hoppo, on the pearl fishing coast. She kept quiet for a while, but she never resigned her orders and always remembered that she was a priest for her lifetime. Her time in Hoppo was far from peaceful because in 1950 Mao Tse Tung's liberation army reached Hoppo. Many people were killed and the church was closed. Li Tim Oi journeyed for 1600 miles to join a course at the Three Self Theological College in Peking, where the 'Three Self Movement', still practised in the Church in China, was promoted. The three referred to are self-support, self-government and self-propagation. When she was at the college Li Tim Oi was very unhappy because she was suspected of being a spy and was ostracised. She had times when she felt that God had abandoned her. She later said, 'I thought about jumping into the lake to drown myself . . . but I told myself that I am an ordained priest, and that if I kill myself it will give the Church an evil name.'

Li Tim Oi went from Peking to Canton for four years until the 'Great Leap Forward' in 1959, when she went to work on a farm and became 'captain of chickens'. She also worked in a factory. She, like many other educated people in China, lost all her books during the Cultural Revolution between 1966 and 1970. She was forced by the Red Guards to cut up her robes. She was given the work of a labourer and had to dig and wear a placard which read, 'Backward Priest. Opposed to the Revolution.' She was allowed no religious 'things' at all and had to depend upon her memory.

In 1970 the Anglican Communion stated that it would not prevent the ordination of women, and the Diocese of Hong Kong and Macau was the first to ordain them. Li Tim Oi's licence was restored. She retired in 1974 at the age of 67, and, along with other Chinese Christians, was able to worship freely again in 1979 when she became a consultant pastor.

Li Tim Oi came to Westminster Abbey in 1984 to celebrate the 40th anniversary of her ordination as a priest. She received a message from Archbishop Robert Runcie: 'Your selfless ministry is an example to us all.' A year later Archbishop Runcie stated in public that he could see no reason against the ordination of women to the priesthood.

Li Tim Oi was a pioneer in many ways and she was an inspiration for women all over the world and an encouragement for women who became priests in the Anglican Communion. She was an inspiration for many people, men and women alike. She lived a hard life but though she came close to it at times, she never lost heart. She trusted God and focused on him who made everything else possible.

SECTION SEVEN
Special Times

Drawing by Jane Walton-Loxton

Introduction

There are for most of us special times that are important to us, some times to celebrate and others to mourn and remember. Most people in most countries, religions and cultures have special times, including family times, community times and national times. The most important family times in the UK perhaps mark the births of its members. Birthdays are important for many families and not just for the children. A religious family, of any of the world faiths, may celebrate important festivals, including the initiation ceremonies of its members. Communities also have their special times, from the history of the people. If we attend a church, there will be special times also, such as its Foundation Day or its Saint's Day, and of course the calendar of events through the Christian year, at the height of which is the celebration of Easter Day, following the fasting of Lent and Holy Week. The festival which Western society has adopted as its own, however, is not Easter, though people do buy Easter eggs, but Christmas. Christmas, the time of the birth of Jesus, is perhaps the most special time in the year for most people in the Western world, when Christians attend church, and most families gather, and there are presents and good food. In many parts of Africa, Christians spend the whole of Christmas Day at church, with the community, and it is there that, following the services, a feast is held.

As members of a country there are collective special times that we all share. In some countries these will include the day of independence for the country. Many members of the British Commonwealth, for example, have a special holiday at this time. When India celebrated 50 years of independence the whole sub-continent, from richest to poorest person, celebrated. In the cities there were exhibitions, dramas, dancing, speeches and feasting. The people who had won independence were specially remembered.

Every world religion has its special times which have grown

up usually over many hundreds of years. The festivals are often the glue of the community, times of celebration but also times of reflection and commitment. For example, Jewish people are required to attend at least three pilgrim feasts each year. These are the Passover celebrated in mid-April to remind people of the delivery from Egypt, the Feast of Pentecost held at the end of the wheat harvest (this is also used to celebrate the giving of the law) 50 days after Passover, and the Feast of Tabernacles, an eight-day celebration that takes place in the autumn at the final harvest of olives and fruits. During this feast, the people make shelters, or 'booths', to remind them of Israel's time in the wilderness when the nation lived in tents.

Some events are celebrated at lengthy intervals. In this section of our book Judith has written of the walk undertaken in her deanery to celebrate the Millennium. This deanery is in West Yorkshire within the South Pennines, where steep-sided valleys made by the melted glacial waters from the Ice Age dominate the land. Above are the bleak moorlands bordering the Haworth moors of Brontë fame, where, in *Wuthering Heights*, Cathy cries into the wind, mist and rain for Heathcliff. As Judith says, in this deanery the only way to really celebrate the Millennium was to walk through the hills – which meant going up and down these long steep-sided valleys many times. This was not a walk for the faint-hearted, nor the faint-footed!

Other events are occasional, such as the Year of Pilgrimage that was celebrated in 1997. In that year Christians were encouraged to travel in pilgrimage, and one contribution to that was a walking pilgrimage organised by Christians Aware across the North York Moors. For some of the pilgrims, this was their first experience of a walking pilgrimage of any length and it gave them a new insight into the continuity of such a pilgrimage. Whilst the deanery pilgrimage mentioned above may have been over much more difficult terrain, walking for each day over a whole week has a very different feel to it.

Many people can make a supreme effort for a short day, but having to repeat it again and again is not the same. It's not that you put less effort into each day but rather that you start the second and subsequent days with your body already slightly used. There are some parts of the feet that are already getting sore, bits of the old body you didn't know you had that are beginning to ache, and in your mind you know what's coming. Now, to those who are used to repeated walking that's fine, but to those new to it these sensations are not always very comfortable. It's not the occasional special event that is the hardest thing to cope with – most of us can rise to a challenge when we must, but rather it is the everyday tedium and dreariness for which we need to be prepared. But the everyday, ordinary life is what makes the special times possible, just as the Lenten fast leads to the rejoicing of Easter Day.

Some anniversaries are best celebrated in 50- or 100-year spans. The Year of Pilgrimage, 1997, was used to recall the 1400th anniversary of two events: the death of the Irish missionary to Scotland, St Columba, and the beginning of the mission of St Augustine to England. 'The Northern Saints', later in this section, gives a clear account of Christianity in Northern England, and in particular Celtic Christianity. It leads one to consider not only what we can learn from the saints of old, but also how different styles of worship and evangelism, as well as different denominations, could and should relate to each other today.

John and Diana Hargreaves have written about how they celebrated the life of St Dunstan in 1988, the millennium year after his death. This was originated by a church leader in the United States in a church dedicated to the saint, who suggested that churches dedicated to Dunstan all over the world should be represented at a celebration in Canterbury Cathedral where the saint had been the Archbishop. The journey was long and over several days of continuous walking, and John and Diana have described the lessons that were learned during this time in language that all walkers will know only too well: 'Everyone's blisters hurt, whether you are a Bishop or a bar tender.' Continuity leads us all to trust more and more in God, partly because we come to realise how merciful he is in really practical ways. A shoeless Buddhist monk once spoke about the bliss of being able to stand in shade on a hot day when the ground burned his feet. There is also nothing else we can do. It is almost in this giving up of control and self-sufficiency that we learn most of God and feel his nearness and presence that was already there anyway.

A more recent anniversary is described later in this section by Stan Lane who carried out a pilgrimage walk in 1995 to mark the 50th anniversary of the death of Dietrich Bonhoeffer. The walk was 375 miles in length and gave Stan the opportunity to talk to many individuals and groups along the way not only about Bonhoeffer and his times but also about the contemporary issues of today. Stan's conclusion is that the Church today needs to be readied to speak out in times and circumstances of 'trouble'. We also need, in our own lives, to be ready for times of difficulties and hardships. This does not mean that we should all wait for trouble to arise and then rush in to do what we can. Rather it means that people of faith should so live and work in the everyday world that a positive and loving climate emerges in society at large. If this can only be done, then the troubles every thinking person fears are less likely to arise.

It is also vitally important that society at large never forgets the hard times in the history of the world, the terror of Hitler being an excellent example, but also more recent atrocities, including the massacres of Cambodia and Rwanda, and the cruelties of many wars. The establishment of an annual national Holocaust Memorial at the end of January is something to be grateful for, because it allows the people of the UK to think about what happened and why, and to be committed to a better future for the whole world. Memorials may also be a thanksgiving that horrors ended.

Oberammergau in Germany has been the setting for a passion play acted out between May and September every ten years as a thanksgiving for the survival of some of the people from the plague of 1633 which followed the Thirty Years' War. The play goes on, and the local people, all amateurs, still take part. The next time will be in 2010. Many churches and groups organise pilgrimages to see the play.

As a worldwide Church, Christians of all denominations, we share a number of special times with each other every year. We share not only the major festivals of Christmas and Easter but also the reading of the same passages of the Bible for many occasions. Members of a denomination will normally share a common prayer book. Anglicans, for example, have a new prayer book, Common Worship.

John and Anne Gould write in this section of taking part in an annual pilgrimage to Bradwell to the place built by St Cedd. To visit a place of such age and history is a special time, as is a visit to Lastingham where we have been in a group of pilgrims celebrating a Celtic rite of Holy Communion. There was almost a stepping back in time particularly when we felt the cold of the place through its thick walls, and realised that little has altered through all the years that have gone by.

There are times each year when it would be suitable to design a special pilgrimage book if one could only stand back and think about it in advance. We can only be grateful for those who do provide some of the resources we need at the special times. The times of Advent and Lent are obvious annual times for this, but so also are special anniversaries or special events, such as a visit from a special person or group of people. Other occasions might be when there is a group of people all undertaking the same or a similar piece of work or journey. An example of this was a group of students following a theology course who wished to pray for each other in between the times they were together. Each gave a passport-sized photograph of themselves and a prayer or thought that they particularly liked or had written themselves. These were then put on a page together with an empty box that could be written in. All the different headings for the course modules were added, one to each page, and so the book was put together. Each person was given a copy and asked to use it in their quiet times. Some have since written in it as if it were a prayer diary with thoughts and memories for that person or that course topic.

Another example was a book for Christmas and the New Year organised by a local 'Churches Together' group. Each church was asked to provide three different-styled articles to be included in the finished book. These were then collated with a number for the day of the month given to each, and distributed and sold through all the participating churches. As always with these collaborative efforts, a certain amount of chasing for items has to be undertaken, and having a couple of people who can 'run something up quickly' also helps for those well-intentioned and promised articles that never do appear!

There are also special times to be recalled and celebrated each week. Some Christians have for many years remembered that Christ died on a Friday by not eating meat on that day, and all churches recall Christ's rising again on that first Easter morning each Sunday. Even during the time of Lent, Sundays are still celebrated for that reason and so are not included within the 40 days of fasting, penitence and preparation.

The Church calendar sets down the pattern for the liturgical year and even suggests the colours for each season. The colour used for each service is intended to reflect the predominant theme and is reinforcement for the readings, the prayers and the service style that is used.

Throughout the day there are a number of key moments that one can use as special times – 12 noon is traditionally the time to say the Angelus. The Angelus has been prayed for many centuries to celebrate and honour Christ's incarnation and the Blessed Virgin Mary. It used to be said morning, noontime and evening, but it is now more commonly used only at midday. During Easter-time the Regina Caeli is used instead of the Angelus. Meal times can be a special time to say Grace: to give thanks, not just for the food in front of us but for all the things we wish to recognise at that time.

The devotion of the Stations of the Cross was first used during the Middle Ages to recall the special times and places of Jesus on that last day. Pilgrims retrace the steps of the Via Dolorosa, the distance from the Praetorium where Jesus was condemned, to Calvary, where he was crucified. Since the sixteenth century there have been fourteen stations used for this meditation, and these have been marked along the probable route in Jerusalem, and they are also shown along the walls of many churches. The idea is to move physically from the beginning to the end, stopping at each station along the way and meditating on different aspects of the Passion of Christ at each one.

Special times are milestones along the path of life, some of them are linear, and having celebrated them we never do so again, including all our birthdays and one-off events in the history of our community, country or the world. Some of the special times follow a circular path, so that we repeat them, day after day, week after week, year after year. The circular pattern is an important reminder of the need every human being has for regular ritual and the security it brings with it. The linear pattern is a rather more stark reminder that life does move forward, from its beginnings to its ends. The special times are encouragements and warnings along the way.

Twenty-First-Century Pilgrimage
A Poem for the Millennium Year

Peter Challen

In millennium year 2000
I took a train to Canterbury and back, alone;
yet accompanied by the all inhabited
world about me, near and far,
and observed that –

Attending pilgrims
search minds,
savour cultures,
adjust their focus,
enlarge perspective,
seek creation's local purposes;
their global sensitivities never sated.

Thrill tourists
seek refreshment,
crave exceptional excitement,
delight in the exotic,
ignore mundane realities,
let mobile phones replace
face-to-face communications;
and come away replete,
to plunge unchanged into their own unreal world.

What both see, pilgrim and tourist alike,
they should, in all humility, admit
they do not own or deeply know,
nor for it bear response-ability.
Said the Talented Mr Ripley:

'I had always thought it would be better
to be a fake somebody
than a real nobody.'
Oh! how misguided was he!

Pilgrims travel without pretension,
tourists rarely escape it;
tourists feast myopically
on corporate and consumer cancers.
Pilgrims taste diffidently,
seeking to heal the plague,
to mature as inclusive citizens of Earth
in sustainable liveability,
for the planet's community entire.

Pilgrims see deeply,
where tourists merely look.
This train from Canterbury
carrying both explorers,
not only terminates at London Bridge,
but also starts anew from there.

The Calder Valley Deanery Walk September 2000

Judith Thornton

When you live in the Calder Valley, the only way to celebrate the new Millennium is to walk amongst the hills. The Deanery, which runs from Luddenden in the east to Walsden in the west is about ten miles as the crow flies but if you want to follow the route via all our eight parishes it's more likely to be 20 miles.

We set off from the east starting our journey at Luddenden. Twenty walkers arrived to the aroma of crispy bacon and hot coffee – if this was the way we would be greeted at every church the walking would be easy. Tim Sledge, Vicar of St Mary's, Luddenden, led songs, Bible readings and prayers. At eight o'clock the journey started. Donald Crossley from Mytholmroyd was our walk leader and off we trudged. The climb out of Luddenden was very steep, and Donald set off at a cracking pace. I hoped everybody was experienced at walking because at this pace people would be dropping off by the time we reached Mytholmroyd. We walked up to Midgley School and down to the valley via Brearley Wood, then along the valley bottom to Mytholmroyd Church.

On reaching St Michael's Church, Mytholmroyd, we were joined by 20 more walkers. After a short stop at the church it was a pleasant walk up to Cragg Vale, partly along the road and then joining the River Elphin to St John in the Wilderness, Cragg Vale Church. Bible readings and prayers were followed by coffee and biscuits.

Forty walkers left Cragg Vale heading up towards Stoodley Pike monument. It was very impressive looking down on the walkers as they snaked up through the many stiles to reach the crossroads. The views from here were stunning, and it was such a clear day you could see Todmorden in the west,

Halifax to the east, south to the Stoodley Pike monument, and north to Heptonstall. Heptonstall looked to be so close, but we knew it was a long walk into the valley bottom and then an even tougher walk up to Heptonstall. At the crossroads before our descent into Hebden Bridge, Donald was in fine voice and the hymn singing sounded excellent. Singing God's praises in such fine surroundings was magical; the sheep were a little confused as they are only accustomed to listening to the birds singing.

As we reached Hebden Bridge, people were beginning to struggle. The young people were beginning to hobble and we hadn't reached the halfway stage yet. With the sun on our backs, this climb up the Buttress from Hebden Bridge to Heptonstall was the steepest and longest climb of the day.

At St Thomas' Church, Heptonstall, we were greeted by the church cat, who was quite willing to share our sandwiches. There was also some delicious soup made by the ladies of the church. For the readings and prayers we stood round the altar in a large circle. Sharing the worship was very uplifting and prepared us for the next stage, which was a very short walk down the hill to St James' Church, Mytholm.

We were getting behind schedule now, and there were several people waiting at Mytholm to join the group. We were now halfway into the walk, and for the people who had walked from Luddenden it was the big test: shall we stay until the bitter end? This next phase was over the hills to Cornholme, the longest stretch. The route took us through Rawtonstall, Hippins Bridge and Great Rock where we stopped for a photo call. We then walked along the Calderdale Way, passing Todmorden Golf Club, Whirlaw Common, Hudson Bridge, and down into the valley bottom via Shore Chapel. There wasn't much time to admire the views because we were running late; we were an hour overdue when we arrived at St Michael's Church, Cornholme, to be greeted with cakes and coffee.

The prayers were well received here as we needed revitalising ready for all the road walking that was in front of us. The only good news was it was all downhill to Todmorden. We stopped for quick prayers in St Mary's Church, Todmorden, as it was now beginning to grow gloomy but it wasn't the time to give up as we only had three miles to walk; at least it was nice and flat now all along the canal bank.

Hymns, readings and prayers were sung and said in St Peter's Church, Walsden, with some very tired people. Twelve of the pilgrims had walked all the way, and well over 60 Christians had met up at some point during the walk, ranging in age from 10 to over 70. One or two people had been at each church to make sure nobody wanted a lift home.

I must admit I was very impressed that I had walked the whole route; the fellowship and the spiritual uplift at every church made the day feel just right. We are so lucky to live in an area with such splendid hill walking.

Yorkshire Pilgrimage, July 1997

We offered a walking pilgrimage as the Christians Aware contribution to the Year of Pilgrimage, and we chose a journey across the North York Moors, an area of wooded valleys, of sheep and cattle farming, of wild open moorland and of the North Sea coast. We began in Easingwold, where we were generously given a place where cars could be left for the week, and we walked to Ampleforth Abbey and on to the ruins of the Cistercian Abbey of Rievaulx. From Helmsley Methodist Church we took the road to Kirkbymoorside and Appleton on the Moor, where we were the guests of the Ryedale Christian Council, staying in homes. We shared a Eucharist in the Norman crypt of Lastingham Church, built on the place where Cedd founded his monastery in 654 CE, and we walked from there, over the moors to Rosedale Abbey. The path from Rosedale to Goathland was long, the desolation relieved by the sunshine and the views. An open-air Eucharist and supper with members of Goathland parish and a very sound sleep in the parish marquee ended a full and challenging day.

The final walks, from Goathland to Sleights and on to Whitby Abbey and the United Reformed Church, took us to the end of the pilgrimage

We were at pains to make sure that the pilgrim journey, the speakers, the worship and the pilgrims themselves were as ecumenical as possible. The pilgrims came from all over Britain, from the Middle East and Egypt, and were of all ages and from all the main Christian denominations. We managed to include most of the traditional ingredients of pilgrimage in our week: the simple church hall and camping accommodation, the meeting of people in the communities and along the way, the conversations between the pilgrims, the worship and meditation, the talks, art and music, and the struggle with the weather, aching limbs, twisted ankles and blisters. We learnt one of the lessons of all the world faiths, which was lived out by the Celts, of the value of focusing on the present moment, of appreciating the pathway, the other people, the opportunity of the walk, and the foolishness of thinking ahead to the end of the walk, tempting as that sometimes was to us all.

The pilgrimage created a community of walkers and developed in many of us an awareness of caring, generous and open community at the heart of much Christian life and work. The first day of the walk was perhaps the most difficult. Most people were not well trained, and tiredness soon set in; the weather was poor, with heavy rain in the morning. The warm welcome by the Ampleforth Abbey community, together with the good meal, refreshed the weary and bedraggled group and gave a new spirit which was nurtured by other communities throughout the week. The Celts developed communities around their monasteries, inspired by their understanding of God as community in Trinity, an understanding they shared with the Egyptian monastic desert communities. Above all, however, it became clear to us as we journeyed through the week that what made the Celtic communities strong was the sincerity of their lives lived in the light of the gospel, inside and outside the monasteries, by priests and teachers, travellers and farmers, kings and peasants. The pilgrimage year marked the 1400th anniversary of the death of Columba on Iona and the arrival of Augustine in Canterbury. Both of them built Christian community by sincerely living it for Christ's sake and not by speeches, writing or campaigns. What was true 1400 years ago is true now, we realised. Most people join the Church when it is a community which is caring, generous and open. This truth has been brought out by the research work of one of our pilgrimage speakers, Bishop John Finney. This truth can be seen in the present work of the Whitby sisters, the Anglican order of the Holy Paraclete, founded and continuing in the spirit of St Hilda, the energetic and loving mother whose life was lived for the sake of other people, their welfare, education and general development.

We as pilgrims, and as members of our different churches, are faced with a great challenge to Christian living now. Our pilgrimage has enriched us and must enrich and enable others for work for change, justice and development – or what was the point of it all?

Interconnectedness

The strands of Celtic pattern weave a whole
and bind us in our common goal,
as over moorland paths we tread
with naught but hard ground for our bed.

Those threads stretch back to saints of old,
terrain so harsh, the winters cold.
Strengthened by adversity
they gave their all to follow
thee.

Though many centuries lie in between,
we've visited places they have been;
worshipped in crypt and open air
in fellowship beyond compare.

Strangers have met us on the way
offering welcome and a place to stay:
we've listened to the tales they tell
and our own stories told as well.

And so our journey did unfold,
and looking back we do behold
a fabric of enriching hues
to treasure always, never lose.

Janet Stephens

The Northern Saints

A Benedictine Monk of Ampleforth Abbey

1997 marked the 1400th anniversary of two events – the death of the Irish missionary to Scotland, St Columba, and the beginning of the mission of St Augustine to Kent. These anniversaries sparked a number of celebrations throughout Great Britain, celebrations which focused on the life and works of these two great figures in our Church's history. I have found myself asking several questions. Firstly, what is it that we celebrated when we commemorated these men? Secondly, and perhaps more importantly, what can we still hope to learn from the celebration of the lives of these saints? What can they still teach us about our own Christian lives today?

With regard to the first of these questions, it is clear that the anniversary celebrations meant different things to different people. For some, the celebrations were purely historical – recalling the basic events which have in some way shaped the society in which we live and the great figures who brought those events about. For such people, Columba and Augustine are curiosities, exhibits to be explored, part of the great museum of life which makes up the British Isles. For authors and publishers, such anniversaries are a God-send. For others, the anniversaries were an excuse – and I believe a very good excuse – for grand public events, pilgrimages and parties. Here, perhaps, we are on more clearly 'spiritual' ground, for such events pick up the medieval idea of pilgrimages, those strange mixtures of prayer and holiday, of piety and frivolity, of superficial jollity and deep spiritual purpose. To this extent, they are a 'good thing', as the authors of *1066 and All That* would put it, a way of building our common faith on the sure rock of our own history.

It is here, I believe, that we have our best justification for the celebration of these anniversaries. The stories of the saints and of the conversion of Britain to Christianity are important because they are our story. The tales of heroic faith and miracles are crucial not only because they tell us where we came from, but also because they challenge us to live up to the example which is set before us. As Isaiah says:

> Listen to me, you seek saving justice, you who seek the Lord. Consider the rock from which you were hewn, the quarry from which you were dug. Consider Abraham your father, and Sarah who gave you birth. When I called him, he was only one, but I blessed him and made him numerous . . . (*Isaiah 51:1-2*)

or again, as the letter to the Hebrews tells us:

> With so great a cloud of witnesses around us, we too should throw off everything that weighs us down, and the sin that clings so closely, and with perseverance keep running the race that lies ahead of us . . . (*Hebrews 12:1*)

It would probably take several days even to begin a satisfactory biography of Columba and his successors – Aidan, Cuthbert, Chad and Cedd, Hilda, Caedmon, Bede, Benet Biscop, Wilfrid, Oswald and Oswy, to name but the main figures. I want to try and give some view of the historical context of these figures, attempting to demonstrate some of the reasons for the growth and success of the Celtic missions in the North. Equally, I want to suggest that in many ways the geography of the North is almost as significant a factor in the consideration of the 'northern saints' as is any consideration of theology. It is the places which shape the saints, and which in many ways give them their characteristic witnessing to the truth that God is the God of space as well as the God of time.

Most of us have a rather 'linear' view of the history of the Church. We see the Church as having started in Palestine at the beginning of our era, and then spreading gradually to the edges of the world, sometimes enduring persecution and set-back, but on the whole advancing in a fairly regular pattern. Within the Church, the history of doctrine follows a similar pattern; at each step, the belief of the Church seems to be imperilled by heresy, until a new understanding or doctrinal formula appears which sweeps all opposition from the field and restores peace and harmony. To some extent, such a picture is useful, allowing us to build up a systematic understanding of our faith and its origin. It gives us the familiar pattern of a family tree, by which we can trace the ancestry of our faith. We owe a great debt to St Luke for this approach to Church history, for in the Acts of the Apostles this is precisely the picture which he draws; the faith starts from Jerusalem and then gradually reaches to the ends of the earth (as symbolised by Paul's arrival in Rome), rather like the ripples spreading across a pond after a stone has been dropped into its centre. When Bede wanted to describe the coming of the faith to England, his knowledge of the scriptures drove him to use the same type of model, and throughout his work we see this same pattern of slow and steady advance, with the light of the gospel carrying all before it. The reality of the history of the faith in Britain is much more complex, however, and this is particularly true of the history of the northern missions. In fact, the whole process appears to be much more similar to those processes involved in evolutionary theory than it does to the simple linear scheme of the textbooks.

We do not know when Christianity came to Britain, but it seems likely that it owes its origins to the Roman invasion by Claudius in 43 CE. The inclusion of Britannia into the Empire meant an increase in contacts with mainland Europe, and the constant flow of trade and military personnel seem to have provided ideal conduits for the new faith, much as they had done in the Mediterranean world of St Paul's mission. Certainly, there is evidence that by the third and fourth centuries there was a flourishing British Church. Bede dates the martyrdom of St Alban to 301 CE, suggesting that there were priests around at this time, and a number of archaeological finds have corroborated such suggestions – for example, the Church building at Silchester, the Christian wall paintings at Lullingstone in Kent, and the substantial hordes of Christian treasure recovered at Mildenhall in Suffolk and at Canterbury in Kent. There is also some documentary evidence that there were British bishops present at Church councils in Gaul during the fourth century, including a bishop from York. Traditionally, too, the Emperor Constantine's mother, St Helena, the woman who found the True Cross, started life as a barmaid in York, so that one could say at a pinch that it was from Yorkshire that the western world was converted to Christianity!

However, with the withdrawal of the Roman military presence in 410 CE there began a gradual collapse in both civil and religious organisation. It is particularly important to note here that whilst this collapse was perhaps most obvious in the South (where the level of Romanisation had always been greater), its effects were perhaps deepest in the North. The Romans had never been particularly successful in the North; only the great towns of York and Carlisle had significant populations, and much of the country remained what it had always been – wilderness containing a small and stubborn population, which was always threatened by invasion from Scotland, a threat to which Hadrian's Wall bears mute testimony. Outside York, we have no evidence of Christianity at all. The withdrawal of the Romans, and the consequent severing of the links between Britain and Europe, and particularly between the North and Europe, left this part of the country exposed to the recrudescence of paganism, and probably resulted in the complete destruction of whatever Christian organisation there might have been.

All was not lost, however, for during this period our focus of attention shifts from northern England to Ireland – an island which had never been conquered by Rome and which knew little or nothing of its style of government. Early in the fifth century, a noble British youth was captured by an Irish raiding party, and taken as a slave back to Ireland. His name – Patrick or Patricius – strongly suggests that he was of Romano-British stock, and he seems to have been a Christian. Eventually escaping from slavery, he fled – most probably to Gaul – and completed his education, returning to Ireland to convert the nation which had enslaved him. Whilst in Gaul, Patrick seems to have come under the influence of monastic ideas which were by then spreading through the Western Church from the East, and the Church which Patrick left in Ireland was monastic to the core.

It is important to understand here that the monasticism of these early Irish converts was very different to what we would now recognise as monastic. The monastic impulse itself appears to have begun in Egypt at the beginning of the fourth century, roughly at the time of the 'Toleration of the Church'. With the disappearance of official persecution and martyrdom as the crowning achievements of the Christian life witness, there began gradual attempts to express the same qualities of self-denial for the sake of Christ whilst remaining alive – the replacement of the 'red martyrdom' of death with the 'white martyrdom' of monastic endeavour. Thousands flocked to the deserts of Egypt and the caves of Palestine and Syria to live the gospel life in solitude, in prayer and in fasting; they would live as solitaries, as hermits, often in close proximity to each other and to a spiritual elder or 'Abba', meeting only on Sundays and feast days to celebrate the Eucharist. This style of life became highly influential extremely quickly, and was brought to Gaul by St John Cassian, who had himself been brought up in such a desert monastery in the East, and also by St Martin of Tours.

It is this style of life which Patrick would have encountered in the monasteries of Gaul – a life based on the reading and learning of the gospels and the psalms, on fasting and penitence – and it is this style of monasticism which became predominant in the Irish Church. To this beginning, the Irish monks added much which was characteristically their own. Their own

315

wilderness – their version of the Egyptian desert – was not the arid, parched and almost lifeless rock of Sinai and Palestine but a wilderness of heath and moor and mountain. The desert in which the Egyptian monks learned of the changeless omnipotence of God through constant searing heat changed in Ireland to the wilderness in which God was seen in rushing torrents, in snowstorms and thunderstorms, in lashing rain and the chill of winter. The lack of distraction found in the desert – where there really is nothing but one's sins to contemplate – was exchanged by the Irish monks for the contemplation of God as creator, as builder of mountains, as stirrer of the depths of the sea, as the life and breath of animals and birds. It is very much the same type of monastic struggle, but a slightly different perspective because of the difference in climate and scenery, and a perspective which strongly marks the theology which has come down to us from those times.

Equally, the geographical isolation of Ireland in these times meant that a whole new system of Church government and tradition grew up. The leaders in the Church were the abbots, the fathers of the huge monasteries which sprang up round them. These acted as the religious equivalent of tribal chiefs, each with several thousand monks under their command, often including large numbers of their own relations. Within each monastery there would be a bishop, whose role was almost totally different to that elsewhere in the Church; such bishops were not leaders, but subordinate to the abbot, and carried out their missions of preaching and consecration according to the abbot's bidding.

Last of the characteristic features of this early Irish monasticism is their own special version of the 'white martyrdom'. A fiercely patriotic, fiercely loyal and fiercely tribal people, the greatest form of self-sacrifice which could be offered was considered to be the so-called *peregrinatio pro Christo* – the voluntary abandonment of home and family to go into the world to preach the Gospel. This evangelising zeal – typical of a young Church in its first ardour – made the

Irish monks some of the most important missionaries in Europe during this period, and the missions continued well into the eighth century. Indeed, it was one of St Columba's own followers, St Columbanus, who some 100 years after St Benedict wrote his Rule in Monte Cassino, re-established monastic life in northern Italy and Switzerland, founding monasteries and writing his own Rule, which was to remain the most influential guide to European monasticism until the Carolingian imposition of the rule of St Benedict throughout Europe in 814.

This, then, is the background against which we must view the Celtic missions to the North. The similarities with the Irish situation made it ideal territory for mission work. Like Ireland, Northumbria and Strathclyde were traversed by large stretches of wilderness – sea-coasts, moorland, immense forests, mountains. The populations were closely related, and probably shared at least some elements of a common language. More importantly perhaps, the missionaries themselves were simple men, men who knew only the gospels, but knew them well enough to live them to the full – steadfast in prayer, offering hospitality, giving and receiving love from all whom they encountered, men and beasts alike, and marked – at least according to the contemporary accounts of their lives – by the capacity to work miracles which is also found in the accounts of the early Church in Acts.

The circumstances of Columba's coming to Iona are surrounded by mystery. Some legends speak of feud over a book, others of the violation of a church; either way, Columba, after some 15 years of preaching and founding monasteries in Ireland, took up the challenge of the *peregrinatio* – possibly even as a self-imposed penance for the slaughter which had been caused in the feud. In the early summer of 563, he and 11 companions set sail, and continued on their way until they reached Iona, the first landfall from which Ireland was completely invisible. There they built their first church, and the small beehive cells in which they lived, and to this little island retreat hundreds began to flock – so many that soon they could send monks off to the mainland to begin the task of conversion and the establishment of new houses. By the end of his life, Columba is said to have founded some 100 churches, and to have converted many of the pagan petty kings of Scotland. From Iona, too, came Aidan, sent in answer to the request of Oswald, king of Northumbria. Oswald had been baptised during a period of exile in Scotland, when he had come under the influence of the new teaching of life, and he was most concerned that his people should share his faith. As was commonly the case, once the ruler had become a Christian, the people followed more willingly (the same is true of the conversion of Ethelbert of Kent), and Aidan seems to have been a very powerful example of the simple but profound faith in the gospel which stands at the heart of the Celtic missions. Bede, writing of Aidan's criticism of the first priest who was sent from Scotland to aid Northumbria, puts the following words in the saint's mouth:

> Brother, it seems to me that you were too severe on your ignorant hearers. You should have followed the practice of the Apostles, and begun by giving them the milk of simpler teaching, and gradually instructed them in the word of God until they were capable of greater perfection and able to follow the sublime precepts of Christ . . .*

Despite Bede's evident unhappiness about some of the practices of the Celtic monks, it is quite clear that he sees nothing at all wrong with their faith. Again and again we see him describing these northern saints, the heroes of his own land, in terms which clearly draw on the pictures of the Apostolic Church which he has read about in the Acts of the Apostles. Again and again, too, we see the importance of the simple preaching of the word of God as being the tool *par excellence* in the

* Bede's *Ecclesiastical History* (Penguin edition).

conversion of kings and commoners alike. It is the work of monks to read and learn and live the scriptures, but it is the pattern of the gospel life itself which wins converts to Christ. The Celtic saints, of course, were not alone in this; St Augustine's mission in the south was successful for much the same reasons, as were St Boniface's missions to the Germans. Many centuries later, when St Dominic wished to convert the Cathars of southern France from their neo-Arianism in the thirteenth century, he chose to live out the 'vita Apostolica' in simplicity and community, in poverty and preaching. The same can be said of St Francis and the Franciscans. It is the example of the gospel as preached and as lived which formed the greatest possible introduction to the Christian life, and it is this lived example which forms the golden thread connecting the portraits of all the Northern saints – Columba, Aidan, Chad, the apostle of Mercia, Oswald king of Northumbria, Cuthbert the 'fire of the north' – which we find in the pages of Bede's 'History'.

In many ways the story of the northern missions is more like the process of evolution than it is a simple linear picture of conquest. What drew Darwin's attention to the possibility of an evolutionary theory was the effect of isolation on a population of finches in the Galapagos Islands. He noted that on the islands there were a variety of finches, all with identical bodies, but slightly differently shaped beaks; these differently shaped beaks allowed them to use all the available food resources to maximum effect – some having sharp pointed beaks which are good for catching insects, some with large heavy beaks which are good for cracking nuts and fruit, and so on. His idea was that the isolation allowed the original population of finches to develop in different directions, so that the end result was the best possible use of the available resources.

In many ways, I think this gives us quite a good model for understanding the Celtic missions. Separated from the main-stream of European thought and Church government, the

Celtic Church developed a whole new way of understanding the gospel, and knowing the God who stood behind the gospel. The basic truths of the Christian faith provided the initial impulse for this process, and the basic pattern of life for those who were newly created by baptism, but the way in which that life was lived out – in prayer to God and to Christ, in solitude, in fasting, in silence, in hospitality, in close communion with creation and in the clear delight in creation which is evident from the decorative carving and calligraphy of the Celtic Church – was shaped largely by the available environment, which appealed very deeply to those who came into contact with it. Whilst conditions of isolation continued, the Celtic forms of organisation and thought remained the most successful way to use the available resources of the North.

Of course, such isolation could not last for ever. Indeed, in many ways, it was the success of the Celtic missions which served to bring the isolation to an end, spreading Christianity and peace throughout the north country and Scotland, and fostering links of fraternity between Irish, Scots and Northumbrians. In 627 CE, Paulinus, one of the companions of St Augustine, refounded the See of York, and brought a new exposure to the European and worldwide dimensions of Christianity. Very soon, there were influences from Europe and the North running abroad, and often at cross-purposes within the same kingdom. Bede tells the famous story of the principal difficulty which arose between the two traditions – that of how to fix the date of Easter. Those following the Roman tradition had adopted the decree of Nicaea, the earliest ecumenical Church council and fixed Easter in one way, whilst the Scots and the Celtic Church followed an equally ancient tradition, set aside at this same council, which calculated differently. The result was that whilst the king of Northumbria, brought up under Aidan, was celebrating Easter, his wife was still in the middle of Lent! Clearly, the situation could not be allowed to continue. In 664 CE, a synod was held at the Abbey of Whitby to attempt to resolve the differences, and in the end, after much debate, the proponents of the Roman dating – that dating which was celebrated throughout mainland Europe – were successful in convincing King Alfred to move to the Roman system.

We must be careful how we interpret this 'success'. There is no real reason to see this as Roman triumphalism, crushing the native Church and ancient tradition in its thirst for domination, as at least some commentators have suggested. Rather, we are again faced with our idea of evolution. In the early Church, many forms of tradition, and many variant practices of Church orders were tried and tested, and only gradually did such ideas as orders of clergy, fixed datings for feasts, the authority of bishops and so on emerge. They emerged, generally speaking, because they were the forms of government and organisation which seemed to work best within the Church as a whole. In many ways, the story of the Celtic missions and the Celtic Church is like watching a re-run of the evolution of the early Church, with different forms of organisation being adopted because they suited the environment in which the Church was. When that environment changed, as it did in the mid-seventh century when the North again became part of a greater Christian Britain, it was inevitable that some changes in organisation would occur. What is perhaps most impressive about the northern saints – and particularly Cuthbert and Chad – is the flexibility and calm and humility with which they accepted those changes, seeing the value for the people of a strong and broadly based Church, and happy – at no little cost to themselves – to accept the good of the many as overriding their own particular preferences. Certainly, there is no reason to think that the Celtic Church, its traditions and spirituality were suppressed – it continued to be a vital part of the life of the North and of Scotland and indeed of all Europe well after the Synod of Whitby, surviving the onslaught of the Vikings in the eighth and ninth centuries and still being the predominant form of Christianity in Scotland until the time of the Normans.

321

What can we learn? We can learn from their eagerness to know God through his word, the Word which he has given precisely that we might know him, the Word which they spent so much of their time in reading and pondering. We can learn, too, from their simple faith in putting that Word into practice, realising that the Words of the Gospel are not simply good ideas, or wonderful ethical teachings, but a rule for life, a rule to which we should try to conform and a rule by which we, as Christians, will one day be judged. For the northern saints, the gospel life was not only for themselves, but for others, and it was their practice of it which drew men and women to them to know more. We, too, should perhaps take the effects of our example as Christians more seriously; if we seriously try to imitate Christ, there is no doubt that we will draw the interest of those around us, and in drawing them to the gospel, God will draw them towards himself. Perhaps, too, we should learn from the example of these northern saints that we can find God where we are – in the circumstances of our daily lives, in those around us, in the environment in which we live. Few of us, perhaps, will have strength enough to stand in the sea overnight to recite the psalms as St Cuthbert did, but perhaps we can find something of the power and majesty of God if we spend a little time in quiet walking across the moors, in watching the sea, in thanking God for the endurance and miracles of these saints which are quite beyond our powers, and that may be the case; still, we should not overlook the value of turning the radio off for five minutes and being still, looking for a little wilderness where we can be alone with God, even if only for a few minutes every day. It is, I think, by little steps, little steps patiently and perseveringly made, without too much worry about whether we will achieve the miraculous, that we too can celebrate the anniversaries and follow the examples of these great saints – walking the same roads as they walked on earth, so that we may come to the same great home in heaven.

The Glastonbury to Canterbury Pilgrimage Celebrating the Life of St Dunstan

John and Diana Hargreaves

When Dunstan, the son of a Somerset miller and landowner, began to take Jesus Christ seriously, he did the usual thing for those days and became a monk. That was the tenth century. He was soon known for his artistic skills. He made bells for churches, painted beautifully, composed fine music, and trained fellow-monks to do the same. He was a great leader of men, and became abbot of Glastonbury at the age of 18. This high position brought him into close touch with the Court – too close on one occasion, when he rebuked the 15-year-old king Edwy for leaving his own coronation banquet and making love to a girl in his bedroom, and as a result, had to endure years of painful exile on the continent. But while there he discovered the splendid developments of the Benedictine monasteries, which became the basis of his own great work when he returned to England.

The monasteries were in wretched shape owing to the Viking and Danish invasions, and revival was desperately needed. It meant dealing with those monks who had forgotten their vows (Dunstan was famous for his patience and charity) and meant also creating a whole system of education for the nation through the monasteries.

Inevitably he became a Bishop, first of Worcester, later of London and eventually the Archbishop of Canterbury, and so began a close Church and State link. (We still use the coronation service which he drew up for King Edgar.) For 20 years he and Edgar worked hand in hand and created a unified 'England', previously a group of divided tribes. Many landowning barons were persuaded to share their wealth

Photograph: Diana Hargreaves

Glastonbury to Canterbury pilgrimage
during the Dunstan Millennium

with their local communities, and, in the Church, English and Danish leaders worked harmoniously together. Dunstan talked with kings. He talked also with God. He was saint and statesman in one person.

He was called 'God's light in dark times'. He lived through situations which have some similarities with our own, as we seek in our age a unified Britain, a true relationship between Church and State, the real meaning of education, racial harmony, and a sense of community.

If, then, Dunstan towered over his contemporaries, as the outstanding figure in both Church and State, how was it that his memory has been strangely obscured? This was surely because he was closely followed by the Norman Conquest and by Archbishop Becket's murder by order of the king, both of which steal the limelight in our school history books. So when the millennium of his death, May 1988, was approaching it seemed important to celebrate his life. The Rev Dick Daniels of St Dunstan's, Tulsa, Oklahoma, suggested that churches dedicated to St Dunstan all over the world should be represented at a celebration in Canterbury Cathedral. As part of this, Diana Hargreaves in England offered to arrange a walking pilgrimage from Dunstan's birthplace near Glastonbury to where Dunstan died as Archbishop.

Glastonbury was then an island, with Dunstan's monastery in the centre. Now there is a tor or grassy hill with only St Michael's tower standing. Sixty or so of us assembled in the abbey ruins, many from Dunstan churches. We viewed each other with interest, wondering what sort of people our fellow-pilgrims would turn out to be over the next 125 miles. Thirteen came from USA, six from Canada, two from Australia, and Dunstan Bukenya from Uganda. The rest came from Britain, through Christians Aware, and there were four from the St Dunstan charity for the war-blinded, who brought with them four helpers and two guide-dogs. It emerged that the blind men walked faster than most of us, somewhat to the alarm of weary walkers.

The first day began with Holy Communion in the crypt of the Abbey ruins. Then Bishop Philip Goodrich, the 111th successor to Dustan as Bishop of Worcester, blessed us and led us out to Baltonsborough. This is where Dunstan was born, and where today there stands a fine church. During the long walk that followed, through many fields, we stopped for a break at a manor house, and Susan Sayers taught us her song, which became the 'Pilgrimage Song', being remembered and sung long afterwards:

Sometimes rough and stony, the
way is hard and progress is slow;
then bright meadow flowers, and
sun shines as we go.

God's good world to walk through, and
his the hands that support and befriend,
his still peace enfolding us
all at each day's end.

We walked to Bruton, to the Red Cross hut, where we were grateful for hot tea, sticking plaster, and hot water for our feet, and for supper. That night we slept on the floor (not by any means the last time), although a pilgrim from Pennsylvania chose a table-top. A mini-bus helped us with our loads on our walk to Heytesbury and to Salisbury Plain. Here our driver, a university lecturer, showed us Stonehenge and told us that it was probably dated 3500 BC, which made Dunstan seem modern. So across great carpets of blue speedwell to Figheldean. Here we celebrated Ascension Day in the church, and remembered the pilgrims taking off at about this time from many airports on their way to join us in Canterbury. After an enormous supper, we somehow went on to dance 'strip the willow' with sore feet, and we sang with gusto one of the home-made songs written for this pilgrimage, and we didn't get to bed till 11.

Pilgrims we follow Dunstan, stumbling along his way;
carting our awkward burdens all the footslog day.

Strangers, we meet and parley, stragglers, we greet and stray;
seeking somehow between us to walk in Dunstan's way.

Struggling, we sense our shortfalls (sin-bins of show and
        pride);
meaning to be obedient. Dunstan, be our guide!

Guide us as we journey eastwards, Canterbury our goal;
gather our aching fragments; bless them and make us whole.

From there we walked over many stiles and many bridges,
and felt that the pilgrimage had begun in earnest. So when
we stopped for refreshments and were offered some thoughts
on the meaning of pilgrimage, they made sense, as a sort of
allegory of life. For example:

- Trusting and needing each other
- Accepting the basic elements of God's created world, sun
  and rain, comfort and weariness, differences in nature and
  in human beings
- Travelling with a purpose, aware of the goal
- Discovering people as people rather than as 'roles', since
  the blisters of bishops and bar-tenders feel much the same
- Seeing yourselves as only the latest members of a long line
  of pilgrims
- Risking the unknown, whether fellow-pilgrims or country-
  side
- Trusting God, who has led us far, and will lead us

Every day we had a special theme for our prayers, and as we
made our way to the incredibly beautiful Salisbury Cathedral
our theme was 'Following Dunstan, we glorify God through

suffering', and who better to lead our prayers than Dunstan Bukenya who knows the past and present suffering of Uganda? Our blisters, the five-foot-high nettles, heat exhaustion and the like could be seen in proper proportion. From Salisbury local ramblers took us to St Cross and then to the majestic Winchester Cathedral. There we had a great meal and a talk by the Dean who shared his special knowledge of present-day plight of Christians in parts of Eastern Europe. Cathedral evensong with the full choir was both appropriate to our theme and tranquil. Our visit to Winchester ended with a return to St Cross, to the ancient 'hospital' for 'poor impotent men'. From there we went to Guildford and to St Martha's 'Pilgrim Church', through golden cowslips and woods, covered in bluebells, then through lovely villages like Shere, and Abinger with its little man striking the hours on the village clock.

So we reached Dorking, where we slept among the infants' desks in a school, with a nightingale singing outside, but not before a local craftsman, knowing the fame of Dustan as a metal-worker, showed us how he probably did it. He let us all experiment in making little metal articles. We ended the day using a prayer of Dunstan's: 'Teach us, God of truth and beauty, to see in you the source of all our talents. Move us to offer them for the adornment of worship and the advancement of true religion.'

The next day began at an uncomfortably early hour with a Communion service at which the Bishop of Dorking presided. The day's walk was uphill and over a great many stiles. 'Why stiles and not gates?' asked the Canadians. We told them about sheep escaping when people left gates open. Eventually we were on the ridge, going east, and were thrilled to see signs, 'Pilgrims' Way', realising that generations of pilgrims had trodden this path, focused, as we were, on Canterbury. The rich variety of smells interested us – garlic (lovely white blossom), new-mown hay, manure, petrol, and a fellow-pilgrim's chewing gum. We were collected from Oxted by friends from Sevenoaks in their cars and taken to their homes, where we were given supper and hot baths and real beds to sleep in.

Our route now took us to great ancient houses. There was Knole House where Lord Sackville told us how it was Archbishop Cranmer's house till Henry VIII took it over and left it to his daughter Elizabeth. After moving in such exalted circles, we were brought down to earth as Julia, carrying the banner that went everywhere with us, was chased by an angry sow in the ripening cornfield. At St Dunstan's, West Peckham, we were joined by the Dean of Rochester who told us how much we in the west owed to the Russian Orthodox Church. For a thousand years they had protected us from pagan hordes further east, enduring great suffering and preserving the Christian life.

The theme of today's prayers was 'Following Dunstan, we glorify God through life in community'. Remembering that it was Benedictine Communities to which Dunstan brought new life and of which he was a member, we were glad to visit the Anglican Benedictine community of West Malling Abbey. We slept that night in the medieval barn at Allington Castle, now a monastery and conference centre.

Our next stop was the tiny church at Harrietsham, and then Boughton Lees, where a professional orchestra was practising in the empty church. With their music floating behind us and through us, we began the long trudge in steady rain through the beautiful Challock Forest. It was, incredibly, the first rain we had had, and we all looked different in our coloured anoraks. The mud was deep and some of the American pilgrims had never seen anything like it. As we came down the forest path we felt that we were really nearing our goal, as there before us were the twin towers of Canterbury cathedral, yet still a day's walk away. Then came the warmth of Harbledown Church, where a choir from King's School, Canterbury, sang Compline, using the style of music with which Dunstan would have been familiar. It was simple, but harsh to our ears. This was our last night together, and as we walked in silence and by candlelight to our 'beds', we thought of our fellowship and support over the past days and sadness at having to part. We had become a cohesive band of pilgrims who shared the delights and the difficulties, our food and drink and clothing, our hopes and our fears, and much about ourselves, and it was not easy to say goodbye.

On the last day of the pilgrimage we entered Canterbury. As this was 19 May, the day of Dunstan's death 1000 years ago, it was fitting that we should first visit St Dunstan's Church. Afterwards we went over to St Peter's where we joined the great host of pilgrims who had come by plane and coach, and there was Dick Daniels himself already robed for the final service. So, with hundreds of banners waving in the wind, we went into the Cathedral.

Of the service itself, three things stand out. The first is huge crowds, which seemed to fill the Cathedral even before we arrived, although we ourselves were given special seats in the front – and some of us saw the thirteenth-century 'Pilgrim Window' on our way; then there was St Dunstan's own hymn with which the service began; and thirdly, of course, Archbishop Runcie's sermon.

The hymn was originally translated from Dunstan's Latin by Alfred Noyes; the tune is traditional, arranged by Vaughan Williams:

St Dunstan's Prayer

Thou who never canst err for thyself art the way,
thou whose infinite kingdom is flooded with day,
whose eyes behold all, for thyself art the light,
look down on us gently, who journey by night.

For the pity revealed in thy loneliest hour,
forsaken, self-bound and self-emptied of power;
thou who even in death hadst all heaven in sight,
look down on us gently, who journey by night.

Archbishop Runcie's sermon was special, because we felt as

he spoke that here was someone who really knows what it is to be the leader of the Church and at the same time, like Dunstan, to be in close touch with the heads of state. We recollect here some points from his sermon:

- The monastic communities led to deeper spiritual life at the heart of the Church, but they were not a flight from the world; they worked to shape the character of the world.

- Dunstan wonderfully brought new life into the monasteries, but at the same time had a deep sense of duty to the whole of society, including its leaders.

- Behind tradition we see a very human figure. He knew doubt and hesitation. He suffered serious illness and serious temptation. He had a complicated temperament, which made it hard for him to combine his deep longing for prayer and silence with his artistic gift and public service,

- It is, then, possible for holiness and high office to go together. In Dunstan they did. His life was all of a piece.

- We live in an age of fragmentation and specialisation, and can learn from Dunstan that, on one condition, it is possible to move from one area of life to another. The one condition is that we have a heart in which everything is held together in offering and praise and thanksgiving to God himself.

- In our world, so different from Dunstan's, we are still able to place our innermost heart under the loving authority of God, where all our thinking, planning, acting and willing are brought together.

- It is because this way of life is of such importance to us and to the world that we are here today and that pilgrims have come from Dunstan churches all over the world (here the Archbishop waved vigorously to those who had travelled great distances to be present).

The service was a great climax to the pilgrimage. Afterwards there was a farewell meal together, and we parted, not without difficulty.

Postscript

Looking back on the pilgrimage, it is natural to ask, 'Why did we do it?' It was not because we were historians or hero-worshippers or antiquarians, but because Dunstan is part of our roots. We all need to be in touch with our roots in order to be ourselves, to be nurtured and inspired by the past, that past in which Dunstan shone with such brilliant light.

Walking with Bonhoeffer

Stan Lane, a Baptist minister who has a long interest in issues of community and justice, made his 375-mile walk along the long distance footpaths from Middleton in Teesdale to Bath in 1995 to mark the 50th anniversary of the death of Dietrich Bonhoeffer. Stan was inspired to set off partly because he knew many people who had themselves been inspired by Bonhoeffer's example and teaching on the Christian imperative to confront social and political issues, so that they could do the same in their own day

Stan confessed that he loved walking, and had not, when he planned his walk, realised that Bonhoeffer walked through Germany every year, so that he could meet and talk to people along the way. Stan invited people to join him on his walk, and many did so, mostly for short distances. He also met people along the way and arranged discussion sessions with some of them.

When Hitler came to power in 1933, Bonhoeffer was a young lecturer in theology at Berlin University. He denounced Hitler's attempt to control the German Church and to impose a clause excluding all Jews from office. He warned that Hitler's aims were incompatible with Christian faith. He later said that Christians had no right to sing their Gregorian chants unless they were willing to 'shout for the Jews'. He was banned from public teaching and preaching in 1936. He helped to establish the Confessing Church in 1934 and directed the seminary at Finkenwalde to train pastors.

In 1940 Bonhoeffer was working for German Intelligence, whilst sharing information with others, including the Bishop of Chichester, George Bell, in the great effort to bring the war to an end. He finally joined the plot to assassinate Hitler as he saw this as the only chance to end the regime and war, and to save lives. Hitler survived the explosion of July 1944 and by then Bonhoeffer was already in prison on suspicion of helping Jews to escape. His involvement in the conspiracy against Hitler was revealed and he was executed just before the war ended.

When the Finkenwalde Seminary was closed and some of the students imprisoned by the Nazis in October 1937, Bonhoeffer said:

> Should the Saviour have come only to save us from worries, pain and anxiety and in order to long for a better world beyond this? I dispute that. The Christian resurrection hope differs from the mythological ones because it points to a completely new life on the earth now, much more poignantly even than in the Old Testament. The Christian must live fully engaged in this life. . . . The here and now must not be pushed aside before time, in this the Old and New Testaments meet. Christ grips man in the midst of his life. The deliverance consists in placing our cause unreservedly into the hands of God. . . .When we share in the suffering of God, that is metanoia.*

Stan began his walk in a hailstorm and at his first meeting, with a group of Methodists in Middleton in Teesdale, he encountered what was to be an on-going problem. There was a division between the people who wanted to talk about Bonhoeffer and those who wanted to talk about contemporary problems and social issues. In that first evening the group talked, amongst other things, about single parenting, advertising, attitudes to wealth and anti-Semitism in Christian history. As the walk progressed, with wonderful Pennine scrambles during the day, the evenings varied. Sometimes no one could be persuaded to join a discussion session, whilst on other occasions good meetings were held. In Keld a meeting of the Christian Council focused on the needs of young people, many of whom move away to larger towns.

* *The Cost of Discipleship*, Dietrich Bonhoeffer (SCM Press).

As the walk went on it became clear that many people felt strongly that Christian resistance in rural areas should be against the power of market forces and in support of human and community values. Some groups were very interested in Bonhoeffer, and Stan had the opportunity to tell his story and discuss the implications for modern life. Some of the best meetings were held in schools, and broadcasts were made through local radio. Sometimes local initiatives to improve some aspect of community life took place as the direct result of Stan's visit.

As the walk progressed, Stan became more aware of the power of the Bonhoeffer story to focus attention on social forces against which a determined Christian resistance needs to be sustained. It became clear to Stan as the walk went on that the Church itself needs to develop an ethic of resistance, so that it is prepared when trouble comes. The fear is that a complacent Church may not even recognise trouble.

Stan's journey ended at Bath Abbey. He had spent much of the walk in solitude but in Bath he was surrounded by tourists. It was a good place in which to reflect on points of resistance to the prevailing culture.

It was when Stan was in Broadway in the Cotswolds that his reflection perhaps summed up why he had embarked on such a long pilgrimage in memory of Dietrich Bonhoeffer. He said of Bonhoeffer:

He seemed to be able to maintain both his faith and his integrity, though certainly not without times of struggle, when everything around him conspired to undervalue or ridicule him. In that sense I think he is a twentieth-century saint.

Pilgrimage to Bradwell

John and Anne Gould

The Bradwell ecumenical pilgrimage takes place every year on the first Saturday in July. It begins in Bradwell village in Essex, outside the parish church, and then 1500 pilgrims walk the mile and a half through fields to the chapel of St Peter, an isolated Saxon building which looks rather like a barn and has been used, over the centuries, as a lighthouse and, indeed, a barn. It has also been a smugglers' den.

We learn about the history of this ancient church from Bede's history. Bede tells us of the ministry of St Cedd who became the Bishop of the East Saxons in 653. Ythancaestir is the site of the Roman and Saxon shore fort of Othona, at the mouth of the River Blackwater in Essex. St Peter's chapel was once a cathedral. It was built by Cedd from the old fort materials. It now stands isolated in the flat land surrounding it. There are three large stones on the altar, from Iona, from Lindisfarne where Aidan taught Cedd, and from Lastingham where Cedd built another monastery.

When the modern pilgrims reach the chapel they enjoy a picnic on the grass. They have plenty of time to enjoy the wonderful view north and east over the River Blackwater and the North Sea. People may walk along the beach for a while and then everyone gathers at the chapel for a short service.

Lastingham

The church at Lastingham stands on a Saxon foundation, the site of the place where Cedd fasted before he built his monastery of wood and daub in 654. Cedd and his three brothers were English but they followed a Celtic rule of life, educated as they were in Aidan's monastery school on Lindisfarne. Cedd was Abbot of Lastingham and Bishop of the East Saxons, and he divided his time between Yorkshire and Essex (where he founded the monastery at Bradwell). The monastery at Lastingham was quite large, with the church, huts for the monks, a guest house and a refectory. The pattern of life was Celtic until after the Synod of Whitby, and the monks painted manuscripts, farmed and visited the people. After the Synod of Whitby the Rule of St Benedict was adopted.

The crypt at Lastingham is the site of the altar where Cedd was laid to rest after he died of the plague after the Synod of Whitby in 664. When he died, his brother Chad took over from him. Chad later became bishop in York and then in Lichfield.

The present crypt, entered down a flight of rough stone steps, is early Norman and a beautiful dark, heavy and cold stone place. There are the typical thick rounded arches, most with ram's horn capitals above the sturdy pillars. The original entrance is now walled up. It was at the north-western corner, so that pilgrims to the shrine could enter and worship without disturbing those who were in the church. It is possible that the present altar may have been used by Chad. There is also a large cross head which probably dates from Chad's time. It is said that this cross head was part of the largest pre-Norman monument in England. There are many stones all dating from the seventh to tenth centuries, including a Viking tombstone.

It is exhilarating to remember that very little has changed in the Lastingham crypt since 1088. There used to be a cobble stone floor, and probably an oak panelled roof, but otherwise it is much the same. The church above the crypt has also changed very little.

We arranged a Eucharist in the crypt, as part of the 1997 Year of Pilgrimage celebrations. The service was simple and very moving in such an ancient and atmospheric place. A walk across the moors to Rosedale Abbey followed the Eucharist, and it was easy to think of Cedd, his brothers and his brother monks trekking out to visit distant farms and welcoming people into the monastery in Lastingham.

SECTION EIGHT
Spirit of Place

Photograph: Barbara Butler

Introduction

The places which arouse feelings of inspiration, wonder, amazement, astonishment, dread, reverence and veneration are rarely the places human beings live in day by day. They are much more likely to be the special places of journey, pilgrimage and worship, or places remembered from the past. Sometimes past places are revisited, and then there may be either disappointment or a renewed or fresh inspiration. We have included the story of when John and Muriel Gore revisited the place in Eastern Zambia where they had lived and worked for many years. They found that the spirit was still there, the spirit which had inspired them years ago, and which must have existed in the early years of the twentieth century, when Leonard Kamungu travelled from Malawi and built the great church with Chief Msoro's villagers.

The early Celtic Christians had strong feelings for place and came to talk of finding their places of resurrection. The place of resurrection is not necessarily a place reached after death, but rather a place of heightened awareness of God and where God's will is fulfilled. God is Father, and reaching him is a homecoming, an arrival in a place of love and safety, where he speaks through the ordinary everyday things of life. It is the place where the Spirit is encountered, not in an extraordinary way but through the everyday meetings and care people have for each other. It is the place where the Incarnation may be truly experienced and understood, where we may see the Christ in the middle of the struggle of life.

The gospel story of the prodigal son is the story of a journey to the place of resurrection. The son thinks that he must travel and find a better life than the one he has with his family, only to go to far-off places to make mistakes and to be rejected and to suffer. He finally comes home, in sorrow, for the first time appreciating the place and the love of his father.* Every

* The story is told in Luke 15:17-20.

pilgrim must search for, and find, their resurrection places many times in their lives and in many different places and ways, for they are not places to stay in, but places to visit, places in which to be renewed and places from which to go out in Christian discipleship, well aware that the blessings given, and in turn given again, are the blessings of God.

It is likely that people were first inspired by natural landscapes, including forests, seas and mountains. Many indigenous people continue to be filled with awe in their traditional surroundings. The adivasi or tribal people of India go to the sacred groves or forests. The Australian aborigines are, like many nomadic people, inspired by the landscapes they pass through.

Many people today are inspired by mountains and natural landscapes, which is why they go there. Many also go for physical challenge and for the beauty of the landscape.

When a group of people at a conference on Lindisfarne/ Holy Island were asked to share their special places, places of resurrection, many of them shared natural and often wild places.

A student spoke about her love of being near the sea and of the animation she felt. She always stayed with her grandmother on the North Welsh coast. She felt challenged, but also safe and loved with her grandmother. She felt close to God. Someone else spoke of the inspiration of snow, especially of fresh snow on a normally ugly place.

Two people found the Lammamuir Hills very inspiring and healing. One woman, who lives in a market town, spoke of the hills of North Wales which bring home her insignificance in the presence of God. A man who had recently walked along the Pennine Way spoke of his lifelong wish to do so, of his pleasure as he tackled the physical challenge and was successful, and of his journey as symbolic of a moving on in life.

A woman who is very lame is also someone who loves mountains, and she talked about driving in a car to the top of Plynlimon, where she could see everything for miles around.

On a very special occasion, when a group of British

Christians went to Kenya and climbed up Mount Kenya with a group of Kenyan Christians, it was quite clear that the expectations of the two groups were different. The British people wanted to go up Mount Kenya as a challenge, to see the scenery and certainly to be inspired. They approached the whole adventure with excitement and great happiness. The Kenyans, however, had a different history, for in the tradition of their people, the Kikuyu, the mountain, almost 17,000 feet high, was the home of Ngai, God. They had lived below the mountain all their lives, going to school and college, working in their small farms and going to their daily work. It had never occurred to most of them to climb the mountain before. They approached the journey with awe and some trepidation.

The journey was a wonderful one for both groups, and we became one group, as we climbed up from the forest, through the vertical bog lands and out on to the dark and forbidding scree. The Kenyans had been right to be hesitant, because the journey was never easy, but constantly a challenge, both physically and mentally. It was a Kenyan man who cooked breakfast at 2am so that everyone could begin the last stretch of the climb in the coolness of the night, up the slippery slope of the glacier, to stand together in exhausted but awesome silence on the summit, as dawn broke and the sun came up to reveal the most stunning mountain scenery anyone had ever seen.

When a group of British students climbed Mount Kilimanjaro, the largest mountain in Africa, they set off for the adventure, rejoicing at the changes in the scenery, from the forests where a few monkeys could be spotted and up to the first hut. The mist came down and the seriousness of the project dawned on many people for the first time. The spirit of the place began to be revealed. The second day took the group out on to open moorland and across ravines to a second hut from which there were wonderful views from above the clouds. The summit loomed ever above and beyond. The journey now moved on into the very wild alpine desert; the walking was harder and the landscape very alien. People began to be affected by the altitude and the next hut was 'stone and very cold'. The final ascent was a seven-hour climb up a frozen scree slope. The altitude sickness and the ice meant that progress was painfully slow and some people had to drop out. Those who reached the rim of the volcanic crater managed to summon up the energy to walk round to Uhuru Peak, a special place at the end of a very special journey.

Many people find mental, physical and spiritual challenge and the encouragement to change on mountains. Others find the same challenges and opportunities when they go to wilderness or desert areas of the world. The wilderness has perhaps always been important for those on a spiritual quest. Many religious leaders have gone off to desert areas including Jesus, the Buddha and Mohammed. The Desert Fathers of the fourth, fifth and sixth centuries lived in the desert areas of Egypt, Syria and Palestine.

We have included a wilderness retreat in Yorkshire, and also a pilgrimage into the Sinai Desert which tells something of the history of the desert as a place of pilgrimage and of transformation, including the great story of the Exodus. The mountain in the desert, Mount Sinai, has always had a special role as a place people climbed in search of God. Many of the modern pilgrims go to remote places, where they are alone and not quite confident. There is a mixture of challenge and solitude together with the evening-time community of the pilgrims and their Bedouin hosts.

As people have grown into the world and through the world, they have always sought to change parts of it, to suit their needs. Sometimes places have been made more appropriately spiritual to suit a special understanding of the spiritual quest so that temples, mosques and churches have been built all over the world. Sometimes places have been made more secure for everyday living and working. The Maasai, for instance, have very simple homes which may easily be moved, but they do build a strong thorn fence around them. Some people, like the Maasai, have remained nomadic, but most people have built permanent homes, cultivated the land and built farms, and developed cities to suit their need for creativity and specialised work. It does not necessarily make a place more or less spiritual because it has been created for worship or for a more practical purpose. Sometimes practical places offer spiritual resources to those who would not think of going into a place of worship.

Some of the members of the group on Lindisfarne said that their special places were places of natural beauty which had been embellished by people in some way. Someone who loved mountains was even more inspired by them when a small area had been made more hospitable for humanity. She talked of the long Alpine footpath leading to the mountain hut, a sign of hope in the far distance of a wonderful landscape, and of climbing halfway up Mount Kenya itself to stay on a lonely but very solid farm surrounded by tea bushes.

Lindisfarne itself came into the category of places which have been touched by people over the centuries. One person spoke of the inspiration of the early Celtic Christians, which he could still feel everywhere he walked on the island. He was especially aware of Cuthbert, whose tiny island with its crude cross is there just across the sea or sands from the church, depending on whether the tide is in or out. The island always gives him the urge to go out and do things when he returns home. A woman spoke of the love she felt for the island, which gave her space and time for deep reflection. She could also talk to herself, with no one to hear. She has gone to the island many times, and always builds a cairn of stones. Each stone represents a problem or an issue she has to deal with. She spends a long time holding each stone and all that it represents, reflecting deeply, and then she throws the stones into the sea.

Lindisfarne is one of the few places we have known where the people who live there actually say that they are inspired by their surroundings. One man said that he feels a sense of the presence of God every time he gets up and walks along to the parish church of St Mary with its wonderful view, through the abbey ruins, of the harbour and the castle.

One of David Adam's poems is about Holy Island.

There are times that I need to be an island,
set in an infinite sea
cut off from all that comes to me
but surrounded still by thee.
Times of quiet and peace
when traffic and turmoil cease
when I can be still and worship thee
Lord of the land and the sea.
Full tide, ebb tide
let life rhythms flow
ebb tide, full tide
how life's beat must go.

Lord, I must be part of the mainland
a causeway between me and others.
There are times I can only find thee
in working with my brothers
times of business and industry
freeing ourselves from captivity.
It is when we give a helping hand
we meet you Lord of sea and land.
Ebb tide, full tide
let life rhythms flow
full tide, ebb tide
how life's beat must go.*

A special place for many pilgrims, quite close to Holy Island but more remote in the North Sea is Inner Farne, which once

* David's poem is included in his book, *The Edge of Glory*, published by SPCK.

had a reputation of being infested with demons; perhaps they were the noisy and aggressive sea birds or the great seals which are still everywhere. Cuthbert, searching for a 'desert in the ocean', built his high-walled hermitage on Inner Farne and lived there for ten years and later died there. Inner Farne may be a special place for pilgrims because it is remote and requires a sea crossing which is often very rough, or because of its associations with Cuthbert, or both. Tamara Crabtree was inspired by the island and by the memory of Cuthbert when she wrote:

> We went to where Cuthbert went,
> where a tree was planted alone on Inner Farne.
> Over the sea in a rocking boat,
> grey northern sea, fresh and freeing –
> so that creation of birds both black and white
> red flapping feet, yellow bill became enchantment.
>
> Later strong rocks, deep, deep colours
> masterpiece of Master Sculptor.
> Then on to more sea creatures, friends of Cuthbert
> grey friends, curious creatures
> and I rejoiced in all these things
> sharing faith.*

One woman at the Holy Island gathering spoke movingly about a stone circle in Ireland which was near to a holy well. The well was shallow and rather dirty, but when she stood on a stone in the middle of it and was very still the water cleared and she could see her reflection in the sky.

A woman spoke of her love of the Lake District, but it was a love which was enhanced by her experience of attending a concert in a church in Hawkshead, when she sang 'For the beauty of the earth'.

* Included in publications by Christians Aware.

Someone else spoke of his love of the scenery and the buildings of Northern Cyprus. He always found that the desert-like space with mosques interspersed at fairly regular intervals gave him great energy and also peace.

Some people spoke of special gardens as inspirational for them. These were their own gardens and also gardens they had visited. People's own gardens inspired them because they wondered at the beauty and peace which had come out of the work they had enjoyed doing. Other people's gardens were inspiring partly because they were a refreshing surprise which enabled them to dream of what was possible elsewhere, perhaps even at home. One person spoke of a special garden in Scotland which she always returned to, where the flowers and trees give her a rare feeling of security. We have included an introduction to the Quiet Garden Movement in this section. This movement is a wonderful opportunity for rest and renewal.

There were those also for whom places were inspiring because they were associated with people or filled with people. One woman will always return to the counselling centre she went to when her father died, her niece was killed and she was also facing a divorce. She knew that this was the right place for her. A Quaker member of the group has always liked to sit in a quiet corner of the meeting house, partly because it is peaceful, and partly because it has an aura of the people who go there, the community, silent in worship and active in social outreach. One man talked about his church, in central London, where he is accepted exactly as he is, and is therefore able to flourish.

A Kenyan priest spoke of the Church Army as his community, which he would always carry with him, wherever he went in the world.

Some people spoke of the memory of their childhood homes, places where they felt loved. One woman spoke of her home in Egypt, a centre of community. She will always remember the people who gathered there, especially now that the house is shut up and covered in dust.

Some people said that their spiritual places were their work places. One woman spoke of her work in operating theatres as very special, because of the intensity of the battle for a life and because of the concentration of everyone fighting together in the battle. It was at those moments that she was aware of the sacredness and the fragility of life.

The Viking attacks on Holy Island at the end of the eighth century were a dramatic demonstration of the fragility of life. The monks took the body of Cuthbert, together with the Lindisfarne Gospels, and carried it away, stopping in many places for many years. They went as far as Ripon before the attacks stopped, and then they began to go north again towards Lindisfarne. As they were travelling along by a river, the story is told of how suddenly the coffin became so heavy that they could not move it. One of them thought that Cuthbert wanted to be buried on the hill called Dunhome and they then picked up the coffin, now light again, and took it up the hill. They put it down there and built a small shelter followed by a small church and then a big Anglo-Saxon stone church. After the Norman conquest the Anglo-Saxon church was destroyed and the Normans built the huge Norman church which is Durham Cathedral. After one more journey away from Durham, during the Norman conquest, the body of Cuthbert was finally laid to rest and Durham became a famous place of pilgrimage.

Country towns with churches and cathedrals are special spiritual places for many people and we include a list of some of these at the end of this section, along with other special places. Places of history are always inspirational and we have chosen a pilgrimage to Rome from the many possibilities.

It is perhaps more unusual for the large cities of the world to be seen as inspirational, except perhaps the capital cities with their beautiful buildings. Ordinary cities, however, are often stimulating and elevating for the many people who go there for work and to meet the community. People are the huge inspiration of most city places, many of which may be ugly and even unhealthy in themselves. Calcutta is a good example of such a city. It is large, ugly and polluted, with huge traffic and noise problems and unspeakable poverty. Nevertheless, the beauty of Calcutta, which makes many people go there time and time again to be uplifted, is in the communities of people, who support each other and welcome the stranger.

In Britain the 'Faith in the City' report which came out in 1985 brought out the strength and inspiration of community life. As people visited the disadvantaged areas, they became more and more inspired by the courage of the people, so that the places themselves became places they wished to return to, to be encouraged by in their own work elsewhere.

Wherever the special place may be and whatever it may be, from a hill to a tree or mountain, to a stone circle, a wooden hut, a great cathedral or an inner-city community centre, the journey to it becomes a pilgrimage because of what happens within the pilgrim. The pilgrim goes to imagine, to pray, to think and to meditate perhaps, or simply to be open to new ideas and directions in life. The aware pilgrim may meet God in the special place, but they will also move on, knowing that God will be in the new place, inspiring, challenging and upholding.

Return to the Bush

John Gore

The plane had been delayed on the way, and we were late touching down at Lilongwe International Airport. The late afternoon sky and the air of Central Africa were familiar, even after a 20-year absence.

We had expected to be taken straight to our hosts for our two-week stay in Zambia, but there was a further delay. Our late arrival meant that to travel through Malawi and on into Zambia would mean travelling after dark. This was deemed inadvisable. It would not be safe. This was the first of many differences Muriel and I were to discover from a Zambia we had left 20 years before.

We had been invited, through the kind offices of James Cairns, Medical Superintendent of St Francis Hospital, Katete, to attend the consecration of the first bishop of the newly inaugurated Diocese of Eastern Zambia. It was an offer that could not be refused.

One of the delights of expatriate life in foreign parts is that you can turn up unexpectedly at anyone's home and be given hospitality. So it was that, with Faith Cairns who had come to meet us from the plane, we turned up at the home of the daughter of someone we had known in Zambia, now living in Lilongwe. The food was stretched. Beds were found.

The next morning was spent going around the stores in Lilongwe with Faith, buying things not available in Zambia. These were mostly from South Africa, with whom Malawi had long been on good terms, even in apartheid days.

And then, at last, the journey to Zambia.

Now, we were to attend the consecration of a bishop, and there are various accoutrements that bishops need to have, like episcopal rings and pectoral crosses. These are not readily available in Central Africa, and so we were asked to bring these precious items with us. The question was, would they be allowed through the Zambia customs? It was therefore with some apprehension that we approached the stern-looking officials at the border posts. But they couldn't have been nicer!

My mind went back to another visit to this frontier post between Zambia and Malawi, when I waved goodbye to a friend who had been deported from Zambia by an over-zealous immigration office, many years previously.

So we arrived at Katete, a few hours' drive from the border. But the roads! Full of potholes, so many of them that they are impossible to avoid. No wonder it was thought not to be safe to drive through the night. Here, indeed, was a difference. When Muriel and I had lived in Zambia in the 1970s there was an extensive road-building programme. During that time the Great East Road, linking Lusaka, the capital, with the Eastern Province and its regional town, Chipata, 400 miles away, and then on into Malawi, was tarred. It was a superb road. That was when there was money about, loads of it, offered by the developed countries on loan – loans that have never been repaid, that will never be repaid because they cannot be.

The scandal of loan repayment, demanded by the richest countries, was much in our minds as we saw the cost to a country like Zambia. We had left a country beginning to build up a modern infrastructure. We found all around us evidence that these signs of development had declined drastically. Roads were breaking up, school buildings were in need of repair, the cost of basic foodstuffs was soaring. We heard stories of schools without equipment, hospitals without drugs and dressings. All because Zambia has to honour its debt repayments before considering the needs of its people. It reinforced our determination to work with others in Jubilee 2000 and similar campaigns 'to drop the debt'.

St Francis Hospital, which was to be our base for our two-week visit, had retained its character as a mission hospital, originally laid out around a central reservation, the staff houses around two-thirds of the circle, and the hospital wards and the chapel taking up the rest. But beyond those original wards, the hospital had expanded enormously. Here, in quite an isolated part of Zambia, had grown a district and referral hospital offering medical facilities of a high order, together with a nurses' training school. It is not that you would find the sophisticated equipment of a hospital in England, but within the limits of what was available, here was a centre of medical excellence.

My mind went back, as I am sure Muriel's did, to the delivery ward in the 1970s, where our two children were born. Through the holes in the roof you could see the sky!

What we had not known in Zambia in our time there, but which was now cruelly evident, was the scourge of AIDS. It is decimating the population, and leading to a new problem – large numbers of children with no one to look after them: orphans. The ideal of continence is promoted. Practical advice about safe sex is given. Those with full-blown AIDS are cared for. Orphans are looked after and given skills to help them as they grow up. It is a tremendous task that encourages the concern and the energies of the hospital staff.

The staff had worked wonders developing the hospital. They were continuing to work wonders in the face of limited funds and resources, and new challenges.

But there were other differences, too – signs of growth. There was now an African priest as chaplain; there were African senior members of staff. And the hospital was now a joint venture, Anglican and Roman Catholic.

Moreover, because we were here for a purpose our fellow guests were arriving, bishops from the other dioceses of Central Africa; and they were African bishops, coming to consecrate – unusually nowadays – a white priest as bishop. But the consecration was not to take place at Katete. St Francis Hospital had been a newcomer on the mission scene, in what was then Northern Rhodesia. It had been founded in 1947 by a priest/doctor, Francis Trefussis.

The consecration itself was to take place at Msoro, deep in the Luangwa Valley. For it was there that the Anglican Church was first planted in the Eastern Province, back in 1910. In 1910, in thanksgiving for 50 years of blessings to the Universities Mission to Central Africa, it was decided, as an act of faith in the future, to found a new missionary diocese. This was to be the diocese of Northern Rhodesia. One of its first mission stations was founded in the Luangwa Valley, an extremely remote part of the country, and its first priest-in-charge was appointed. But he was not a white missionary. He was the first Malawian to be ordained priest, Leonard Kamungu.

Leonard was a remarkable missionary, not only for his total dedication to the spread of the gospel, but also for the manner of his life. He built and lived in a mud and thatch church at Msoro, which also served as a school and his own living quarters. More remarkable still, he embraced the celibate life for the sake of his work. He was said to travel the area by night because there were not enough hours in the day – and that was something no normal person did! The area was – and is – alive with dangerous animals.

But it was not wild animals but his manner of life that led to his death. It is said that he was offered a female companion by the local chief, and refused. The chief, insulted, caused his food to be poisoned, and he died. His grave, in a grove of trees, has become a place of pilgrimage, much revered.

The blood of the martyrs is the seed of the Church. From those beginnings grew a mission station serving an area the size of Wales, the centre of an educational system that has supplied many of today's leading figures in Zambia, a centre of healing that has improved the quality of life of countless people, a centre for the faith, for the challenging of God's grace through the sacraments of the Church.

This was the place where we had lived and worked, and which we had left behind us 20 years before. This was the place where the consecration of the first Bishop of Eastern

Zambia was to take place. From its humble beginnings, Msoro was to be the spiritual centre of the new Diocese of Eastern Zambia, and the Church of St Luke, at its heart, was to be its cathedral.

Returning to a much-loved place which had been your home for 13 years, after a long absence, is never a comfortable experience. Muriel and I were glad, therefore, of the opportunity to make our way down to Msoro for a private visit before the day of the consecration. With the generous loan of a truck we carefully negotiated the ruts and the boulders and streams of the 50-mile track.

Communication is difficult in those parts, and our visit was unannounced. No one knew we were coming. It felt strange arriving at the mission station, not, as when we lived here, coming home, but coming as strangers – or pilgrims? But African hospitality had not changed, and we were welcomed warmly and generously as honoured guests. A house was prepared for our use. Food was brought. A few friends we had known were at hand, called to spend time with us and share news.

Night falls early in the tropics. For us in the old days nightfall was the time to light the tilley lamps. But electricity has reached Msoro – a long, slender power cable sneaks across the valley quite close to Msoro, always vulnerable, of course, to the attention of elephants. So we were interested to see this march of progress, out here in the bush. Mind you, it was only available in the hospital and in the secondary school.

The hospital is officially a health centre, but in reality it is a small hospital with 40 beds and an out-patient department. It began life as a collection of huts, but over the years has grown into a fine modern medical facility for the area. This was where Muriel had worked, and we were delighted to see that everything was clean and tidy and well run – no longer by an expatriate staff.

St Luke's hospital staff has to deal with everything that comes to it. The doctor visits from Katete twice a month.

Difficult cases, often maternity cases, have to be taken to Katete by the hospital Land Rover. This is a rough journey in the dry season. In the rainy season it is a nightmare.

St Francis Secondary School was new to us. There had been upper schools at the mission station both for boys and for girls in the old days, where children would be termly boarders. There were also lower schools scattered around the mission district, which fed into the upper schools. The administration of education over such a wide area was an enormous undertaking, and regret was mixed with relief when the newly independent government decided to take direct responsibility for primary education. The only Anglican secondary school was a thousand miles away. So it was heartening to see a new secondary school at Msoro, for both boys and girls. Of course, it was struggling, like all institutions in developing countries, but it was there – and it was a bold new church venture.

The church people always said St Luke's was like a small cathedral, and now it is! Built at the top of a rise, it is a noble building, built by local people from local materials, and has survived the ravages of white ants, bats and owls, and has been hallowed by the devotions of countless people. It holds many memories. Sunday Eucharists, full of warmth and robust vitality. Saturday night Benediction with a church full of school boarders, songs of adoration within the stillness. Ordinations, confirmations. The daily office – Morning prayer by early sunlight, Evening prayer by kindly tilley light.

To digress, tilley lamps are one of the wonders of the world – once they are lit. The secret is to keep them in good order. Then they will serve you well, for you carry a pool of bright light wherever you go. Comforting and reassuring, especially for medical staff going out in the middle of the night to the delivery room in the hospital. Thank God for tilley lamps!

But we were here for another kind of birth, the birth of a new diocese, and of its first bishop. John Osmers, a New

Zealander by birth, had been elected for this office – a man of courage and dedication. As a priest in South Africa, he had incurred the wrath of the authorities, and as a result, had lost one hand through a letter bomb. Not deterred, he continued his ministry in Zambia, encouraging lay leadership in the Church and caring for refugees fleeing to Zambia.

When the new Diocese of Eastern Zambia was formed, such was the trust that he had won from the people that he was elected as its first bishop. The consecration service was to be in Msoro. Conscious of the significance of the event, the people of Msoro pulled out all the stops. They repaired the roadways – a mission station is rather like a large village – tidied up the buildings, used gallons of whitewash, swept and polished until the place gleamed.

People began to arrive from all over the Eastern Province and from the rest of Zambia, tired, hot and dusty from their long journeys by foot or whatever transport could be found. And, of course, bishops. Ten African bishops of the Province of Central Africa, together with their archbishop. The skies are clear and the sun is not over-hot in June, and in any case the church, with its new honour as cathedral, large as it is, could not accommodate so large a gathering. So the consecration was to be outside. Nor was there a table large enough for an altar for all the bishops to gather around. This was not a problem. A brick dais was erected, and a brick altar built upon it, all connected with quick-drying mud.

People gathered, singing as they came. Prominent among them was a large number of women dressed in the distinctive blue and white uniform of the Mothers' Union. And, not to be outdone, a very well-turned-out band of men from the Copperbelt, with the blue jackets and white trousers of the Fathers' Union! Youthful choirs sang and sang. And then the service began with the entry of the bishops and the bishop elect. The great liturgy unfolded with high ceremony, and the sun shone on the proceedings like a blessing from God.

And then, of course, there was rejoicing and feasting. We

were invited to a feast of meat and rice, mountains of it, in the house that had been the Ladies' 'Hotelo' (or mess) in the days when there were white women missionaries. Now it was a public building and put to very hospitable use. Of course, with such a gathering it was the time for reunions with friends we had known and worked with and lived among. There were cries of recognition and much vigorous handshaking – but no kissing and hugging, not in Africa! Language, now grown rusty, was dredged up from the depths of memory and brought back into use – the lovely soft local language of Chinsenga, amazingly logical and consistent, first reduced to a written language in this very place by the priest who followed Leonard Kamungu, Sidney Ranger – 'an angry man', people said.

And so, when all was over, bishops returned to their dioceses. People from far-off parts of the country set off on their long homeward journeys. Local people drifted back to their villages. The newly formed Diocese of Eastern Zambia, now with its bishop, girded up its loins for a task that would engage all their faith and all their energies.

We ourselves could not stay on long in Zambia because of pressing developments at home – we were moving to another parish. But we did have the opportunity to worship on ordinary Sundays in St Luke's Cathedral and in a little church far out in the bush. What struck us there was a new vitality in the worship. The last stages of the 'missionary' period of the Church in those parts had left a feeling of uncertainty. But a new confidence has taken its place. We found that churches were full. We found indigenous music to the accompaniment of drums, once thought to be unsuitable for Christian worship, widely used and enjoyed in church. We found people taking on responsibility for administration.

We had the feeling that for all its poverty – the diocese is run on a shoestring – here was an authentic Church, trying to live out the gospel within its environment. Here were none of the trappings of an established Church, none of the bureaucracy of an institutional Church, but a Church true to the tradition but free from its clogging history. Was our return to the Eastern Province of Zambia a visit or a pilgrimage? It is difficult to say. For us there were elements of both. It was a visit with a purpose, certainly. But it was also a pilgrimage to places that will always be holy, special places for us because of those with whom we associate them. And special for the signs of God's kingdom that they are, signs of his grace and his presence in this little-known corner of the world.

To revisit such a place in which so much of our lives had been invested was for us an enormous pleasure – and also a great encouragement. Perhaps that is what a pilgrimage should be.

The Cheviot Hills

David Adam

We had wandered to the Cheviot Hills, through one of the loveliest valleys I know, the Breamish. The morning had been spent watching the dipper, at noon a buzzard circled overhead, the afternoon was full of the sound of the cuckoo. In the valley the gorse stood out like gold and there we saw the goldcrests play.

Now the valley was becoming darker as the sun was going behind the hills. We believed that if we climbed the hill we would see the sun again. But it was not to be. It did not take us long to climb up the steep hillside over a great pile of stone and into a bronze age fortress on the hilltop. Really it was only a circle of loose stone. From here we could see a storm was brewing, dark clouds skudding in from the North Sea. Yet somehow I felt safe on this hilltop surrounded by a defence that had given people in the past protection from evil.

I had found a sanctuary, a safe place; somehow this circle would keep evil outside and goodness within. Now I knew what Columba was doing when he drew a circle around himself in a time of evil and oppression. This was no thin line traced by hand; this was affirming the encircling power of God. As the Cheviot Hills surrounded me, as the stones of the old fort went around me, so did the power of Almighty God. St Patrick describes the presence of Christ in this way:

> Christ be near at either hand,
> Christ behind, before me stand.
> Christ with me where'er I go,
> Christ around, above, below.

I discovered later that the Celtic people call the circle the 'caim' and draw it round them in times of trouble, not as magic, but as affirming the ever-abiding presence and protection of the Almighty. So sitting there, I wrote this prayer:

Circle me, O God,
keep protection near
and danger afar

Circle me, O God,
keep hope within,
keep doubt without.

Circle me, O God,
keep light near
and darkness afar.

Ayers Rock

June Tillman

Red, massive, forbidding,
it rises straight from the plain,
not cleft,
like the gentler
more mysterious
Katatjuta nearby.

In these I could hide myself
and get friendly with the redness.
Without that,
the ascent might have been impossible.

In the arc of the coach lights
we set off.
I was determined to get there
in my own time,
aware that other people's time might be
the death of me.

Up the black crocodile on hands and knees
to the start of the chain.
'I am the way
up the steepest part of the climb.'
(Which would have been impossible without it.)
The upward path was indeed not always smooth,
although the very roughness of the rock
enabled us to get a grip.

'Lean into the rock!'
called the brash American travel agent in his Brunnhilde hat,
as the wind threatened

to dislodge us
from our narrow strip of rock,
and deposit us
down one of the yawning chasms
that beckoned on either side.
I used the rock to combat the wind,
and frequently sat
holding the chain
where the gradient was gentle enough.
So I reached 'Chicken Rock'.

The travel agent had thought of everything.
He offered us water:
'Rinse out, then drink!'
he commanded,
as we lay spread-eagled in the bed
of a welcome old dry water hole.
His wife wore a black sweat shirt
which I thought said 'St Francis'.
'We could do with his help,' I muttered.
Closer scrutiny revealed 'San Francisco'.
In such circumstances does language matter?

If previous wayfarers had not said
that after the chain
it was smoother,
I would have joined the ranks of the descenders.

However, a gentler, more undulating terrain
occasionally tricked me into thinking
it was a Sunday morning stroll in the park –
but for the bright red colour,
the occasional precipices,
and, of course, the view.
The flat plain stretched as far as the eye could see,
broken only by the strengthening friendly Katatjuta.

On her heads I saw the sun rise,
for I was not quick enough to the top of the Rock.
The only indication of the sun on the Rock
was the vast black shadow
spreading over the plain,
sign of the presence of Uluru –
the shade-giver –
friendly or formidable.

'My love for you is strong like fire,
(or was it wind?)
I will guide your steps by my promise.'
I had read that night.
I went on.
At times I slithered down gently on my bottom,
using a movement I had practised
in place of crawling.
(I knew it would come in handy someday.)
By this time others were returning,
victorious.
'Only a couple of blocks!'
called a passing American.

Jean came with them –
she to whom I had said I would do it alone,
in the days when I dreamed of
a magnificent transcendental experience.
Such high-minded thoughts
had vanished.
Brute strength and dogged determination
was needed
to push forward the rubbery limbs
that seemed to have a will of their own.
There had been other helps –
a purple desert plant called Thryptomene
and cooling water from one of the water holes.

Jean offered to join the last few ups and downs.
I was glad she could perceive my need of a companion.
Together we reached the upper cairn.

We stood at the top,
a motley assortment of nationalities,
sharing our drinks
and screaming with delight.

There was little time for exultation –
just a psalm of thanksgiving for answered prayer
and an offering of family and friends
to the eternal keeping of
a love
that filled the unyielding rock,
now aflame with fiery sunlight,
the wind that had been my ally,
the refreshing water,
and the companion strangers
who gave a helping hand
and then moved on.

Ayers Rock rises from the plain near Katatjuta. Its aboriginal
name is Uluru, meaning 'Shade-giver'.

© Copyright 1988 June B. Tillman.

Wilderness Weekend

Paul Valleley

This retreat was in the remote Yorkshire Pennines. Members stayed in a scout hut and walked, mostly through thick mists, for most of the weekend.

At first sight we seemed ill-equipped, that is to say over-equipped, with our Karrimor rucksacks, High Force anoraks, Gore-Tex boots and cars parked handily outside the hostel. But the talk by the spluttering wood stove after the evening meal gave the lie to that. A number of oblique shafts in the conversation, as it ventured out into that territory where people hint at their own vulnerability, intimated that the wilderness can be a psychological as much as a physical state. Spiritual journeys begin with an awareness of a sense of inner need. In our cars we had brought our wildernesses with us from the city.

Next morning we set out in heavy hanging cloud and fine drizzle up the side of steep bracken-clad hillsides which veer steeply up from the higher tributaries of the River Calder. All around, the purple flowers of the moorland heather were fading into crumbly ochre husks which crackled in protest underfoot. The route took us across the surmounting heath past a farm called Egypt and along a rough, pathless high valley called Noahdale. With admirable restraint, the leaders of the party made no forced allusions.

Instead, we began a long tour of the ruined farmhouses of these upper reaches. They were once handsome buildings of fine-cut stone with elegant archways and mullioned weavers' windows to give extra light to the upper stories. Changes in the market for wool had forced their abandonment in the mid-nineteenth century. Wilderness, the ruined habitations seemed to say, can come to places which least expect it.

At the valley top we struck out on a compass-bearing across a deep bog. An hour later we stopped and stood in silence on the blasted heathland. All round the barren, brown heather stretched to the horizon. The vista was broken only by the odd windswept bush whose bare branches were curved like the spine of a bent old woman. It is on mountain tops, the traditions of so many religions have it, that as the mist lifts, an awareness breaks through of something we can only half-grasp. Back in the hostel, at the end of the hour's trek the silence continued. The wood fire crackled like a live animal as the wet boots steamed gently before it. But otherwise there was nothing to interrupt the shared silence as some slept and others read or watched the flickering flames.

Of course, there was nothing here to match the privations of the real wilderness. And yet we were perhaps as far from the norms of our daily routine and the rush of noise and activity as were those Desert Fathers from the harsh facts of everyday life in fourth-century Judea. Silence is not an austere preference for aloneness, the early fathers believed, but the opportunity to listen. It is a lesson in which our modern world is showing renewed interest; the National Retreat Association lists over 200 centres with year-round programmes in its handbook.

Finding wilderness, as with so much else about the contemporary search for the spiritual, is a question of finding new vehicles for the old verities. So it did not seem odd the next day, Sunday, to share a service of Communion high on a hillside by a broken stone wall. The words were quite conventional and the actions simple, with one of our number, an Anglican priest, celebrating. It was understated yet apt. The mist descended with a vengeance. We walked in swirling cloud through the knee-deep heather but along a path that one of our party had reconnoitred some time before. We strode on, with our mist-shrouded eyes fixed on the uncertain ground and our thoughts occupied with unarticulated metaphor. It was late lunchtime when we arrived at our destination, Top Withens, the ruined farmhouse that was the inspiration for *Wuthering Heights*. The place was full of sandwich-stealing sheep and Japanese tourists, for the Brontë town of Haworth was not far the other side. But it did not matter. When it comes to hearing the voice of God, it is the journey rather than the arriving that counts.*

* Paul's writing first appeared in *The Independent*.

A Pilgrimage into the Sinai Desert

Janina Macdonald

A person who chooses to embark on a pilgrimage journey is seeking something deeper than a surface impression, something that will alter their lives in some way; in short, a journey that will offer a spiritual, mental and sometimes even physical transformation. This 'transformation' can happen in many ways, but it is often connected to being challenged in some way and struggling to find the inner strength to work through this challenge. For centuries, the Sinai has played an important role in pilgrimage, acting as a place where the lives of everyday Christians and their relationships with God have been transformed since biblical times.

I work for a small UK-based company which has specialised in the Sinai for ten years, striving to carry on the important tradition of the Sinai pilgrimage. As the new Millennium begins, we are taking a step back and looking more closely at the reasons we, as Christians, are so affected by a journey through this land. Having worked with so many different groups we feel we have a special insight into the many different reasons a Sinai pilgrimage affects our spiritual lives so deeply. Some of these reasons are ancient, shared through time with pilgrims who pressed their feet into the sand of the desert so many centuries before us. Some of these reasons are unique to our time and place as Christians in an increasingly globalised world. However, in order to fully appreciate all of these reasons and to understand our distinctive perception on this subject, it is important to look at the background of our company, the ways in which it has evolved, and the careful way we plan, organise and offer our pilgrimage journeys to those who seek us out.

Emma Loveridge, Director of Wind, Sand and Stars, set up the company ten years ago when she was doing doctoral research on early Christian art at the sixth-century Greek Orthodox monastery of St Catherine's, located in the central high mountain region at the foot of Mount Sinai. While there she began to make some friends among the local semi-nomadic Bedouin communities who have been living there for centuries.

It was a time when many local indigenous communities around the world were beginning to feel the effects of tourism and the growing need to earn tourist dollars. The Bedouin of Sinai were no exception. Coastal resorts were being built to serve tourists looking for a new place to enjoy the sun, the sea and snorkelling. Roads were taming the desert landscape that had once made places such as St Catherine's Monastery and Mount Sinai only accessible to those who could endure a bumpy ride in the back of a four-wheel-drive jeep, or, before the arrival of the jeep, a long journey on a camel. These changes meant that more and more tourists were arriving in the area and tourist dollars were quickly becoming a much needed commodity in Bedouin communities in which traditionally goods were exchanged through trade. When Emma met the Bedouin, they were struggling to work through these changes and to understand ways in which their semi-nomadic desert culture could evolve to incorporate them.

With a degree in theology and as a non-stipendiary minister in the Church of England, Emma is very aware of the draw this desert has for Christians, both past and present. It was this awareness, coupled with her growing relationship with the Bedouin families, that helped lead to the formation of Wind, Sand and Stars; a company set up to bring together western pilgrims and local communities in a way that is mutually beneficial. It has proven to be an interesting combination to say the least, and through it we have come to realise the important role a challenge plays – spiritual, mental and even physical – in the pilgrimages of Christians past and present, and why the Sinai is a place of such challenges, where every-day lives and personal relationships are changed, sometimes dramatically.

Our business partner in the Sinai, Dr Rabia Barty Tawfeek, is a Coptic Christian and he has been working with the Bedouin for many years. Like us, he has built up many long-lasting friendships among them and we work closely with him on each of our journeys. The way in which we try to ensure that our presence in the Sinai benefits the Bedouin is by getting their permission to travel through their desert lands and using their desert skills and knowledge in order to take pilgrims safely away from the coastal resorts and the roads into the very heart of the desert, an important part of our pilgrimage journeys as we shall see later. In this way the Bedouin are able to earn direct trade and we, and the people who travel with us, are able to gain a valuable in-depth insight into the everyday lives, culture and religion of these semi-nomadic Islamic desert tribes. It also allows the Bedouin children to realise that their desert skills and lifestyle are valued by those outside their community, thus encouraging them to remain in the desert instead of going to live in poverty in the cities.

It has been an essential part of our time in the Sinai to learn how to work closely with the Bedouin, particularly as our aim is to ensure that anyone who wants to come on a Sinai pilgrimage, even those who are unsure about travelling in such a different environment, can do so in safety and comfort. Today it feels as though our relations with the Bedouin are fluid and easy. However, it has taken us many years of patience, understanding and inner struggle as individuals and as a company to reach the stage we are at now. Sorting through the challenges of working cross-culturally has tested our capacities to live and work with all peoples, learning how to see things from sometimes totally different perspectives, particularly in a hot land like the Sinai where the heat of a temper can sometimes match or surpass that of the temperature!

However, despite the frustrations, we have had the privilege of witnessing first-hand how Christians can work together with people of other nations, other cultures and other religions, and that relationships can positively affect everyone involved

– Christian and non-Christian alike – and set an example for the adventure tourism industry. And for those who travel with us, their pilgrimage experience reaches a deeper level, as they feel that their presence in this area can contribute to changes that are not only important in their own lives but also in the lives of the people whose home they are travelling in.

Of course, Sinai has hosted many visitors throughout the centuries and another part of working in the Sinai that has been particularly rewarding for us has been the opportunity to examine why earlier pilgrims chose to come into the Sinai, and to see the similarities and the differences between their reasons and those of the modern-day pilgrim. What we find when we look back through the boundaries of time is that even more than 1500 years ago people were coming into the Sinai in order to meet the challenges of the desert and thus come to understand themselves, their lives and their relationship to God in a different way.

For example, around 390 CE there was a young man who worked as an officer in the court of Constantinople and chose to leave behind this life, not to mention his wife and son, in order to make a pilgrimage into the Sinai desert to pursue the religious life of a monk. This man was St Nilus, and he later became one of the most well-known people in the Eastern Church. People as powerful as the emperor would write to consult him on various ethical and moral matters. He left behind a great many writings and in one of them he describes how it was the solitude in the Sinai that so contrasted with his busy worldly life in the court of Constantinople that was perhaps the most important part of his pilgrimage in the Sinai. He writes:

A powerful longing towards Sinai seized me, and neither with my bodily eyes nor with those of the spirit could I find joy in anything, so strongly was I attracted to that place of solitude.

For St Nilus the solitude of the desert, where you can strain your ears but hear nothing but a crushing silence, and feel as though you are the only person on the planet, transformed his life. For many of us, who have very busy modern lifestyles, the idea of worshipping in a place where there are no worldly distractions almost seems like heaven on earth!

However, St Nilus also pointed out that this solitude was not simply about getting away from worldly distractions, but it was also about facing the challenge of being alone in an unfamiliar and somewhat harsh environment, and reaching through that to gain a higher spiritual level, needing to rely more and more on his faith in God.

The Sinai has also attracted many pilgrims simply because of its close associations with our Christian heritage. Here is the desert where Moses and the Israelites camped; here is the mountain upon which God spoke to Moses; and here is where Elijah fled when he feared that Jezebel would kill him. Through the writings of Egeria, a rather pernickety though enterprising Spanish abbess, we understand that this need to pray and worship at Holy places such as Mount Sinai is something that we also share with those who came before us. Egeria writes of her experience of climbing the 'Holy Mount of God',

These mountains are ascended with infinite toil, for you cannot go up gently by a spiral track . . . but you climb straight up the whole way, as if up a wall . . . until you reach the very foot of the middle one, which is . . . called Sinai. By this way, then, at the bidding of Christ our God, and helped by the prayers of the holy men who accompanied us we arrived . . . at the summit of Sinai, the holy mountain of God, where the law was given, that is, at the place where the Glory of the Lord descended on the day when the mountain smoked. Thus the toil was great, for I had to go up on foot, the ascent being impossible in the saddle, and yet I did not feel the toil . . . because I realised that the desire which I had was being fulfilled at God's bidding. . . .

> When the whole passage from the book of Moses had been read in that place . . . they showed us the cave where holy Moses was when he had gone up again into the mount of God . . .

Egeria speaks of how much she was affected or changed by actually being on, the 'holy mountain of God' where Moses had received the Ten Commandments. Much like St Nilus, she was also able to reach beyond her physical experience saying she 'did not feel the toil' for her faith in God, strengthened by being in such a holy place and witnessing 'her desires' manifesting themselves, carried her through any physical pain she may have been experiencing. The record of her experience is actually extremely moving, particularly as, having climbed the mountain many times, we know it is not an easy journey! Judging from her diaries it is possible to imagine that many of her acquaintances hoped that she would not only be spiritually transformed by her experience but that perhaps some of her more annoying habits would miraculously disappear as well, although we have no records of this for her diary ends before she returns home!

The tradition of a Sinai pilgrimage fostering a transformation dates even further back than the experiences of St Nilus and Egeria. Indeed, we only have to look into the Bible to find stories of life-altering experiences happening within the desert and mountains of Sinai. The story of Exodus, for example, tells of the journey of the Israelites, a journey that changed almost everything about their lives, transforming them from slaves into free men and women, and laying down foundations and rules for a new culture to develop and for their religion to take shape.

The story of the Exodus is filled with the challenges the Israelites faced once Moses had freed them from slavery and they had begun their journey through the Sinai – physical and mental challenges that for many were overwhelming. For example in Exodus we read:

The whole Israelite community set out from Elim and came to the Desert of Sin, which is between Elim and Sinai, on the fifteenth day of the second month after they had come out of Egypt. In the desert the whole community grumbled against Moses and Aaron. The Israelites said to them, 'If only we had died by the Lord's hand in Egypt! There we sat around pots of meat and ate all the food we wanted, but you have brought us out into this desert to starve this entire assembly to death.'*

However, in the desert God reveals himself to the Israelites by relieving their suffering as we see later in the same chapter in Exodus:

I have heard the grumbling of the Israelites. Tell them, 'At twilight you will eat meat, and in the morning you will be filled with bread. Then you will know that I am the Lord your God. That evening quail came and covered the camp, and in the morning there was a layer of dew around the camp. When the dew was gone, thin flakes like frost on the ground appeared on the desert floor. When the Israelites saw it, they said to each other, 'What is it?' For they did not know what it was. Moses said to them, 'It is the bread the Lord has given you to eat.'†

Part of the physical challenge of living in the desert abated with this manna from heaven; the next challenge the Israelites came up against was a mental and spiritual one. When Moses went up the mountain in order to meet with God, his people lost their faith and, weakened spiritually, they called for Aaron to build them another god:

When the people saw that Moses was so long in coming down from the mountain, they gathered around Aaron

* Exodus 16:1-3.
† Exodus 16:12-15.

and said, 'Come, make us gods who will go before us. As for this fellow Moses who brought us up out of Egypt, we don't know what has happened to him.'*

God was so angry by their deception that he almost destroyed them. However, through the intervention of Moses, they were not destroyed and were instead transformed into a different people, as they accepted the commandments laid down by God as the basis for a new way of living and worshipping.

And what of Moses whose first encounter with God in the Sinai changed the course of his life, transforming him from a simple shepherd into one of our great Christian leaders and saints? His first meeting with God in the desert sets his life on a totally different course as we read in Exodus.

> . . . and he led the flock to the far side of the desert and came to Horeb, the mountain of God. There the angel of the Lord appeared to him in flames of fire from within a bush. '. . . So now, go. I am sending you to Pharaoh to bring my people the Israelites out of Egypt.'†

Through his experience of meeting God in the Sinai desert and rising to the challenge that God set before him, Moses becomes a servant of God and successfully leads the Israelites out of slavery in Egypt into the desert of Sinai. When they are camped at the bottom of Mount Sinai, Moses meets personally with God in order to put together the commandments that would begin to govern the people – commandments that we still follow today. The inward spiritual changes of Moses, which happened during his time of meeting with God, are reflected in his outward physical appearance as we read in Exodus:

> Moses was there with the Lord forty days and forty nights without eating bread or drinking water. And he wrote

* Exodus 32:1-2.
† Exodus 3:1-2, 10.

on the tablets the words of the covenant – the Ten Commandments. When Moses came down from Mount Sinai with the two tablets of the Testimony in his hands, he was not aware that his face was radiant because he had spoken with the Lord.*

The role that Mount Sinai plays, as a place where humanity encounters God, continues in the story of Elijah. 1 Kings 9 tells us that when Elijah's life was threatened by Jezebel, he lost his faith in God's protection and fled into the desert. Physically weakened, he collapsed under a broom tree and could go no further until the Lord, much as he did for the Israelites, provided him with bread and water. Strengthened by this he travelled further into the desert to Mount Sinai and, as 1 Kings records, found shelter in a cave on the mountain:

He travelled forty days and forty nights until he reached Horeb, the mountain of God. There he went into a cave and spent the night.†

Then, once again, Sinai plays host to a life-altering experience for on Mount Sinai, much like Moses, Eiijah encounters God, and through this encounter finds the strength to meet the challenges before him and thus change the course of his life. 1 Kings continues:

And the word of the Lord came to him: 'What are you doing here, Elijah?' He replied, 'I have been very zealous for the Lord God Almighty. The Israelites have rejected your covenant, broken down your altars, and put your prophets to death with the sword. I am the only one left, and now they are trying to kill me too.' The Lord said, 'Go out and stand on the mountain in the presence of the Lord, for the Lord is about to pass by.' Then a great and

* Exodus 34:28-29.
† 1 Kings 9:8-9.

powerful wind tore the mountains apart and shattered the rocks before the Lord, but the Lord was not in the wind. After the wind there was an earthquake, but the Lord was not in the earthquake. After the earthquake came a fire, but the Lord was not in the fire. And after the fire came the crushing sound of silence. When Elijah heard it, he pulled his cloak over his face and went out and stood at the mouth of the cave. Then a voice said to him, 'What are you doing here, Elijah?' He replied, 'I have been very zealous for the Lord God Almighty. The Israelites have rejected your covenant, broken down your altars, and put your prophets to death with the sword. I am the only one left, and now they are trying to kill me too.' The Lord said to him, 'Go back the way you came . . .'*

And, strengthened by his encounter with God, Elijah does.

Thus the Sinai as a place of renewal and transformation is an idea that is rooted deep in our Christian history, and we continue a tradition that was started by prophets such as Elijah and Moses and carried on by pilgrims such as St Nilus and Egeria. Although encountering God in the desert is not an easy experience, it is the challenge, both mental and physical, that leads to an inner spiritual transformation and a life-altering experience.

Bringing this history to life and making connections with the experiences of the pilgrims of the past and Christians today is part of the joy for us of working in the Sinai. Time and again we have led weary but determined pilgrims to the top of Mount Sinai, and witnessed their awe when they reached the top. Many of them, much like Egeria, are overwhelmed by the feeling of being in a place inextricably and historically tied to the very core of our belief system, and where Christians have come to worship for centuries,

* 1 Kings 9.

It takes a day to climb the mountain. The view becomes increasingly majestic until you reach the peak and gaze at range upon range of mountains stretching to the horizon. It is difficult to put the experience into words for here is the dwelling of a God of majesty and beauty.*

Bringing alive the sights and sounds of the stories that many of us have been reading since we were small children infuses them with an extra level of meaning and poignancy.

However, one of the major differences between pilgrims who travelled through the Sinai centuries ago and those of us who are coming now is, of course, our reliance on creature comforts such as running water and a cosy bedroom. Many of us tend to feel that travelling in an unfamiliar environment such as a desert, even if it is important to us as Christians, is something that should be left to adventurers such as Wilfred Thesiger or Ranulph Fiennes. It is for this reason that many Christians did not come into the Sinai until roads and four-star hotels were built so they could travel to holy sites on a level of comfort similar to their lives back home.

Unfortunately, by doing this they miss out on an extremely important part of a pilgrimage in Sinai, the part that St Nilus spoke so passionately about – the challenge of worshipping in a place of solitude and the importance of being in a place with which one is physically unfamiliar and perhaps not entirely comfortable. This brings us full circle to Wind, Sand and Stars' work with the Bedouin. For by using their desert knowledge we are able to take people safely away from the roads and coastal resorts in order to experience the challenge of worshipping in the solitude of the desert and to meet with the physical challenges of living in such a different environment.

Of course, this experience is not as challenging as St Nilus' may have been, for we try to ensure that anyone can travel with us and we have taken 8-year-olds and 80-year-olds

* *Sr Elizabeth Rees, Wind, Sand and Stars Pilgrimage Journey.*

safely into the desert. Not only do we have a full support system in place, but we ensure that experiencing the solitude of the desert is complemented by sharing the company of fellow pilgrims and the Bedouin around the campfire at night, for to travel with people of a very different culture can add another layer of meaning to their pilgrimage. For this experience can also lead to a transformation as they get an in-depth insight into the traditions and lifestyles of another culture, an insight that inevitably teaches them something about our own.

The Bedouin of Sinai are a kind, gentle and hospitable people with a very strong community spirit. Their lives seem simple when compared with ours, and many of their concerns are basic: for example, ensuring they have clean drinking water and proper shelter. Access to medical help and education is, at the moment, still quite limited, and at times their lives can be filled with physical pain and frustration. However, although their lives can be quite difficult, they also live with a sense of freedom, a freedom that we do not often experience in our own lives back home where a huge 'to do' list often awaits us, filled with endless tasks, papers to fill out, telephone calls to make, and bills to pay. Major Jarvis, a British administrator in Sinai at the beginning of the twentieth century, encapsulated this feeling perfectly when he observed that,

> . . . to the Bedu, civilisation is hateful because it means he must live in a house and is not free to wander at his will . . . we ourselves are hopelessly tied up by the bonds of civilisation.

Travelling with the Bedouin and experiencing their very different lifestyle causes us to reflect upon our own lives and re-evaluate what is important to us and what we need to make more space for once we return home.

And thus the pilgrimage through Sinai today affects and transforms people for many different reasons: by visiting historical biblical sites, through worshipping in the silence and solitude of the desert and by travelling with the Bedouin. As one of our recent pilgrims expressed it to us,

> 'Thank you' seems an inadequate phrase to express the very real gratitude I feel for last week's amazing pilgrimage which your organisation and execution made so memorable. I'd long wanted to visit Mount Sinai and St Catherine's monastery so achieved those ambitions. But the manner of our doing so – making our way through the stunning beauty of the wilderness, experiencing the depth of silence, the majesty of the surroundings, the grandeur of the mountains, the space of the desert places, meeting with the Bedouin and in a little way sharing in their way of life, receiving their generous and open hospitality – all this gave a depth and dimension to the experience which will long remain with me.*

Within the magnificent sixth-century monastery of St Catherine's, which is nestled into the foot of Mount Sinai is something that helps symbolise the important role the Sinai has played in transforming the lives of pilgrims both old and new. In the church of the monastery hangs an Apse of the Transfiguration – completely unrestored from when it was first built in the sixth century. This important biblical event is a story of a transformation as we read in Matthew.

> After six days Jesus took with him Peter, James and John the brother of James, and led them up a high mountain by themselves. There he was transfigured before them. His face shone like the sun, and his clothes became as white as the light. While he was still speaking, a bright cloud enveloped them, and a voice from the cloud said, 'This is my Son, whom I love; with him I am well pleased. Listen to him!'†

* *Rev Peter Boulton-Lea, Wind, Sand and Stars Pilgrimage Journey.*
† Matthew 17:1-2, 5.

Underneath this sixth-century Apse of Transfiguration the monks celebrate the Eucharist through which Christians past and present have 'met' with God on earth:

> And as we follow his example and obey his command grant that by the power of your Holy Spirit these gifts of bread and wine may be to us his body and his blood who, in the same night that he was betrayed, took bread and gave you thanks; he broke it and gave it to his disciples, saying: 'Take, eat; this is my body which is given for you; do this in remembrance of me.' In the same way, after supper he took the cup and gave it to them, saying: 'Drink this, all of you; this is my blood of the new covenant, which is shed for you and for many for the forgiveness of sins.'

And so our Christian history blends with our present, coming together on a pilgrimage through the Sinai, transforming us through various physical, mental and spiritual challenges, and giving us a better understanding of our role as Christians today and how we relate to people of other nations and religions.

Many people, such as St Nilus and the monks at St Catherine's are so affected by this land that they choose to make it their home. But what happens to the things we have learned on our pilgrimage when we leave this land to re-enter a familiar life at home? It is a difficult question, and many people feel they need to make more than one pilgrimage to the Sinai. However, others like Moses, the Israelites and Egeria do leave and never return. Perhaps it is best to remember that the experience of a pilgrimage through Sinai does not ever leave you. For as God said to Moses, 'My Presence will go with you, and I will give you rest.'*

* Exodus 33:14.

The Quiet Garden Movement

Sheila Walters

The Quiet Garden Movement* sprang from a simple meditation in a garden. In that stillness the founder of the movement
reflected on the way Jesus spent time away from the crowd,
sometimes with his disciples, often alone. He chose gardens,
hillsides and a boat on the sea to be still, to reflect on his life,
to speak to God and listen to his voice. God spoke in that
stillness through the medium of natural environments, and
Jesus was restored and re-energised for the task ahead. The
parables were charged with the energy of the insights gained
from paying close attention to blades of grass, ears of wheat
and sowing of seeds.

The person meditating in the garden was the Rev Philip
Roderick. He progressed from there to shared silence in a sitting
room, and then to the first garden in a room at Stoke Poges
Farm and the initiation of the movement. There are now
many gardens offered for hospitality and prayer in what has
become a worldwide movement. The individual size of the
garden does not matter and may only consist of a small place
in an inner-city churchyard, but the dynamic of the day will
be an offering of space for people to take time for reflection
and prayer.

Modern life is full of clamorous demands on the time and
attention, and as attempts are made to meet them, energy levels
may become exhausted and depleted. Individuals are called
to make time for God and to follow the example of Christ by
setting aside a time for reflection and for stillness. In that
quietness the insistent demands that bind, hinder and exhaust
can be put aside for a day or an hour and be replaced with a

* Information is available from the Quiet Garden Trust, Stoke Park Farm, Park
Road, Stoke Poges, Bucks SL2 4PG. E-mail: quietgarden@ukonline.co.uk.

Photograph: Barbara Butler

sense of the presence of God. As the pace is slowed, the attention becomes focused on less, just the word of God, the natural environment and the immediate surroundings. It is then that connection is made between our story and the word of God, and in the making of our own parables we continue the journey of faith.

The pilgrimage undertaken at a Quiet Garden day has more to do with the inner world of the individual and the inner journey. It is a journey of developing awareness of the presence of God and is about taking time to step into God's time so that the inner world may be refreshed, re-energised and attuned once more. This pilgrimage is not just for those of a reflective disposition or for any one particular age group; the journey has to be undertaken by every individual. As Jesus Christ called his disciples to a hillside, a garden or a boat on the sea, so he calls each individual to a meeting place with God. In that place God's voice speaks to the individual soul, drawing it ever closer into a more defined and loving relationship with him.

Yorkshire Abbeys

David Bryant

I leave the busy A64 and plunge through a wooded lane into another world. Frost-covered fields drop down to the 1000-year-old ruins of Kirkham Priory. Ice crackles under my feet as I walk to the monastery gateway, which rises up in splendid isolation. Crumbling stone shields bearing the arms of de Clare, England, de Roos and Vaux jostle with a gryphon and leering gargoyles. A seated, headless Christ broods over the silent monastery site. A window is set into the gateway and I half expect the cowled head of the janitor to appear. 'Good-day, traveller. What brings you to this holy place?'

Kirkham was an Augustinian Priory whose monks based their rule on the teaching of Augustine of Hippo.* It was a liberal order, and the monks were allowed to leave the house, administering parishes, looking after churches, running hospitals, and caring for the sick and dying. Their hooded black cloaks and black tunics gave them their name, 'Black Canons'.

I follow a path beside the River Derwent. Water froths and bubbles; fish break the surface; patches of brown cropped reeds huddle by the icy bank. Reflected in the water, the monastery ruins shimmer and ripple like some forgotten Avalon. For a brief moment, I seem to hear the distant chanting of plainsong. There has been holiness here for centuries.

It's on to Jervaulx Abbey, one of Yorkshire's less-known treasures. Whale-backed hills tinged with fading purple announce the Yorkshire Dales. Jervaulx is a wild, unfettered place, unspoilt by modern accretions such as ticket offices, museums and shops. It is owned by the Burdon family, who leave it open all year round and trust wayfarers to pay an entrance contribution and leave money for a guidebook.

* Katy Hounsell-Robert has written about her journey in the footsteps of Augustine of Hippo on page 250.

Inside, the ruins are a maze. I make my way through a narrow stone gap and climb a precarious flight of steps that leads nowhere. Ivy twines heavenwards; birds twitter and hop on mossy stones; bushes thrust and brambles grow. In spring and summer, unusual plants like wall rue, maidenhair, spleenwort, pellitory of the wall, shining crane's bill and weld grow here. In the roofless nave of the once great church, pillar-bases squat, free of the weight of the vaulted roof. Where the altar once was, tufts of grass and dead leaves flutter. Empty sarcophagi gape. I peer inside, but there are no skeletons to be seen. I walk through a four-foot-high doorway and wonder whether all medieval monks were tiny.

The monks' living area is cold and bleak. What must the winter nights have been like, with that wind howling off the tops, and only a hard cot and a rough serge blanket to keep it at bay? Jervaulx was a Cistercian house founded in 1156. Its monks led a harsher life than the Augustinians; they sought out wild places, and spent time in work, devotion to God, and study of the scriptures. Lay brothers did the heavy work, freeing the monks for prayer. The abbey prospered, and grew into one of the leading religious houses in Yorkshire. The monks had a healthy income from sheep farming, and coal- and iron-mining. They also bred hardy workhorses.

Jervaulx came to a terrible end. Adam Sedbergh, one-time Abbot, unwisely became involved in the revolt against Henry VIII known as the 'Pilgrimage of Grace'. He was arrested, imprisoned in the Tower, and hanged at Tyburn. The King's militia descended on the abbey, drove out the monks, stripped it of its valuables and blew it up.

On a spring day I drove 40 miles south-east, to the North York Moors National Park and the remote and beautiful Rosedale. The moors were bursting out into green. Smoke rose from village chimney pots; and the high moors stood foursquare round the village, on guard. I plunged vertiginously down Rosedale Chimney, at 1-in-3 England's steepest hill. Rosedale Priory stands in a field next to the church. All that is left of it now is a fragment of the old convent, a stair turret in meadow, which was possibly the south-west transept of the nunnery church. It was a small house of the Cistercian order, founded by Robert de Stutevile in the late twelfth century. Its church was tiny, a mere 60 or 70 feet long, and 18 to 20 feet wide. The buildings housed nine nuns, overseen by a prioress, and a few lay workers who farmed and shepherded. In a good year, it produced 12 sacks of wool for sale. Over the years, the nuns were given stray sheep, a toft and craft (house and field), and several small plots of land.

All was not peace and tranquillity with the order. An iron forge next to the priory infuriated the nuns with its noise, fumes and smoke. Matters took a darker turn in the fourteenth century, when Archbishop Greenfield was summoned to deal with financial troubles and to issue chastisements and penances. (What on earth had the sisters been up to?) The priory was destroyed at the instruction of Henry VIII and Thomas Cromwell. At the end, all that remained were two small bells valued at ten shillings, some gilt plate and chalice and goblet worth about £37. Several stones from the priory can still be seen bedded in the present church, together with a stone coffin and a sundial on a wall. The motto on the north door of the church reads 'Omnia Vanitas', 'All is Vanity'.

The last of my visits was to a magnificent ruin in the Hambleton Hills. I reached it with a ferociously dangerous turn off the A19, and through a huddle of farm buildings. Mount Grace was a Carthusian monastery, and we are talking heavyweight spirituality here. There was none of the homely squabbling of the Rosedale nuns at Mount Grace, none of Kirkham's strolls by the river, nor of the bustling life of busy Jervaulx. Carthusian monks lived, worked and prayed in separate cells. Contact with fellow monks took place in church or in the refectory only on Sundays and feast days, and in strict silence.

My first impression was of the high wall that shut out the world beyond the Carthusian house, and enclosed all who set foot inside. The remains of the church stood out as bleak orange-brown stone, capped by a tower that looked faintly Gothic against the irony-grey sky. At the east end of the aisle is a delight: a superb modern statue of the Madonna of the Cross. Malcolm Brockelesby, the sculptor, has done a wonderful job. As I look at her, I feel the slow stir of holiness. Cell 8 was rebuilt in 1900 by Sir Lowthian Bell. It is surprisingly roomy, with two floors, a loom, a cot bed and chair. Outside, an ambulatory leads to a courtyard flanking a small self-contained vegetable patch, and on to a stone lavatory. I am amazed to think that drainage and clean water was laid on for each monk, in an age when sanitation topped no one's list.

Time to go. I ease my way back into the hurtling traffic and rejoin the twentieth century. Yorkshire's abbeys and priories are the very weft and warp of its rich and holy heritage.*

* David's paper was published in *The Church Times* on 12 January 2001.

Drawing by Jane Walton-Loxton

A Cycling Pilgrimage

Martin Parrot

I went on a cycling pilgrimage with a friend, Andrew Ashdown. We cycled from Iona on the west coast of Scotland, to Lindisfarne on the east coast of England. We covered over 200 miles on bicycles, averaging about 50 miles a day, and spent our evenings and nights at various youth hostels.

My overwhelming impressions of the trip were, first, the stunning beauty of Mull and the enormous privilege of cycling through the island. Iona is a little gem off the western tip of Mull. We spent a couple of nights there at the Anglican hostel, the Bishop's lodge, exploring the island and learning a lot about the community of people who live there and who, including the Iona community itself, have a tremendous impact not only in Scotland but throughout the world. A quarter of a million people visit Iona every year.

As we crossed Scotland and went further south into England another impression was the sense in which the Scottish saints – Columba in particular – started to lose their influence, and at a certain point the Northumbrian saints took over and we started to read about Aidan and Cuthbert. One of the highlights for me was arriving at Melrose and looking down on the site of the monastery where Cuthbert spent his early years.

We arrived at Lindisfarne after about 10 days and spent a couple of nights with Ray Simpson in his retreat centre. It was a thoroughly invigorating experience physically, emotionally and spiritually, and as we left Lindisfarne the wind blew into our faces and tried to keep us there, but eventually we got to the train station at Berwick-upon-Tweed and headed back to our normal lives.

Iona
The island of Iona is reached by ferry from Oban and then

from Mull. It was a holy place for Druids and then Christians even before the great Columba went there around 563 CE. St Oran's chapel, near to the abbey, is named after Oran, a cousin of Columba, who is said to have been buried alive to consecrate the ground. The King's Walk is where Scottish and Scandinavian kings are buried. The Labour Party leader John Smith is also buried there. St Martin's Cross and St John's Cross are wonderful examples of Celtic crosses with knotwork patterns and scenes from the Bible.

The abbey was founded in 1200 CE and rebuilt by George MacCleod in the 1930s. There is a small shrine where Columba was most probably buried. Exploration of the island leads to discovery of an earthwork marking the place where Columba's monks met, and a hermit's cell.

The emphasis of the island, due to the work of the Iona Community, is on justice and peace work. Those who stay on the island are encouraged to recharge their batteries in order to go to work in the world of deprivation and struggle in large cities and around the world.

Pilgrimage to Rome

Brian Hoare

It didn't really start out as a pilgrimage at all. Indeed, to be quite honest I was rather disappointed when the letter came advising me that the official overseas trip during my year as President of the Methodist Conference would be to Italy. After all, others had flown off to exotic places like Sri Lanka, Zambia or Hong Kong, and somehow Italy didn't have the same sort of appeal. Yet how wrong I was! For this turned out for my wife and me to be a trip which not only informed us about church life in Italy today (especially in the Methodist and Waldensian Churches which we were there to visit), but also took us back to the Early Church and the very beginnings of the Christian faith itself.

Rome is a fascinating city in which the ancient and the modern stand cheek by jowl in a largely harmonious coexistence. In the midst of its bustling modern life there are constant reminders of its glorious past as the capital of the great Roman Empire which did so much to shape the whole of Western Europe. New excavations here, old and familiar ruins there, and on almost every street corner evidences of a civilisation long gone, yet still strangely and powerfully alive.

Our hosts for the stay in Rome were the minister of the English-speaking Methodist Church at Ponte St Angelo and his wife, and they made us warmly welcome in their spacious apartment above the church with its roof gardens affording good views of the Vatican. They joked that we could see the Pope's bedroom from there! They had lived and ministered in Rome for some time by now, and were fluent enough in Italian and familiar enough with the city to prove the perfect guides for our stay. So it was that we saw not only all the usual tourist sights, but also some that were off the tourist track altogether.

Two visits in particular stand out in my memory, however,

and will no doubt echo the experience of many who have had the privilege of spending time in Rome.

The first was our visit to the catacombs. These amazing subterranean warrens of tunnels, galleries, tombs and chambers had originally been dug as Christian cemeteries on the edge of the ancient city beside the great Roman roads, but during the years of cruel persecution suffered by the early Christians from the time of the Emperor Nero onwards they became places of refuge and safety. Some of the stories about believers meeting here secretly for worship and fellowship are no doubt more romantic than realistic, but it is certainly true that these tombs, which were the last resting places of many who had died by sword, fire or wild beasts, became places of pilgrimage and worship over the years. Burial grounds were sacrosanct under Roman law, so Christians could meet in these elaborate underground basilicas unmolested, and would do so especially on the anniversaries of the martyrs. It was a moving and a humbling experience to walk those passages, to see the wall-paintings and the scratched symbols of the faith, to stand in the very places where early Christians had gathered to worship and to recall how much our forebears in the faith had endured out of faithfulness to Christ.

The other site that helped to turn our visit to Rome into a genuine pilgrimage was, of course, the ancient city's most famous monument – the Colosseum. This immense amphi-theatre seating some 50,000 spectators took eight years to build and was opened in the year 80 AD with a programme of games lasting for 100 days. It is said that 9000 wild animals were killed during those opening festivities, and thereafter the Romans developed a taste for the most bloodthirsty of sports. Perhaps the best known of these were the gladiatorial games in which men were trained to fight to the death, and lions and other wild beasts were let loose among them to increase the horror of the show. Here, too, the famous chariot races were held, and on other occasions the huge arena was filled with water and mock naval battles were staged.

As we stood and contemplated the still impressive ruins of the Colosseum we were somehow transported back across the centuries and could begin to imagine both the splendour and the horror of all that had taken place here. For us, however, it was not so much the great sporting spectaculars that were uppermost in our minds, for this too was the arena in which countless early Christians are believed to have met their deaths. Here innumerable martyrs had been willing to give their lives for their faith in front of thousands of bloodthirsty spectators, and we were humbled by recalling their courage and commitment to Christ.

It was not until the beginning of the fifth century that a monk named Telemachus had been instrumental in putting an end to the cruelty of the gladiatorial games. Entering the arena, he stood between the gladiators and pleaded with them and the crowd to stop such shows but his intervention was greeted with jeers and insults, and he was stoned to death for his pains. Yet from that day onwards the shows stopped. Centuries later, in 1749, Pope Benedict XIV declared the Colosseum a 'via crucis', a place sanctified by the blood of the martyrs, and erected a dedicatory cross there. Later still, in the twentieth century, a larger cross was raised by the Roman Catholic authorities high above the very section of the arena where the emperor and his imperial household used to sit.

For us it was a parable. The powers of Rome had done their worst. For centuries attempts had been made to stamp out the Christian Church and crush the faith of Christian believers. Many had indeed been killed, but the blood of the martyrs had become the life-blood of the Church. The cross still stands above the Colosseum and all it symbolised, and we thought of the words of John Bowring:

In the cross of Christ I glory, towering o'er the wrecks of time,
all the light of sacred story, gathers round its head sublime.

What scenes of both tragedy and triumph that ancient city had seen. And I for one will never be the same for having been there.

Pilgrim River Poet

Donna Worthington

At the feet of the wanderer
worn hands place palms

Walking
in a garden
I seek out those things fallen
by the wayside
broken palm branches

Eyes gaze
mouths shout the hurried hosanna plea
Pilgrim Messiah
He discovers the anointed pathway
beyond . . .
Disturbed,
he moves onward, always onward

I weave and link the soft brown blades
leaves turning, twisting, circling

Beneath the erring clamorous cheers,
he only hears
the soft murmurings
of the branches
breaking
under the feet of the beast

The mask
creates of itself
It becomes a cross
intertwining palms

enfolded by the circle
creation's pathway
the dancer's crown of red

Crowds surround this man on high
and he . . .
he puts down roots to their very depths

Witnessing green broken palms
through the darkness hidden and unseen
the weaver gathers the fragments
transforming the broken pieces

I place a stone circle
at the foot
of the entwined leaves
red petals
at the crossing
the place of meeting

Tree of life

SECTION NINE
Pilgrim Tools

Pilgrim Tools

In this section we have tried to provide some tools for pilgrims to use on their journey. They are starters to help with the planning and organising of a pilgrimage, either for an individual or for a group of pilgrims. We start with what to wear. It may sound silly, but for pilgrims in the past the correct clothing was an all-essential ingredient for their pilgrimage. It spoke to others and to themselves. So today it is still important and can help particularly in relation to meeting others and in creating a feeling of belonging to a group, where this is relevant.

Here you will also find some suggestions for ways to discover suitable readings and some examples of these, some ideas for writing your own prayers as well as using those of others. There are meditations, thoughts and suggestions for celebrating Holy Communion together, as well as views about pilgrimage tokens and souvenirs. Remember, there are also useful resources within the practical section.

Pilgrim Clothes and Articles

Pilgrims have traditionally been recognised by their clothing and the articles that they have carried. In many ways the items that pilgrims are likely to carry today are not very different from those of the past.

The Scrip

This was a bag in which the pilgrim could keep his relics, food, money and other necessary items. For modern pilgrims this is likely to be a bag that goes around the waist, a handbag, a shoulder bag or a small rucksack. This will vary with the type of pilgrimage being undertaken and the individual pilgrims.

The Staff

This was actually two sticks swathed together tightly by a withy band. Today, for a walking pilgrimage this is more likely to be a stout walking stick, either tall or short, or even two of the telescopic ones! For a town pilgrimage many people still use a walking stick, often with a small seat attached to be used at the pilgrimage site where there are not always handy vacant seats.

Badges

These, again, were specially used by pilgrims who would sew them on to hats or hang them round their necks or even pin them to their clothes. Today in many countries around the Mediterranean you will find metal badges for sale depicting different parts of the body, or the outline of a person, to leave at a pilgrim site. This is particularly obvious in Orthodox churches where you will often find a long string of such emblems hung over a picture within the church. Many pilgrims who are travelling as a group will have their 'logo' sewn or printed on to sweat shirts or T-shirts. This is particularly visually effective to outsiders and does allow easier recognition of fellow pilgrims – especially if they are not well known to each other! There's nothing quite like the same coloured T-shirts with suitable words or a picture on each to help pilgrims see themselves as part of a group; a pilgrimage experience.

The Cross

This was particularly used in the past by those pilgrims who were travelling to Jerusalem. Today many Christians wear the sign of the cross on a chain around their necks, or on their clothes as a part of everyday dress. However, there are so many shapes and sizes of crosses, let alone the different materials that they can be made from, that for a group of pilgrims it may be better to agree on one design.

Bells or Other Instruments of Music

These were often taken on pilgrimage to while away the hours – remember, travelling was restricted to daylight hours only. Pilgrims often travelled together for safety on their journey –

and to demonstrate to others they met on the way that they were on pilgrimage. Many pilgrims today, if asked and encouraged, will bring along an instrument to play. This may range from a guitar or flute to tambourines. The most common form of musical instrument, of course, is the human voice, and groups of pilgrims will often take along song and hymn books.

Walking boots
Original pilgrims would probably have worn a smock either over their clothes, or as their clothing, and as we don't today normally do this we include walking boots here instead, as they are an integral part of today's dress. Footwear is the one thing that separates us from the earth itself, so its very fabric is of great importance. It allows us to follow the pilgrim path whilst at the same time feel the ground beneath our feet, in varying degrees.

Choosing Suitable Bible Passages

You'd think that choosing a relevant Bible passage to use during a pilgrimage would be really easy, as the whole Hebrew Bible is the story of the pilgrimage of the Israelite people, and the New Testament tells us how to follow Jesus. Jews were expected to make pilgrimages to the temple in Jerusalem for the great festivals, as can be seen from the description in John 12:12 about the great crowds who welcomed Jesus being in Jerusalem for the Passover. The Book of Acts opens in Jerusalem, during the Pentecost holiday, where over a million pilgrims were milling about the city when suddenly a group of 120 believers came alive. The term pilgrim is rarely, if ever, used however, with usually the words being translated in the Revised Standard Version (RSV) as 'exiles', whilst the New International Version (NIV) uses 'aliens' and 'strangers'.

Using a concordance is the easiest way of finding or choosing a passage. Don't forget to use one that is matched to your Bible version, and then just look up specific words that link with your theme of pilgrimage, or are included in the text you're trying to find.

There's also a *Roget's Thesaurus of the Bible* that is absolutely excellent for linking passages across themes and for making those connections that one might otherwise never see. You can either look up a specific word at the back, or you can select a category from the 990 given at the front. Either way, it's a brilliant way to find suitable passages that you do not have already in your mind.

Now that there are CD-ROMs of the Bible we have tended to look in these first, but they do not show the connections in meaning between the passages, only that each contains the particular word(s). Sometimes there are too many passages with that chosen word so only the first so many are shown and you never actually get to see the rest. We have found the CD-ROM the better way to get to know our way around the Bible itself and to spend time alone reading and searching, but for making meaningful connections we still go back to the paper thesaurus.

Below are some passages linked to particular words.

Pilgrimage
A computer search through the NIV will come up with two entries for the word 'pilgrimage'. The first is in **Genesis 47:9** where Joseph's father is talking to Pharaoh about his own pilgrimage of life, whilst the second from **Psalm 84:5** is directly about those who go on pilgrimage.

Invitation to Pilgrimage
Often the most suitable readings are those that don't actually have any direct 'pilgrimage' words in at all, for example, **John 1:35-39** where God invites us to 'come and see' and spend time with him.

Paths
The word path comes up 102 times in a computer search,

though many of these are referring to people or angels walking on a path to a certain place, rather than following the path of the Lord or God helping them on their path. These next ones talk of how God does look after each of us, broadening our paths, showing us his paths (his ways) and even going ahead of us to prepare the way. See the following: **2 Samuel 22:31-37, Psalm 25:4-5, Isaiah 40:3-5, Psalm 119:105-112, Jeremiah 31:21a**.

Crossroads, Paths and Boundary Stones

The field described in the Bible was generally not enclosed, but was marked off from its neighbours by boundary markers, so hence there are a number of texts with these markers in them. These can be useful when thinking about decisions or changes. Which path should you chose? Where will you put the markers, the boundary stones? Just how far will you go? How close to the path will you stick?

We had an experience a couple of years ago where we were trying to follow exactly on a path over wet moorland. As we walked, the land become wetter and wetter until it was almost impassable, and we were forced off the path itself and had to walk a few yards to the side of it. We quickly realised that this was very much dryer and easier, and as it was on open land did no more damage than following the actual path. So long as we kept the path in sight so we didn't get lost we didn't actually need to place our feet on top of it all the time. Perhaps that is a thought that will be echoed by many about following a path in life itself. Maybe, like **Jeremiah 6:16**, we should be following the good way rather than slavishly following the path.

Walking with God

There are many texts about walking with God, but they rarely actually mean just a happy little stroll along together. **Proverbs 3:6**, when translated from the original Hebrew, means more than 'in all your ways acknowledge him' but rather 'in all your ways know him'. This implies more than mere reverence but an actual following of God; and how can you follow someone you don't know? Pilgrimage is about trying to know him better, to know him more, and as a result to be able to follow his ways more closely.

Other examples can be found at **Joshua 22:5** and **Deuteronomy 28:9**.

How to walk
There are many passages that tell us how to follow God, to walk honestly, in the light, worthy of the Lord, uprightly, in his statutes, as taught by him, and so on. Have a look at some of the following examples:

according to his commands	**Deuteronomy 5:33; Psalm 1; Jeremiah 7:23**
as taught by him	**1 Kings 8:36; Isaiah 2:3; 30:21**
uprightly	**Proverbs 2:7**
in his statutes and judgements	**Ezekiel 37:24**
in newness of life	**Romans 6:4**
honestly, as in the day	**Romans 13:13**
by faith, not by sight	**2 Corinthians 5:7**
in love, following Christ	**Ephesians 5:2**
worthy of the Lord	**Colossians 1:10**
in Christ	**Colossians 2:6**
by the gospel rule	**Philippians 3:16**
in the light, as God is	**1 John 1:7**
in white clothing	**Revelation 3:4**
in the light of heaven	**Revelation 21:24**

Special Psalms, 120 to 134
At the beginning of these 15 psalms it says, 'A Song of Ascents'. This is commonly thought to be because the pilgrims who came to the three annual pilgrimage feasts of Jerusalem used these particular psalms. Another thought is because there were 15 steps leading from the court of men to the court of

women in the temple, and the final suggestion is because within some of them the thoughts spoken advance from step to step – though not in them all. Whatever the reason you may imagine pilgrims from millennia past using these same psalms and walking in the footprints of history. **Psalm 121** is probably the most well known, giving a real feel of security, safety and firmness. Indeed Jo's mum asked for it to be read at her own funeral, and has the first line on her memorial stone.

Walking in the Light
John 12:35-36 talks of how we should walk in the light and not in darkness. Anyone who has ever been caught out late walking on moorland, woodland, or an area they don't know very well, will know only too well the truth in this. Our only experience was down to a fault of pride – not turning back when it would have been sensible – and it was only because alongside the path there was a stream of water from the lashing rain that reflected the wonderful bright moon that we ever made our way to a firmer path and then a track back to a main road and safety. Who says bucketing rain is bad?

Prayers
The upsurge in interest in Celtic spirituality has brought with it a feast of prayer books in that style that are extremely well suited to pilgrimage as a journey though the everyday and the special events in our lives. We have included some Celtic prayer books in our books section. Many talk of the way God encircles us in all we do, in a manner that is repetitious but also extending. A typical Celtic prayer will use the name of each person in the Trinity to repeat what is going on; each in a slightly different way. An example for a walking pilgrimage might go like this: 'Today I walk in the name of the Father.' This would be repeated for the Son and the Holy Spirit. The pilgrim may then think about the different aspects of the walk, which could be the physical ability to walk, the direction of

the walk, and the safety of the walk. Now add these two together:

> I walk in the name of the Father, who made me,
> I follow your way this day by the teaching of Jesus the Son,
> I am kept safe in all paths today by the power of the Holy Spirit.

Pilgrims can be encouraged to spend time making up such short three-line prayers. Have a short list of activities or issues to choose from, and also state whether you want the prayer to be one of adoration, confession, thanksgiving or supplication. Ask all the pilgrims to choose and spend ten minutes on their own before you then ask them to join together with others who chose the same subject. In this way it is relatively easy to create longer prayers that flow together and can then be used later in group worship times.

The Practical Section gives some ideas for prayer books. The following North American Indian prayer follows a pattern very similar to that of the Celtic one described above. It was found on an internet site after typing in the two words 'Christian' and 'Prayer'. You do need to take care when you look at some of the sites, they're not always what you might expect!

> *As I Walk with Beauty (Traditional Navajo Prayer)*
> As I walk, as I walk,
> the universe is walking with me.
> In beauty it walks before me.
> In beauty it walks behind me.
> In beauty it walks below me.
> In beauty it walks above me.
> Beauty is on every side.
> As I walk, I walk with Beauty.

Morning and Evening Prayers
Included at the end of this section are the morning and

evening prayers we used for a weekend's pilgrimage in Haworth where the Brontë family lived. The weekend's theme was centred around their lives and the 'passion' that this area had brought out in different people who had lived there and written about the place. The formal prayers were written to reflect the era of the Brontë family who lived when the Book of Common Prayer was still in its heyday.

Different forms of formal prayer are available from a variety of sources – Celtic, Orthodox, modern and traditional. Some suggestions for use are included within the Practical Section.

Meditations
There are a number of books available giving meditation in different styles, and details of some of these are given in the Practical Section. If possible, it is a good idea to use items you have seen or places you have been to, to plan your meditation. Examples for a walking pilgrimage would be around the natural environment you have passed through that day. Pine cones, wheat fields, wildflowers in the verges, birds and their songs, wet and dry paths, and so on.

An example that was once used for a weekend was the introduction into the group of a bunch of yellow roses that were still in tight bud. Thanks to Gillian Houghton for this one, included later in this section.

Holy Communion Service

Holy Communion is not only key to worship for most Christians; it is also a pilgrimage in its own right – the physical journey that we make to receive the wine and the bread, the sharing with others as one family, the preparation beforehand, not only of the table but of ourselves, the clearing-up of the table afterwards, and the consideration within ourselves of how this act has changed us. We are not the same after we have received Communion as we were beforehand. It's like climbing to the top of a hill; the journey and the view are never the same two days running, and we who travel do not come down precisely the same person who went up. We say Communion, though we have sometimes held an 'Agape' service where not everyone in the pilgrimage group was agreeable to sharing Communion together. Whichever you do, these thoughts will apply to both.

With pilgrims it is good to involve them as much as possible within the service, not just by the writing and reading of prayers, or reading from the Bible, but also in the preparation of the 'table'. One suggestion is that each person, as they enter the room or area, places a piece of bread on to the Communion plate. You just need to make sure that the pieces are of a suitable size and quantity beforehand. Another idea is to pass around the jug with the wine in and the Communion cup and ask each person to pour a small amount of wine into the chalice. At the same time they might give thanks out loud for one thing. Do, though, measure the amount of wine beforehand so there is enough for everyone and make sure that the cup will hold it all! This can encapsulate the time of prayer in the service and could be amended to be a time of supplication or praise as you wish.

John Gore's contribution at the end of this Section is a Holy Communion that was used by a group of walkers in a desolate spot. He had given each of us a small stone at the beginning of the walk and asked us to hold it or put it in our pocket during our journey to the site where we would celebrate Communion. The day was wet and misty and there were no views over what was in any case a desolate moorland area.

We stopped to celebrate by the most intact wall on the route in order to have at least a modest amount of shelter. The Eucharist was wonderful. We sang along with the curlews and the sounds of the reservoir water lapping on the banks. We replied along with the sheep munching the grass close to us, and we shared the bread and wine John had carried. It was a celebration of all that life could hold and has the capacity to hold if we but open ourselves to it.

Our offerings were the small stones that we had carried, and as we left them in that place, a small part of each of us was left behind. We received so much from that Communion service.

Pilgrim Tokens

In earlier days pilgrims wore or carried 'tokens' of their particular pilgrimage. In this way people would not only recognise that they were on pilgrimage and hopefully not molest them on their journey, but also would be able to know at a glance to which pilgrimage site they were heading – and even in some cases the nation to which they belonged: the English white, the French red, and the Flemish green.

The signs were usually badges sewn on to the hat or hung around the neck or pinned on clothes. There are still several moulds from which these medieval signs were cast: there are a number in the British Museum. Also there, are some tokens that have been found which were cast or dropped into rivers.

The cross was traditionally used for those travelling to Jerusalem, and this would also have two crossed leaves of palms on it; to St Catherine's tomb on Mount Sinai, the wheel; to Rome, the heads of St Peter and St Paul, or the keys; to St James of Compostella, the scallop or oyster shell; to Canterbury, a bell or the head of the saint on a brooch, or a leaden ampulla filled with water from a well near the tomb; to Walsingham, the Virgin and child; to Amiens, the head of St John the Baptist; and so on.

These symbols have continued through time until today, and travellers to any of the places listed above will recognise the symbols being used then as still being used.

The second aspect of 'tokens' of pilgrimage is those items that are collected during the pilgrimage itself. Most of the routes that people take to a pilgrimage site are well-known ones, and those along the route anticipate the travellers and their needs, so will already have such items for sale. One example is along the 100-kilometre route of St Cuthbert's Way in the north of England, which starts at Melrose and finishes at Lindisfarne – Holy Island. No matter how small the village on that route, wherever there is a shop they would be selling something with the St Cuthbert's cross on it. This might be a postcard, a book, a sew-on badge, a route map, and even tea towels: the route itself is anticipating the goal.

Many pilgrim sites have become incredibly commercialised over the years and it is easy to be overtaken by buying souvenirs. We might distinguish between souvenirs and pilgrimage tokens for a moment. We see a pilgrimage token as being something that reminds the pilgrim of the real meaning of their pilgrimage. This could be water taken from a holy spring, such as one of the wells in Wales, or the waters in Lourdes; it could be a shell from the beach at Lindisfarne, or even a prayer card from the site itself. It could equally well be a piece of expensive jewellery bought in a shop in the town. The actual article is not important, nor is the cost itself, but it must help the pilgrim to go back in time and place to that moment of pilgrimage: that moment or moments when she or he perhaps heard God, knew his presence, even saw him face-to-face; when there was a time of change, of hope, faith and love. A souvenir, on the other hand, is something pretty that reminds us of an outing or holiday.

Some pilgrimage tokens are available today over the internet and we have noted in the Practical Section a website where one can order items that are guaranteed to have come from Jerusalem. The set includes:

1. An olive wood crucifix
2. Holy anointing olive oil pressed in Bethlehem
3. Purifying holy water from Jordan River
4. Holy earth from the hills of Bethlehem
5. Frankincense from Jerusalem

Prayers at the start and end of pilgrimage

The prayers used later in this section are based on those of pilgrim blessing in the Sarum Missal (London 1868, 595-6), and can be used to mark both 'ends' of the pilgrimage. The purpose of the prayers in the Dedication Service is to strengthen and bless the pilgrim(s) and to make a clear starting point to the pilgrimage – this is no longer preparation; it is the pilgrimage itself. Therefore, it is best taking place as near to the departure date as possible. Churches where members are going to undertake a pilgrimage as a group may like to include these prayers within their normal Sunday service on the week before they depart. In this way it will also help to involve the other church members who are staying behind, as will be seen from the continuing request for their prayerful support. It has been written for a number of pilgrims but if there is only one pilgrim it is simple to change it.

The returning prayers are not just to thank God and the congregation for their support, but they are a way of recognising that the pilgrims who have returned are not the same as they were when they left and that they will also continue to change, grow and develop.

Morning and Evening Prayer

Adapted from The Book of Common Prayer

Morning Prayer

Leader   Rend your heart, and not your garments, and turn unto the Lord your God;

All   For he is gracious and merciful, slow to anger, and of great kindness, and repenteth him of the evil.

Leader   Dearly beloved brethren, the Scripture moveth us in sundry places to acknowledge and confess our manifold sins and wickedness; and that we should not dissemble nor cloak them before the face of Almighty God our heavenly Father; but confess them with an humble, lowly, penitent, and obedient heart; to the end that we may obtain forgiveness of the same, by his infinite goodness and mercy.

And although we ought at all times humbly to acknowledge our sins before God; yet ought we most chiefly so to do, when we assemble and meet together.

Wherefore I pray and beseech you, as many as are here present, to accompany me with a pure heart, and a humble voice, unto the throne of the heavenly grace, saying with me:

All   Almighty and most merciful Father, we have erred, and strayed from thy ways like lost sheep. We have followed too much the devices and desires of our own hearts.

Leader   We have offended against thy holy laws. We have left undone those things which we ought to have done; and we have done those things which we ought not to have done; and there is no health in us.

All	But thou, O Lord, have mercy upon us, miserable offenders. Spare thou them, O God, which confess their faults. Restore thou them that are penitent; according to thy promises declared unto mankind in Christ Jesu our Lord.
Leader	And grant, O most merciful Father, for his sake, that we may heareafter live a godly, righteous, and sober life, to the glory of thy holy name.
All	Amen.

Leader	O Lord, open thou our lips.
All	And our mouth shall shew forth thy praise.
Leader	O God, make speed to save us.
All	O Lord, make haste to help us.

Leader	O come, let us sing unto the Lord; let us heartily rejoice in the strength of our salvation.
All	We praise thee, O God: we acknowledge thee to be the Lord.
Leader	All the earth doth worship thee: the Father ever-lasting.
All	To thee all Angels cry aloud; the heavens and all the powers therein.
Leader	O Lord, let thy mercy lighten upon us: as our trust is in thee.
All	O Lord, in thee have I trusted: let me never be confounded.

Old Testament Reading and/or New Testament Reading

A time of prayer

Leader	O be joyful in the Lord, all ye lands: serve the Lord with gladness and come before his presence with a song.

415

All   O go your way into his gates with thanskgiving, and into his courts with praise: be thankful unto him, and speak good of his name.

Leader   For the Lord is gracious, his mercy is everlasting: and his truth endureth from generation to generation.

All   Amen.

Leader   O Lord, shew thy mercy upon us.

All   And grant us thy salvation.

Leader   O Lord, save the Queen.

All   And mercifully hear us when we call upon thee.

Leader   Endue thy ministers with righteousness.

All   And make thy chosen people joyful.

Leader   O Lord, save thy people.

All   And bless thine inheritance.

Leader   Give us peace in our time, O Lord.

All   Because there is none other that fighteth for us, but only thou, O God.

Leader   O God, make clean our hearts within us.

All   And take not thy holy Spirit from us.

Leader   O Lord, our heavenly Father, Almighty and Everlasting God, who hast safely brought us to the beginning of this day; defend us in the same with thy mighty power; and grant that this day we fall into no sin, neither run into any kind of danger; but that all our doings may be ordered by thy governance, to do always what is righteous in thy sight; through Jesus Christ our Lord.

All   Amen.

All   The grace of our Lord Jesus Christ, and the love of God, and the fellowship of the Holy Ghost, be with us all evermore. Amen.

Evening Prayer

Leader   Harken to these words from the Psalms: I acknowledge my transgressions, and my sin is ever before me. Hide thy face from my sins, and blot out all mine iniquities.

All   O God the Father of heaven, have mercy upon us miserable sinners.

Leader   Remember not, Lord, our offences, nor the offences of our forefathers; neither take thou vengeance of our sins: spare us, good Lord, spare thy people, whom thou hast redeemed with thy precious blood, and be not angry with us for ever.

All   Spare us, good Lord.

Leader   From all blindness of heart; from pride, vainglory and hypocrisy; from envy, hatred and malice, and all uncharitableness.

All   Good Lord, deliver us.

Leader   From fornication, and all other deadly sin; and from the deceits of the world, the flesh, and the devil.

All   Good Lord, deliver us.

Leader   From lightning and tempest; from plague, pestilence and famine; from battle and murder, and from sudden death.

All   Good Lord, deliver us.

Leader   By the mystery of the holy Incarnation; by thy holy Nativity and Circumcision; by thy Baptism, Fasting and Temptation.

All   Good Lord, deliver us.

Leader	By thine Agony and bloody Sweat; by thy Cross and Passion; by thy precious Death and Burial; by thy glorious Resurrection and Ascension; and by the coming of the Holy Ghost.
All	Good Lord, deliver us.

Leader	In all time of our tribulation; in all time of our wealth; in the hour of death, and in the day of judgement.
All	Good Lord, deliver us.

All   Our Father, which art in heaven, hallowed be thy name. Thy kingdom come. Thy will be done, in earth as it is in heaven. Give us this day our daily bread. And forgive us our trespasses, as we forgive them that trespass against us. And lead us not into temptation; but deliver us from evil. For thine is the kingdom, the power, and the glory, for ever and ever. Amen.

Leader	O Lord, open thou our lips.
All	And our mouth shall shew forth thy praise.

Leader	O God, make speed to save us.
All	O Lord, make haste to help us.

All   Glory be to the Father, and to the Son and to the Holy Ghost. As it was in the beginning, is now, and ever shall be, world without end. Amen.

Leader	Praise ye the Lord.
All	The Lord's name be praised.

Old Testament Reading and/or New Testament Reading

A time of prayer

418

Leader Lord, now lettest thou thy servant depart in peace: according to thy word.

All For mine eyes have seen thy salvation, which thou hast prepared before the face of all people.

Leader Almighty God, Father of all mercies, we thine unworthy servants do give thee most humble and hearty thanks for all thy goodness and loving kindness to us and all people. We bless thee for our creation, preservation and all the blessings of this life; but above all, for thine inestimable love in the redemption of the world by our Lord Jesus Christ; for the means of grace, and for the hope of glory.

And, we beseech thee, give us that due sense of all thy mercies, that our hearts may be unfeignedly thankful, and that we shew forth thy praise, not only with our lips, but in our lives; through Jesus Christ our Lord.

All Amen.

All The grace of our Lord Jesus Christ, and the love of God, and the fellowship of the Holy Ghost, be with us all evermore. Amen.

A prayer written by Anne Brontë

Oppressed with sin and woe,
a burdened heart I bear;
oppressed by many a mighty foe,
yet will I not despair.

With this polluted heart,
I dare to come to thee –

holy and mighty as thou art –
for thou wilt pardon me.

I feel that I am weak,
and prone to every sin;
but thou, who giv'st to those who seek,
wilt give me strength within.

I need not fear my foes;
I need not yield to care;
I need not sink beneath my woes,
for thou wilt answer prayer.

In my redeemer's name,
I give myself to thee;
and, all unworthy as I am,
my God will cherish me.

A Meditation on a Bunch of Yellow Roses Still in Bud

This meditation, led by Gillian Houghton, was designed for a group of pilgrims who were very much looking for their 'ways'. Each wanted to know where to go next in life, and although they all had some idea, they were looking for a time of reflection and peace to hear God's will for them. This time of meditation was just one part of the whole weekend's pilgrimage.

Gillian spoke fairly quietly and slowly about the following things, as we all looked at the bunch of roses and thought about what she was saying. Not everything was relevant to all of us, but there were one or two things that struck a chord in us all. At the end we were asked to choose a rose to take home with us. These were the headings around which Gillian spoke:

How roses grow

- Manure is good for them, though not something that we necessarily would choose.

- They bloom in the most unlikely places and are still absolutely beautiful. They don't need anywhere special to grow. They don't have to have a certain place or background or inter-planting arrangements.

Consider their growth

- They have thorns which can make them hard to hold – sometimes we, too, are difficult.

- These have tightly curled buds, there's no telling what they may yet come out like, or even if they will come out.

- They need light to get this far and to continue to bloom – the light of the world.

- Their flower is one of beauty, they give joy to others and to God.

- They could go on to complete fulfilment of their potential and to live life in all its fullness, or they could stay as they are; this will depend on many things.

We are called to flourish as roses and to tend the roses around us and, yes, it is a bed of roses – sometimes it's very painful!

Eucharist on the Hoof

John Gore

The day was dull and cold and promising rain. Ten of us set off on a walk with a difference. We were to stop at various points along the way, previously planned, for short meditations. So we were walking prayerfully. But it was also a Sunday, and so we planned to stop about halfway to celebrate the Eucharist together.

We were a mixed bunch – Methodists, Roman Catholic, Anglicans. The fact that I, the only priest in the group, an Anglican, was to preside at this open-air Eucharist did not seem to be a problem.

We walked for a couple of hours, deeper and deeper into the wild moorland between West and North Yorkshire. We looked around for our Eucharistic venue. No perfect spot presented itself, so we gathered at the lee of a wall in a rough semi-circle, placing a plastic plate with a bread roll, and a plastic cup with wine on a not-too-flat stone. A simple order of service was handed around.

We turned to God in penitence and received the assurance of forgiveness, we prayed the Collect for the Sunday, proclaimed the Gospel for the day and drew from it some salient points to carry with us. Bread was taken and wine poured. A form of the Eucharistic prayer was led by the president. Communion was shared, passed from one to another. We thanked God, shared a blessing, packed up, and went on in the peace of Christ.

For those planning an open-air Eucharist your needs are: a suitable rite, bread, wine, water, a plate and cup.

The Rite and Minister

It would need to be a rite authorised by one Church or other, and acceptable to the group. Some Churches have a suitably short Eucharistic prayer authorised for use at home communions for the sick that could be used. The minister of the Eucharist would need to be someone authorised in his/her own Church for this purpose and, again, acceptable to the group. The rite would need to be pared down to the essentials: preparation/confession, Collect, Gospel reading, short sermon or meditation, prayers, short Eucharistic prayer, taking of bread and wine, thanksgiving, and then a final blessing. It has to be borne in mind that it is very likely that the wind will be blowing and the rain falling; so wordiness is to be avoided.

Bread and Wine
Any piece of bread and any kind of wine will do.

Plate and Cup
A plastic plate to hold the bread and a plastic cup to hold the wine are all that are required.

Water
Water from a little plastic water bottle will be needed to wash the plate and cup after use.

The venue
This will be dictated by the circumstances, but shelter from the wind and rain helps with the management of the bread and wine.

Services Before and After a Pilgrimage

Dedication Service at the Start of a Pilgrimage

In order to follow the blessing service below, it is suggested that each pilgrim brings with them the items that they will each have marking them out as pilgrims together. These will almost certainly include at least one of the items included below, but could also include flight tickets and luggage labels, depending on the pilgrimage.

Each pilgrim should also bring a small card with his or her own name on it. This should be folded in half so that it can stand up.

Leader   The Lord be with you.
Pilgrims   And with thy Spirit.

The Leader invites all the pilgrims to place their tokens of pilgrimage together at the front.

Leader   Let us pray.
              O Lord Jesus Christ, you came here and walked upon the earth to seek all who were lost and bring them to everlasting life. You showed us your Father and when you left you sent your Holy Spirit that we might never be alone. You told us that we should always try to live holy lives, and to seek to follow you in all things. We call upon you now, to bless these tokens of pilgrimage that these pilgrims have chosen to wear at their side or hang around their necks or carry in their hands.
              May your hand protect these pilgrims on their journeys so that they may reach the joys of

425

everlasting vision through you, O Saviour of the World, who lives and reigns in the unity of the Holy Spirit, God for ever and ever.

Pilgrims Amen.

The leader gives a bag to each pilgrim, saying:

Leader In the name of our Lord Jesus Christ, receive this scrip, the bag of pilgrimage, for holding things that will support and comfort you in your pilgrimage. With it, may you overcome all hardships and reach your goal; and when your journey has ended may you return to us in health. Through Christ our Lord.

Pilgrims Amen.

The leader gives a walking stick to each pilgrim, saying:

Leader In the name of our Lord Jesus Christ, receive this walking stick, the staff of pilgrimage, for your support in travelling. With it, may you overcome all doubts and fears and safely reach the place where you desire to go; and having obediently finished your journey, return again with joy. Through Christ our Lord.

Pilgrims Amen.

The leader gives a badge to each pilgrim, saying:

Leader In the name of our Lord Jesus Christ receive this badge (T-shirt) as a sign of your pilgrimage. Wear it to remind you of the solemn journey that you are undertaking. Remember that as you wear this, it is not a holiday that you are on; it is something that is far more refreshing than that. May your soul be refreshed and filled with the Holy Spirit during this time. Through Christ our Lord.

Pilgrims   Amen.

The leader gives a pair of boots or shoes to each pilgrim, saying:

Leader   In the name of our Lord Jesus Christ receive these boots/shoes for your use in your pilgrimage. With them, may you walk in the paths of righteousness and truth, justice and mercy. May you follow the right path to your journey's end, and then by the grace of God be returned to us. Through Christ our Lord.

Pilgrims   Amen.

The leader blesses the sign of the cross that each pilgrim will carry, saying:

Leader   O God, whose power is invincible and whose pity cannot be measured, you are the aid and sole comfort of pilgrims. We ask you to bless these crosses which will be worn and carried, to remind each pilgrim of that ultimate journey that Jesus made to the cross, and which will be to them a sign of your strength against temptation, a defence against all difficulties, a protection along the journey, and a security to them on every side.

Pilgrims   Amen.

The leader gives a cross to each pilgrim, saying:
(If no crosses are to be carried, the leader could make the sign of the cross on each pilgrim's forehead.)

Leader   In the name of our Lord Jesus Christ, receive this cross of our Lord Jesus Christ, that through it you may be given protection, blessings and strength during your pilgrimage; and that you will return to us in safety and wealth of spirit. Through Christ our Lord.

Pilgrims   Amen.

The Pilgrims are invited to place their name cards at the front where they will stand until the pilgrims return. As each steps forward to do this, they should say just a couple of words about (a) what they are looking forward to most on the pilgrimage and (b) what they are most fearful about.

The concluding prayer is said by those who are staying behind only.

All who will stay behind

With these tokens of pilgrimage we, who stay here behind, give you also our love and support. We will pray for you on your journey, that this time will be very special and bring you ever closer to the Lord God; that you will not return as you are now but be forever changed and more like him. Through Jesus Christ, our Lord, who with the Father and the Holy Spirit, lives and reigns one God, world without end. Amen.

Prayer on return home from pilgrimage

This follows on from the short prayers given above said at the start of the pilgrimage and, again, you may just want to choose those parts that are relevant to your group.

Leader   The Lord be with you.
Pilgrims   And with your Spirit.

The Leader invites all the pilgrims to place their pilgrimage tokens (this refers to tokens the pilgrims have gained during their pilgrimage and not to the articles that were blessed before they went on pilgrimage) together at the front.

Leader   O God, whose power is invincible and whose pity cannot be measured, you are the aid and sole comfort of pilgrims. We give you thanks for bringing home safely to us these pilgrims, who are not the same as they were when they left us last *(day or date)* for they have journeyed with you and towards you. We praise you for your mercy and graciousness to them, for meeting their needs in ways that we could never have dreamed of, let alone have asked for. Your bounty is beyond our human understanding. Through Christ our Lord.

Pilgrims   Amen.

The leader calls pilgrims out in turn to the front to receive back their name card. As they come forward pilgrims should say just a few words about (a) what was the most important thing that they gained from the pilgrimage, or the best thing, or the thing they liked most, and (b) what, if anything, they didn't like, or liked least: in this way the congregation, who have been praying and support-ing them, hear some of their news.

Leader   We thank you for those tales of travel, of excite-ment, of new experiences, and also for those things that, whilst not wanted or enjoyed were somehow part of their pilgrimage. We pray that through them the pilgrims may be drawn yet closer and nearer to you. We ask you to bless these tokens gained by the pilgrims whilst on their journeys that they may be to them a lasting memory of a time that was very special and holy, and given to you, Lord Jesus Christ, Son of God, Lord of heaven and earth.

Pilgrims   Amen.

The pilgrims retrieve their tokens at the end of the service after the congregation has had time to see them.

SECTION TEN
Photographic Meditation

Planning a Photographic Meditation

A photographic meditation can help pilgrims in two ways. Firstly, it draws their attention on the day itself to a specific view or object, and, secondly, it gives pilgrims a record of the pilgrimage to take away with them and think about at a later date.

There are many meditation books which are written to be read by individuals, either on a daily basis or as a short series. Some of these use illustration stories from the Bible or from daily life; others use simple drawings or artwork. Some use photographs of stained glass showing religious pictures from around Europe to illustrate the theme for those days.

In photographic meditations photographs of the actual place of the pilgrimage, its surroundings and key features are included to act as illustrations and to draw pilgrims closer into God.

There are two key ways to begin designing a photographic meditation: to use the sights of the pilgrimage journey in a free-flowing way to draw out a variety of issues, or to have a theme already in mind and find opportunities for images that reflect aspects of that theme. Both are equally valid and helpful and it will depend on the style of the pilgrimage and on your own preference.

Where the pilgrimage has the walk as central, then the free-flowing style works best while the theme style is more contrived. God talks to us in the everyday if we just open our eyes and ears, but if we try to put him in a box it's not always successful.

On the other hand, if the pilgrimage is being combined with other activities, then the theme approach can be used to hold them all together.

Using the sights of the pilgrimage journey in a free-flowing way to draw out a variety of issues

What is key to this type of designing is to spend considerable time in planning beforehand and then to spend quite a lot of time in the place where the pilgrimage will take place. It's about being open to God and allowing him to use our eyes to see what he would have us see. We may all remember visiting a village and thinking to ourselves, 'There's nothing here. Why have we come?' On one occasion, having walked through the village, we looked back on it and saw that the last house had a very vigorous climbing plant growing up the side of it. As there were windows on that side – two up and two down – the climber had been cut so as not to obstruct the views from the windows. This gave it a clearly cut cross shape, a cross made out of a living plant, a trained plant. The prayerful thought came: 'Lord, make us living crosses for you. Let others look at us and see you.'

When planning a pilgrimage over a large space of time or place, such as a 100-kilometre walk, it's really essential that we read as much about the area as we can beforehand. The pilgrims who come on the pilgrimage will already know some things about the area before they come, because they will have been doing some preparation too, and it's important that what we include in the meditations does not conflict with some local history or facts.

A tall tower could be used to illustrate God's greatness, but if it was actually built for some negative reason, then pilgrims will find it hard to forget that negative and this may even rub off into their thinking of God. The 'Why did he let it happen?' argument. Not that there should not be those discussions, but they should not happen by careless planning. There's so much conflict in the world and in our lives that the whole issue of conflict and pain often comes into a meditation.

The other thing that is key to a good photographic meditation is having the opportunity to spend time in the pilgrimage place. Again, this needs to be done in a prayerful manner, rather than just going there on holiday to take a few snaps. It's more about getting a feel for the place and allowing the atmosphere of the place itself to get into us.

When Jo did a series of meditations based on a garden, she spent time sitting or standing in different parts of the garden to feel what it was like. Parts of the garden had more wind movement than others, parts were noisier – and this varied at different times of the day. Some parts had deliberately been set aside for quietness and being solitary, and there were other parts that were more like a train station with people rushing through on their way to somewhere else. As Jo sat, huddled in two jumpers and a coat against the North Yorkshire March weather, she was able to notice the movement of the ants, enjoy the company of the frogs, and gaze at the wonder of a group of flying doves and pigeons circling above in low swoops for at least twenty minutes. She remembers that she could almost feel the bulbs growing not very far underground.

By spending this time in quietness – and we could either call it 'openness' or 'contemplation' – ideas may come flooding in about how these different aspects may be conveyed through the twin images of photographs and words to visitors to the garden. We don't think the end results would have been the same without time being spent. As it turned out, the whole day was cloudy and overcast and not much good for photos, especially as they would be printed in black and white only. So Jo made a list of what she wanted to take, where from, the angles, and so on; then returned the next morning in glorious sunshine to whip around to take three rolls of film.

Finding what to photograph

We are always very conscious when walking with a group of pilgrims that much of the positive experience comes from members of the group talking with each other. The only trouble

435

with a pilgrimage walk is that we can spend so much time talking with our neighbour that we don't actually look around and notice what is going on. By using photographs this encourages pilgrims to be looking out at the same time as they talk.

It's important that the photographs are not of such tiny or out-of-the-way things that pilgrims won't find them: there's nothing wrong with photographing the obvious. The only time to avoid doing that is when it is a landmark that is shown in absolutely every tourist guide of the area; in that case take a prominent detail of it or take the view from it.

If, when out walking, pilgrims don't naturally find the place or item photographed, it's important to point it out to them; otherwise it becomes a strange sort of competition, and much is lost if not damaged. Pilgrims will also, hopefully, look back at the photographs and be able to recall the moment they saw it and how they felt at the time, and so on.

Designing with a theme in mind

If you are planning a themed pilgrimage, you will need to explore all aspects of that theme as widely as possible, so that as you visit the place(s) you will see how the different aspects will link together without that feeling of being forced or artificial.

An example might be the following for the theme of forgiveness:

- Running water to symbolise cleansing.
- Rubbish heap, bin or pile of rubbish.
- Still dirty water.
- Publicity for special offers – for example, 'Get something free with xxx here.' This could be used to symbolise forgiveness being available.
- Broken chains to symbolise freedom following forgiveness.
- Saw, chopper or similar to symbolise the breaking of those chains.

- Sign on shop door giving opening times to symbolise that God's door is always open.
- Cleaning materials.
- Recycling bins to symbolise that nothing is wasted, even our mistakes.

How to express the meditation

The challenge of using real photographs is that the same item will bring different thoughts to different people. If you have, for example, a residential home for older people, what does it make you think of? Partly this will depend on our own experiences. If we have a relative who lives in a home, we are likely to think of it differently from someone who has never been in one. Not that even then everyone would have the same thoughts. Let's just explore what people could be thinking of about the residential home. Here are some starters for you, but I'm sure you can add to the list:

- Being looked after well.
- Being content.
- Being with other people and not alone.
- Having to give up your own home.
- Losing your independence.
- Being away from your usual friends.
- Not being well enough to go out or do what you want.
- Having activities you can enjoy.
- Sharing with people you don't like.
- Being badly treated.

So, realising that the place could be viewed positively or negatively, we could write a thought that thanks God for the positive and asks for help with the negatives – for example:

Dear God, as you give us shelter in your love, as a bird

hides her chicks under her wings, we thank you for places where those who are elderly and need to be looked after can have a safe and friendly home. We ask your blessing on this place, for all who live and work here, that it may truly be a place of rest and peace. Amen.

When deciding what to write it's important to consider in what ways it could be misinterpreted or could hurt someone reading it. To thank God for something that we all take for granted is OK if we all do take it for granted! However, to thank God that we are healthy, or have a job, or live with people who love us, can hear and see, ignores and offends all those who aren't, don't or can't. When putting meditative thoughts down on paper, we need to be sensitive to the possible diverse circumstances of the different pilgrims who read and use it.

Places to use a photographic meditation

We can use this idea of photographs for a pilgrimage in any place where we can go on pilgrimage. The only absolute essential is the ability to visit the place first in order to take the photographs! The length of the pilgrimage or the number of photographs used for each day does not matter; it's simply a tool to help pilgrims.

Yorkshire Pilgrimage
Hutton-le-Hole, Lastingham and Rosedale Abbey*

I on thy path, O God,
thou God in my steps.
Bless to me, O God,
the earth beneath my foot.
Bless to me, O God,
the path whereon I go.

1. Lord, may your cross live in my life.

* Photographs for the photographic meditation: Jo White.

439

2. I can see your path, Lord – but the other one looks a lot easier.
(The path began to go uphill.)

3. Psalm 23
Even though I walk in dark places I will fear no evil.
Wherever I go you are with me, Lord.
(The path went inside a densely wooded area.)

4. Luke 24:13-35
As I walk today, Lord, make your word alive to me.
(*Both sides of the path were blooming with wild flowers.*)

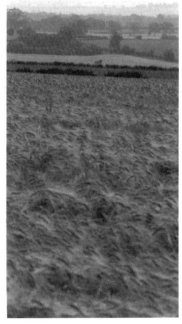

5. Matthew 12:1-14
There are rules and rules. Lord, let me understand.
(*The path went alongside a ripe cornfield.*)

6. Luke 15:1-7
Lord, if I get lost, I know I can trust you to come for me.

7. Luke 6:46-49
Lord, help me to build my life on solid ground – you.

8. Holy Spirit, blow such a wind through my life that I shall never be the same again.
(There is a derelict wind turbine in the field.)

9. Help me to sort out the rubbish from what's important, and then to dispose of the rubbish.

10. Lord, let me rest at your feet and renew my strength in your shadow.
(This cross was set up on a circular stone seat.)

11. John 7:37-39
Holy Spirit,
flow in me,
through me,
and from me.

12. John 18:15-18, 25-27
Lord, help me not to deny you
by the way I act. But when I
do – just bring me back to you.

13. Lord, may your light
shine through my life in all
I do and say.
(*Lastingham Crypt.*)

14. John 4:4-26
Lord, let your water in me become a
spring welling up to eternal life.

15. Father, I pray for those who do not know you, who do not know your love, joy and peace. Give them opportunities to hear and see your word.
(Site of an old cross now removed and only the base is still present.)

16. Lord, help me to play my part in bringing in your harvest. Help me to work with others as one team – your Church.

17. 1 Corinthians 13:1-13
Love never fails. And now these three remain: faith, hope and love. But the greatest of these is love.

18. At the end of my life, Lord God, take me home.

Mount Cross, Todmorden

SECTION ELEVEN

Children

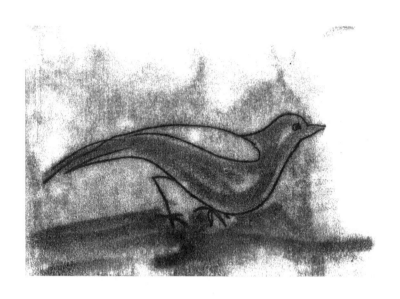

Drawing by Jane Walton-Loxton

Pilgrimage for Children

Children can take part in and benefit from the majority of pilgrimage activities that adults undertake, but it's important that the child's age and abilities are taken into account. Anyone who has ever gone for a long journey with a young child will know how tedious the cries of 'Are we there yet?' can be.

It's therefore crucial that activities are as age-appropriate as possible – though this can be difficult with a mixed-aged party of pilgrims. Even more essential is listening to the children about what they would like to do and the pace they would like to do it. Have a variety of activities so that there are plenty of changes in body positions – sitting, standing and moving around – and in levels of silence and noise; these are all key to helping children stay involved and in encouraging them to get the best out of any activity. One only has to watch a small amount of children's television to realise that concentration spans are short, information-giving time is kept to only a few minutes, and this is then reinforced by carrying out an activity.

An example of this would be talking to children about the pilgrimage that Jesus made on Good Friday when he carried the cross. This could then be reinforced by the children walking as if they had a heavy burden to carry to a place where they could lay it down. Finally we could conclude with a discussion of how it felt while carrying the load, and how it felt when it was put down.

Walking Pilgrimages

Age and experience make a huge difference to how each child reacts to a walking pilgrimage. In our experience children often have a lot more short-term energy than adults. This means that they love to run ahead to be the first, but then will stop and rest for quite a while until the rest of the party has passed them. When this happens, most of the adults will make a comment to the resting children as they pass, which gives the children a lot of positive attention, which they usually enjoy, so this encourages them. Then they will quickly catch up and go to the front again. It's only when this pattern gets disrupted, usually by those who wish to keep a closer eye on them or who want to have them close so they can point things out to them, that they become irritated and then can be 'difficult'. So, if we can somehow combine the elements of safety and learning with allowing children to go at their own intermittent pace, everyone is more likely to enjoy their day!

One way to involve children is to use photographs of objects on the walk for the children to find, rather like the photographic meditation described earlier. For this purpose the photograph needs to be very clearly of something that is quite obvious. If children find it too hard to find the object they will get frustrated and will be likely to give up the game. We could have clear directions on the paper also showing places that the children must stop and wait for the rest of the pilgrims; in this way they won't get too far ahead or even out of sight if we pace it beforehand. A simple map giving the obvious landmarks could be used with the photographs marked for where they should be found.

Another way of doing this would be to go out earlier in the day and 'hide' things along the route for the children to seek and find. We should avoid putting them out too far in advance of the walk itself or some joker is likely to remove them! For younger children these could be very obvious like a brightly coloured piece of material on the end of a four-foot pole put in the ground close to the path. For older children they could be harder to find or we might give them cryptic clues for where to look.

When they find the object the children could be asked to stay with it until the rest of the pilgrims arrive. Again, this keeps the group together so there is less risk of losing people's attention and there is also the sense of doing this as a group.

To keep children's attention during a walk, another method is to give them something to be actively and continuously looking for. Clearly whatever this is has to be of interest to the children themselves or they will soon get bored and give up. This is rather like the time-honoured long journey game we play in our car during the last few weeks coming up to Christmas, where the children (and us parents) keep a running total of how many Christmas trees we have seen in people's houses. In the last couple of years we have modernised the game to include outdoor lights, and last year we counted the number of the indoor electric candle displays in the shape of a pyramid, that are reminiscent of the Jewish menorahs used during Hanukkah.

What you count or look for will depend on where you are walking. Along a canal bank there are usually markers to show how far significant places are, or signs to show where anglers can fish from. In wooded areas we could look for a certain type of tree or birds' nests. In open fields it could be mushrooms, certain grasses, animals, or even the types of gates or stiles used. Whatever it is gives an opportunity to talk a little about it whenever one is spotted.

Making Things

Whenever children make something as part of the pilgrimage we should always put their work out on show so that everyone can see. This encourages conversation again and gives everyone ideas. Although we may need to mark each item to know who has made what, we might try and do this in a way or in a place that others will not see. Remember, this is not a competition but a pilgrimage together.

Miniature Garden

One activity we have often used is that of collecting things along the walk in order to make a miniature garden when we arrive back home. This makes the whole activity a pilgrimage

Photograph: Barbara Butler

Children find many things on a walk

– and not just the walk itself. With this we have to think carefully beforehand about the container in which each child will make their 'garden'. As the chances are that the objects used will not last long, we can assume that this is going to be a temporary garden, in which case we can use a temporary container. The temporary status is also something to tell the children about right at the very start of the activity as otherwise there can be misunderstandings and upset later.

A favourite small container is a round cheese box, one with deep sides being the easiest to keep it all together. But this does mean eating quite a lot of Camembert! These days we might equally eat lots of that delicious ice cream that comes in those nice oval dishes (just for the sake of the children, you understand!). That way the child has a lid also so can more easily take the garden home with them. You might be surprised to find out how hard it is to throw away the most temporary garden when children have taken time and effort to make it.

Before starting out, we should talk with the children about what sort of garden they could be planning as they walk along, and so what type of things, colours and textures they could be looking out for. Will it be the garden where Mary meets the 'Gardener' after the resurrection, or the Garden of Eden? Is it the garden that Jesus talked about where the mustard seed grew into a tree, or where there are birds that his father knows the number of their feathers? Of course it could be their 'own' garden, for God, of course, is everywhere, isn't he? It is in this discussion that we can either try to link what each child chooses to a biblical theme or actually give them all a theme and let each child interpret it in his or her own way.

The only thing each child actually needs to take with them on the walk is a small bag in which to put their treasures. If we can use a see-through bag this gives adults more opportunity to have a look at what each child has, and to talk about their finds as they walk along together. So often it can be difficult for adults to know what to chat with children about. Giving them something tangible to focus on can really help here, and so much teaching and learning can take place about what they have found in a relaxed informal way.

At the end of the walk we would give the children a sufficient supply of suitable earth material and somewhere to make their gardens. This can be done as a group around a suitably covered table or on their own. Again this will depend on the children, but we could use the time as an opportunity to be quiet and thinking about the garden each is making – 'Think of the care that God took when he made the earth, when he made you', for example. We should give the children a set amount of time to make their garden, and try to judge this so some aren't finished ages early and others feel rushed. In other words, we mustn't make it too long or too short, depending on the children themselves. If that does happen we should have something for those who are finished earlier than expected to be doing, such as a picture or puzzle, but we mustn't give them the clearing up – that's more likely to discourage children finishing early ever again!

We can also cut out pictures of people and animals from magazines, glue them on card, attach a small stick (lollipop stick) to the back of each and stand them in the garden if you wish. Small pieces of mirror (as long as they have smooth edges) make good 'water' features.

Talking of water features, just one last tip about gardens in small containers: don't let the children water them, or you'll end up with one very messy, sloppy garden!

Other ways to use items found on the walk

The treasures the children find on their walks can be used in a variety of ways to extend the experience of pilgrimage and to give them a tangible item at the end of the time. Here are just a few suggestions:

- *Decorated Candles*
  Use plain candles with a large diameter and cover the outside of them with a thin painting of PVA glue. The children can then press flowers, leaves and small items on to this.

When finished they may paint a thin layer of the glue over the items; it will dry clear and shiny and act as a seal over the vegetable material to stop them decomposing.

- *Leaf Plate*
This is good with strong autumn leaves that have not completely dried out and gone hard and brittle. Choose a small flat plate or even a saucer, and grease the inside of it with Vaseline and paint the back of a leaf with some PVA or paper glue and lay it on the middle of the plate. Glue on more leaves so that their edges protude a little beyond the edge of the plate. Keep the stems pointing towards the centre of the plate. When the plate is completely covered, glue some scraps of paper on top of the leaves. This will give strength. Apply about three layers of paper and glue, and more leaves to cover the paper, and finally paint glue, thinly over the whole top surface to protect it. When dry ease it off the plate and attach a small 'calendar' hanger to the back of it so that it can be hung.

- *Leaf silhouettes*
Collect different shaped leaves and different colour water paints. Place a leaf on a sheet of paper and hold it in place with your finger. Sweep the paintbrush from the middle of the leaf to over the edge of it. That way you avoid getting paint under the leaf. Do this with different leaves to build up a pattern. The end result is that the sheet of paper becomes a picture of different silhouettes, some alone and some overlapping, in different colours.

Indoor activities

When thinking of planning indoor pilgrimage activities for children, we really need to be clear in our minds what point we are trying to make, what we'd like them to learn from the activity. The activity itself is usually the last thing that we need to get right, because with the right amount of talk we can make most activities work for us. It's getting that initial thinking right that is so crucial.

Most of the aspects of pilgrimage that this book includes are equally suitable for children, but the key difference is about making it all very focused: not to let ourselves be sidelined for too long or too far, or the children are likely to miss the point. We need to balance allowing the children to talk and contribute their own ideas with keeping to the necessary timetable and to the central theme. We should try to make the pilgrimage point in a way that means something to them. The term 'global warming' may have little if any meaning, but they may already have experienced directly having their homes or places near to where they live being flooded. Here are a few examples:

Making a picture based on a circle

Patterns based on circles are not restricted to any one faith. Celtic patterns and mandalas both share the use of the circle.

Celtic patterns use three basic designs – spirals, birds and animals, and knotwork. Probably the best-known examples of Celtic patterns are in the Book of Kells housed in Dublin and in the Lindisfarne Gospel held in the British Library, London.

Mandala is a Sanskrit word meaning *centre* and *circle*. It is said to convey the notion that any centre is tied to its circumference and any circumference is always determined by its centre. Together they represent a wholeness which may be meditated on.

Examples of mandalas abound in nature. Every cell in our body, for instance, is a living mandala. So is the iris of our eye, a snow crystal, a bird's nest and the planet earth itself.

Individual designs in mandalas vary greatly, but they always have the following characteristics: a centre, cardinal points that can be contained in a circle, and some form of symmetry.

They can be very simple or extremely complex as in ancient Tibetan religious designs, Navajo sand paintings, and huge stained glass windows in medieval cathedrals.

Some suggestions for making circle patterns:

(a) Circle pictures

Skills needed: an ability to pick up small pieces of paper or string.
Material needed: Cut-out 8-inch diameter circles in strong paper, coloured paper (this could be from magazines), pieces of wool, ribbon, lace, paper glue.
Time needed: Approximately 5 minutes.

The children decorate their cut-out circle in any way they choose. This can be as simple or as complex as their abilities and time allow. You could make much smaller circles and ask children to make a number of them. These, when dry, could then be hung from a metal coat hanger as a mobile; use a needle and thread to sew through each circle and then hang each at different lengths on the hanger.

(b) Colouring already printed patterns

Skills needed: An ability to colour inside the lines.
Material needed: Pre-printed pattern within a circle.
Time needed: Approximately 5-10 minutes.

There are a number of pre-printed patterned colouring books that are available in good stationery shops. These can be used just as they are, as they allow the children to colour creatively what they see within the pattern and are quite unlimited in the possibilities. For less able children you could draw more simple designs and photocopy them.

(c) Collage of circles

Skills needed: An ability to draw round things and cut out.
Material needed: Strong background paper to glue circles on to, coloured paper, magazine pictures, different-sized circular articles to draw around (saucer, small plate, eggcup), Sellotape, paper glue, scissors, dark felt-tip pens.
Time needed: Any length depending on abilities of children and how much preparation you have completed beforehand.

Circle painting by Hannah, aged 3 years

The children draw round the different-sized circular objects with a dark pen so that it is easy to see, on the different magazine pictures or coloured paper. Then cut out each circle and place them on the background paper to make a pattern.

(d) A simple lacy pattern in a circle
This is similar to the snowflake patterns children make out of white paper and hang by a thread in the window at Christmas time, but here it is the holes that we will be 'keeping'.

Skills needed: It needs care not to tear the newspaper when colouring through it. If this is likely, use a slightly stronger paper such as from a magazine.
Time needed: Approximately 15 minutes.
Material needed: Newspaper or magazine, plain paper, felt-tip pens, Sellotape and scissors.

Using the newspaper draw as large a circle as you want the finished picture to be. Cut it out and fold it into 4 or 8 parts. Draw a lacy pattern on the folds of the circle and cut it out. Open out the paper circle and Sellotape it firmly on to a sheet of plain paper. Colour the pattern on to the paper with felt-tips. Very carefully draw around the outside of the newspaper circle in a dark pen. When completely coloured carefully remove the newspaper.

(e) High-technology circle T-shirt
This is for those who like the high-tech approach! You will need a scanner and a printer on your computer for this. You can iron the finished transfer on to any material; here we've suggested the children bring their own T-shirts. The finished result is a 'plastic' coloured picture (or black and white depending on your printer) on the material. There is also a low-tech way of putting paper pictures on to fabric available from most good art and craft shops. This is sold in a tube that you spread over the picture and almost glue on to the fabric. It takes longer than the high-tech way so do allow for that.

Skills needed: An ability to draw or colour already printed patterns.

Material needed: Felt-tip pens, paper, a pair of compasses, computer with scanner and printer, special transfer paper available from most good stationers and craft shops (this is placed in the computer printer and can then be ironed on to material). The children should bring their own T-shirts.

Time needed: Approx 15 minutes to do picture, but then time is needed to scan each one using a standard drawing package, or even using drawing tools within the word processing software. Then you need to iron the transfer on to the T-shirt – though children could take their picture home for an adult to help them there.

With a pair of compasses draw a circle on a piece of paper. Draw concentric circles inside it. Colour the different bands in different colours. The brighter the colours used, the clearer the finished picture will be. When the picture is complete, scan it into the computer and print it on to the special transfer paper, following the manufacturer's instructions. Iron it, as given on the instructions, on to the T-shirt.

(f) Celtic knot pattern in a circle as a picture or a cushion cover pattern

The essence of Celtic knotwork patterns is that the 'ribbons' have, like God, no start and no end. They also entwine all the time – they go over and under in turn each time they meet another ribbon or even a different part of the same ribbon. One part never dominates the other but there is a sharing and a sense of taking it in turns.

Skills needed: This activity needs persistence as the item has to be traced a number of times, and then gone over again. Also the child must understand when a line goes 'over' or goes 'under' another. To make the cushion cover we have suggested using Wonderweb that needs ironing with a warm iron, but you could sew the ribbons in place.

Time needed: Approximately 30 minutes for a picture, and up to 2 hours for a cushion front.

Material needed for a picture: Greaseproof or tracing paper, dark felt-tip pen, pencil and rubber, coloured crayons or felt-tip pens, and scissors.

You will also need for a cushion cover: Material for the cover itself, one colour of decorative material (this could be binding, lace, ribbon, or similar), Wonderweb (or similar) that will hold material to material when ironed (you can buy this in most supermarkets and sewing shops).

Cut out a circle in the greaseproof paper as large as you want the finished design to be. Fold into 8. On one side draw in a dark pen a ribbon-like pattern that travels from one side to the other. Draw in a dark pen a second ribbon pattern that crosses the first but still travels from one side to the other. Open out the paper one fold only and trace the design on to the blank side. Open out the paper one more fold and trace the design on to the blank side. Continue to do this until all the paper has the design on it. Place the design under the piece of paper you want to have as the final picture and with a soft pencil trace the design. Take away the tracing paper – do *not* throw it away until the end though, just in case you need it! Make a faint mark at the beginning of one of the ribbons, and following that one ribbon, mark each crossing so that it goes alternately under and over until it gets back to where you put the mark at the beginning. It should always come back to the start in the right order. If it hasn't, then check that you haven't missed a crossing somewhere. If you have only two ribbons, then the second ribbon's 'unders' and 'overs' should automatically be completed when you did the first ribbon's. But do check those just in case. If you have used more ribbons then mark these in the same manner. With the chosen colour, colour in the ribbons so that you can clearly see where the crossings are and which goes 'over' and which goes 'under'.

A Celtic knot may be in many shapes

To make the cushion pattern, cut out individual lengths of the decorative ribbon to match the lengths of the ribbon from where it emerges from an 'under' to where it goes down to the next 'under' starting at where you have marked the 'beginning'. Pin it to the right place on the cushion material and, using the Wonderweb, iron it in place. Continue in this way, completing one piece at a time, and making sure you go under and over, until all the ribbon is in place. Finish making the cushion in the normal way.

Other Activities

Painted eggs or pebbles

Eggs have often been painted at Easter time, and many of the symbols used have mixed Christian symbols of the Church with the earlier pagan emblems of healing and new life. However they are applied, the basic symbols put onto eggs contained the same message: the sun for good fortune, flowers for love and charity, and an endless line for eternity.

Birds featured prominently, especially the phoenix – used to symbolise the Resurrection in medieval Christian art. Today they are often overtaken by the peacock or the lily plant.

In areas of the Christian Orthodox church they would put the letters XV meaning Christos Vaskrese – Christ is risen.

In pilgrimage, decorating an egg could be used to allow children to experience for themselves the time and attention to detail that is needed to make something so detailed – a sign of creation, the detail of God still at work in the world today.

Skills needed: Must be able to handle a boiled egg in its shell without breaking it, or you could use large pebbles that the children could collect first.

Time needed: Approximately 10 minutes.

Material needed: One hard-boiled egg for each child. (Remember this egg is *not* for eating and you need it to be uncracked and as hard as possible or it may break when the child presses on it. Put the egg in cold water and bring it very slowly to a simmer and leave it at that heat for approximately 30 minutes, then take it off the heat and let it cool in the pan in the water. Only take it out when it is absolutely cold.) Newspaper or plastic cloth (a flattened, clean rubbish bag will be fine) to place them on afterwards, cardboard egg boxes cut up to be a stand for each individual egg when dry, pencils, felt-tip pens, or paints, methylated spirits.

Preparation: Whether you use paint or felt-tip pens, they can only be applied successfully to a grease-free surface, so clean the eggshell with methylated spirits first. You can buy it at most chemist or hardware shops.

Give all the children a specific theme – for example, draw a picture of a bird or an animal, colour a pattern that has the sign of the cross somewhere in it. Tell them how much time they have to complete the task. Remind them what the object of the activity is – not a competition, but to get an idea of attention and time passing. Talk with each child as she/he is working so that you have an idea of what each is planning and thinking. When completed, ask each child to talk about their work, prompt them if necessary from your own conversations with each.

Footprints

This is an activity related to our pilgrimage to the communion rail: to allow children a sense that the walk which they take on a Sunday morning alone, or with their family, up to the altar to receive a blessing or the bread and wine is itself a pilgrimage. We choose to make that journey; we walk to receive a special sign of God's presence and love for each of us; we travel where many others have walked before us and many others walk behind us; we are a part of the family of God.

Before beginning, we should check with the church leader that he or she is happy for us to place the paper there during the next Communion Service. It is possible that the paper could make it slippery for less stable people, so they may need to be accompanied across it.

The finished paper will be placed on the approach to the altar from the nave area – the aisle that is at right angles to the altar where people normally walk and wait their turn to kneel or stand at the rail.

Skills needed: Must either be able to stand still for a couple of minutes or take off their shoes.

Time needed: Approximately five minutes per child or less if they are able to colour for themselves.

Material needed: A long length of wallpaper or lining paper, different coloured felt-tip pens.

Measure the length of paper needed. Ideally it should be two widths of paper wide so that one is for the pilgrimage to the communion rail and the other is for the pilgrimage back into the world. Give each child a different colour pen. Ask them to draw around their foot or take off their shoe and put one shoe at the start of the paper. Then they draw round their other foot or shoe, moving up the paper and so on until they reach the altar. They repeat this, going back from the altar on the other piece of paper. You should finish with rows of over-lapping footprints in different colours all going in the same direction on each paper. Place the finished paper in the church at the measured spot. When people next go up to the altar rail we should ask them to walk on the paper and 'feel' the footprints of those who have gone before – those that can be seen, and others that we cannot but whom we still remember.

Candle holders

The use of lights and candles is very popular in pilgrimages. The symbolism of light is used in all religions as a positive force against evil, and something to celebrate. These candle holders could be used to help celebrate the season of the year, such as Diwali or Christmas, or they could be used in their own right as a sign that the children are not alone in their pilgrimage but that they have the light always with them: a reminder of the everlasting light, that light will overcome darkness, Jesus the way, the truth and the light.

Skills needed: Little skill is needed, but the candle holder is completed in stages so children need to be able to wait for the completed item and to come back to them a couple of times. The children could take them home and cook them there, but they need to be brought back for painting and varnishing.

Time needed: Approximately 15 minutes for initially making each, overnight to cook, then 10 minutes to paint, one hour to dry, then two minutes to spray varnish.

Material needed for each holder: 8oz plain white flour, 3oz salt, half-tablespoon cooking oil, water for mixing, kitchen foil, blunt knives, forks, shaped cutters, Blu-Tack, one candle approximately 2 cm in diameter per child, paints and a spray can of clear varnish.

Sieve the flour and salt together. Mix in the oil. Add enough water so that the mixture is easy to handle but not sticky. If it is too sticky just add a little more flour. Take off a small amount of the mixture to use for decoration later if desired. Roll the mixture into a ball. For Christmas this shape could be a log, or for Easter an egg shape. Flatten one surface so that it will stand firmly. Place it on a piece of kitchen foil that is approximately 4 cm in diameter bigger in size. Press the candle into the top of it until it is held upright and firmly. Roll out the remaining mixture quite thinly and use the cutters or the knife to make suitable shapes to decorate it with. Undecorated, it could be likened to a stone or a pebble from a beach. The children could imagine the life story of their 'stone'. To add the decoration use a tiny amount of water on the surfaces that will be touching, and press them firmly together. When completed, remove the candle and put the holder on an old baking tray (thin trays or cake tins are likely to brown and spoil). Bake overnight in a very slow oven, gas mark ½, 250 F, 130 C. Don't worry if the inside is still a little spongy when removed from the oven. The salt acts as a preservative and the centre will air dry and harden after a while. The thicker the item, the longer this will take. If the oven is too hot it may crack the holder. This is usually under-neath so should not spoil the finished article. Salt dough expands on baking so if the candle hole distorts shave a little off the base of each candle with a sharp knife until it is held flat and firm. If necessary, put some Blu-Tack in the holder. If wished, you can paint the candle holder with ordinary poster paint after it has been cooked. Try not to get the item too wet or this can affect the dough. When the paint has fully dried, you can glaze it by spraying it with clear varnish.

Young Jesus on Pilgrimage

Harry Haas

Until the age of 12 the boys of the village were with the mothers, just like the small girls. Then they switched over to the men's company. Young Jesus was one of them. He was generally pious. That he was different, at times mischievous, also showed itself soon enough. The first major occasion was his maiden trip to Jerusalem, just after he had outgrown his boyhood and now aspired to manhood.

The prelude to the event was the rehearsal of the traditional pilgrim hymns. The boys sang them, sometimes at the tops of their voices, once they mastered text and melody. The girls' voices, harmonious but soft, sometimes got drowned by the young men's volume. These demonstrated by their sound the pride they took in joining the men's department. Women were softly spoken at home and in the village. Not so, however, at the well, which was their territory. If the girls' voices formed the background, the women were the prima donnas. The boys were in the middle. A song is in three parts, sung by the mixed choir. The hymns aroused different feelings among the singers, apart from the devotion which they all had in common. They sang of the strong and sweet presence of God in the Temple. The young girls also trained for their background role. The young men presented their manhood. The women relished God's distant presence; there was a tinge of desperation in their voices, of subdued anger, of hidden taste for revenge. Jesus, a clear voice among the breaking ones of his contemporaries, had forebodings of the trouble to come. How did he long to see the ramparts of Jerusalem! These ramparts, however, also kept his village out. If the gates narrowly opened, then what? He grew elated and felt giddy.

Young Jesus went on his first pilgrimage to Jerusalem with three distinct expectations. They were interconnected.

He had a great longing to be in the house of his Father, as was called the magnificent edifice of the Most High he was going to.

Furthermore, he could meet the men of God called scribes. Who were they and what did they do? He was not supposed to know. Once he asked his father, after he had picked up the name scribe by chance, what it meant. The answer was uneasily vague. Twice he overheard a group of men talking about the subject. They hushed their voices and then fell silent until he had passed them. He was puzzled for a while but forgot about it. He could not find out what a scribe was and could not figure out what he had to do with it. The male part of the village talked about him and his future off and on. He was a particularly bright boy. He spent much of his time asking questions. Many were embarrassing. They were not meant so, the men agreed, but they put them to shame, as none of them knew the answers. At times the boy also was reticent. He was seen sitting on a stone, all to himself. A few times he did not come home for the night. He never told his parents where he had been. A boy of that brightness was at a loss in the village for sure. In the village there was no school to go to and nobody to coach him. Becoming a carpenter like his father was in the wings. The village had no repute. Now there was a light to be kindled to shine beyond the fields around the cluster of simple houses. There was more. An endless stream of unanswered questions would turn the boy into a source of unrest in the community. One old man had a bright idea: find a scholarship to become a scribe! The listeners were enthusiastic about the proposed solution but the high mood dampened. They scratched their heads and stroked their beards. None had a scribe in the family or knew such a person. Would they accept crude village boys for study? Where would that be? Nobody came forward. But they kept on discussing the matter. The more young Jesus grew up, the more impossible questions he asked. For instance, why did he have to leave the group with the women at the well after the pilgrimage to Jerusalem? Why men were men and women were women? If there was a God father, which was a disturbing point in itself, what about God mother? Why was the village poor and Jerusalem rich? Somebody suggested that once they were in the capital, they would try to get some pertinent information. But nobody came forward to do the job. The thought of the town paralysed them like a mouse facing a cat.

There was still another point which intrigued Jesus. In between the hymn sessions, the women at the well lowered their voices and exchanged whisperings. The secretiveness, of course, aroused the curiosity of the forward boys and girls. They stayed around at hearing distance, pretending to busy themselves with washing clothes. At times the whispers blew up in fireworks of indignant shouts, hushed down immediately by the group. What Jesus could make out, and later checked with the girls who had been near and knew more about the subject, was that the talk was about a comparison of prices at the different stalls in the temple's outer premises. Shouts of indignation filled the air when extravagant differences came to light. At the same stall different women were given different prices. The women were convinced they had to pay more than other women – townspeople, for example. There also had been cases where goods obtained at particular stalls were of low quality, if not unusable. The group was sure that they had been victims of cheating. Young Jesus formed the strong resolution to find out whether in actual fact his mother and the other women were victimised, and, if that was so, for what reason. Was it because they were from the mountains?

What an ambitious agenda for a young fellow, still a child, when pilgrimaging for the first time of his short life to what looked like another world! Close to heaven? But could heaven be so full of unanswered questions as he had in mind?

Jesus spoke to nobody, not even to his parents, about his city programme. In town he soon found his own way and for the duration of their stay in Jerusalem his parents did not see him.

Although he had been instructed on how to conduct himself

in the Temple, he wanted to walk straight to the inner sanctuary. He did not get far. Officials and priests kindly but firmly soon stopped him. How sweet a boy from the mountains was who walked in as if this was his father's home. When he offered to sing a hymn by way of entrance ticket they tapped him gently on his shoulder, and showed him where he could stay. Since the whole house was his Father's, the boy settled in a corner and felt at home. The fumes and aromas neither impressed nor stimulated him, just as he took the smells from his mother's kitchen and his father's workshop as belonging to the house.

The place where the scribes had their headquarters was not difficult to find. It was close to the temple. When Jesus walked into the entrance he was stopped by an unfriendly guardsman. An old man with white hair and flowing garb appeared from the deep corridor. He welcomed the child as if he were his own grandson and asked him what message he was bringing. The uninhibited answer was 'None. I just came.' The man laughed loud, approvingly, and ushered the boy in. There was a bright courtyard and his host presented him to a group of seriously talking colleagues. 'What is your name?' 'Jesus.' 'From where?' 'Nazareth.' 'Where is that close by?' 'Oh, in Galilee. Jesus from Galilee.' The scribes did not show much interest, but when the man started intimate conversation, they stealthily threw glances towards the boy, who stood waiting and did not show the shyness they expected. The 'grandfather' took the lad into an inner room and asked him whether he wanted to know where he was. 'I want to see the place and you people,' Jesus said. 'What are you really doing in a big place like this?' the old man asked, and then took him to the library with its impressive collection of scrolls. He explained to the eager boy what all this was. 'Is that the whole Bible?' the boy asked. His guide shook his head and explained that those were only the ideas which his predecessors and colleagues had been having when reading the Bible. He tried to find an example which the boy would be interested in, but could not find one straightaway. 'Better come back tomorrow. I wanted to go to the Temple when you came. Do you want to come along?' They went out.

In the evening the guide told his sceptical colleagues that he was enchanted by the innocence and the shrewdness of the village boy. 'Totally unspoiled. An unpolished diamond. Good for our school. We have not many recruits anyhow. Let us have some kind of interview. We can keep in touch thereafter when the village boy returns home.' Three men, one of whom was his host, were seated at a table on which a few scrolls were placed, one of them half rolled out. They kept the boy standing. They explained their profession: 'God has given the rules,' they explained to him. 'Take the Ten Commandments. There is the one about not stealing.' Jesus jumped at that: 'Then you can explain why my mother and the women were cheated by stallholders in the Temple premises.' They looked surprised. 'What do you mean?' The boy told them what he had heard about the way the women, including his mother, were cheated by stallkeepers in the temple premises. The scribes exchanged glances of mutual understanding. One of them asked, 'How do you know?' Jesus innocently said, 'From the women.' The men burst into loud laughter. 'Women from the village! Women from the mountains! Women from Galilee!' Some slapped their thighs or hammered on the table in delight. When they calmed down they looked for the boy. He had disappeared. They asked for the janitor. Yes, the boy had run out full speed. In which direction? Temple? The men looked at each other. Had they lost a promising recruit? 'Do not worry. He is in God's hand,' said the senior scribe who had introduced him. He looked really distressed. 'We have gone a bit too far. Such a courageous boy,' he sighed.

Three days later Jesus was back. He walked beyond the janitor, greeting him like somebody of the house, and went to the library, sure to find the men there. His mentor greeted him like a lost son. 'Can I talk?' the young boy asked, almost commanding. 'I have found the truth.' He briefly recounted that he went to the Temple market and made friends with the sons of the stallkeepers. Soon he was behind the counters. He heard the stallkeepers instruct their personnel to increase the prices when mountain women came. He mentioned names and described locations. When one of the scribes wanted to intervene, Jesus cut him short: 'There is more.' He mentioned the names of the priests who were shareholders in particular stalls. The men looked at each other. By the nods of the others, one was designated to say something. 'My son, you did an excellent job of research indeed. You passed your first exam to enter this institution with the highest marks. We know about all that. We can tell you more. Let this suffice. Now we scribes come in. What does God say about such a godless situation? And what do we scribes have to do?' The speaker paused and rolled out a text. It spoke about corruption in the temple. 'This is God's voice.' There was a pause. Jesus seemed to listen to a voice which the men did not hear. 'Now what is our task? We should first of all know what God has to say. He spoke clearly and we know. We also must know the situation in detail. God sent you to offer us details of which we were not fully aware. Now you must understand one thing for sure. We are God's appointed keepers of the Law. Look around. It is all in the books. It is not our God-given role to take action. We pronounce the Law, and quote in this case the prophets. If some of our listeners do not listen, we cannot compel them to do so. A scribe, as the voice of God, should detach himself from direct action. If we do not keep out of daily dealings and have our ears too close to people's mouths, we will become partial, even partisan. Then where does the word of God go? We do not speak any more in his name, but in ours. That will be the end of the Law. It will be anarchy, civil war'.

When he wanted to explain to the boy that this is not cowardice but courage, he did not find him. During his speech he had his eyes lifted unto heaven. The boy was gone. His colleagues hardly saw him disappearing, so smooth had his movement been. 'Gone,' the men sighed in unison.

Jesus' anger in the Temple
Etching by Francis Hoyland

The young man was sure that becoming a scribe was not his deal. First of all he wanted to pursue the track he found. He had his new friends. He needed more figures and more names. Perhaps also scribes were making money out of his people. He was warmly taken in by his comrades and the street urchins belonging to their youth gang. He slept with them on the pavement, and they shared whatever they had. This was different from life in Nazareth. He did not like the smell of the city but loved the smells he shared with the street children. They became his smells.

His parents sought him in vain. They missed him on the way back and the village pilgrims gathered for a rest. They went to the Temple but not the market place. One of the scribes saw the desperate couple and asked if he could help. They went with him to the scribes' place and there a scribe told them what their son had done, carefully concealing the Temple market episode. They knew now where to find him. The street children welcomed them as their family members. From the little money Jesus' parents had left they bought delicacies for the whole gang in a sweet stall.

Two decades later the rage of the women, which had kept burning in Jesus' stomach, burst into flame. In the same Temple market, Jesus had come on his own and for the first time went to Jerusalem with a mission. He had not forgotten what had been his adventure with the street children and the women of his village. It had been simmering in the background. He did not see his friends, except a few, grown up as he was. They had replaced their fathers behind the stalls. Jesus moved in among a group of mountain women. Nothing had changed as before. In his rage Jesus turned the tables, opened cages with pigeons and sent a rain of coins all over the place.

Harry Haas is a Roman Catholic priest who lives in Bandarawalla in Sri Lanka and works with the Woodlands Community.

EPILOGUE
Going Home

Photograph: Barbara Butler

The return home from any time with friends can be difficult, especially for those who are returning to a very different style of life from the time away, perhaps living a lonely life in very different circumstances. Our coming home from a pilgrimage may also bring an added dimension to these potential difficulties of settling back into daily life and relationships: it can be very hard to leave our fellow pilgrims.

Our fellow pilgrims have shared our experiences with us, no matter how different their understanding of that experience. They heard our laughter, and they shared our tears. They struggled up the hill with us, waited for us when they were far ahead, and thanked us for waiting for them when we were ahead. They borrowed our suntan cream on sunny days and lent us their spare walking socks when ours were still wet from washing them overnight. We dressed each other's blisters, held hands as we crossed boggy places, and all in all there really isn't much we don't know about each other's hopes and fears. In a very short space of time we have come to a point where not everything needs to be said. But now we're leaving each other and going home.

The difficulties are heightened for those pilgrims who have been away from home for some time, really relaxed, and spent time with God, and then returned without thinking through what life at home will be like now they have 'changed'. It is important that pilgrimage leaders spend some time with pilgrims talking about how each will meet the challenges of everyday life. If they recognise that they are not the same person as the one who left, how will this new returning person face and meet the people and tasks that lie ahead?

Part of the planning for any pilgrimage should include the returning home stage. What difference has this pilgrimage time meant to each pilgrim; how has each been changed? It's important that each pilgrim is encouraged and enabled to think these issues through for themselves, and then, ideally, talk about them with someone in the group – perhaps the pilgrimage leader and perhaps someone else. Included in this section are some questions, a returning home checklist, to help pilgrims think through the returning home issues.

Often the hardest part of returning from pilgrimage is the longing to share all the details with someone at home who, by the very fact that they were not also on the journey, may find the details unnecessary and just want to know the overall story, or may even be busy when the pilgrim returns and so not have time to hear or listen properly. This longing to share experiences with friends and family is not confined to pilgrims, of course, but may be the experience of any traveller away from home, for whatever reason.

In an ideal world the return home should be a time of rejoicing, with time actually set aside for the pilgrim to be listened to, and for the pilgrim in turn to listen to what has been happening in their absence. This is often best done away from the home, over a meal or a drink somewhere. An hour or two at home to catch up with friends and family is essential, to return a few phone calls, get everything back in order, and so on, but then we should all try to find some time together with our family and away from all the practicalities. Probably going out and leaving the mobiles at home is the only way these days!

Where this isn't possible, we should at least try to spend a number of short times together over the next day or two, just chatting about the pilgrimage time, rather than letting it pass and slipping back into the everyday routine. Yes, routine things have to be done, but the benefits of sharing the pilgrimage experience far outweigh the drawbacks, and it is better to do this whilst it is still fresh in our minds, hearts and souls.

It may be that the person the pilgrim lives with is not the most appropriate person with whom to discuss all the fine detail of the pilgrimage experience, and that a soul friend, spiritual adviser, parish priest, or trusted friend would be more suitable.

Even without a major change in the pilgrim, the return home can be quite a blow to the system. Pilgrimage can leave us on a spiritual high that can plummet to the depths when we come back to earth. It's almost like an addiction that is quickly succumbed to but if not maintained, then drags us into withdrawal. One way to overcome this is by thinking through what it is about the pilgrimage experience that you particularly enjoyed and benefited from, and how you can take that home with you and share it with others.

If it's the music, then we may buy and play a CD or tape; if it's the times alone with God, then we may set aside a time at home for this. We could also make a part of our home a 'worship area'. We may not have a spare room to do this, but we could have a prayer mat (any small rug will do) that we could lay out in a suitable place. We might tell the family that when they see the rug out we are 'praying' and do not wish to be disturbed for so many minutes. We should always keep to the time so that family members may trust us to be available when we say we will be; in that way they are less likely to disturb us. Always put the rug away between prayer times so that it comes to symbolise that special time for you and the Lord. If the rug is not practical, then we could put a small cloth on our table and sit at that. In this case we might want to also use a candle or incense, or an incense oil burner to combine the two.

If the pleasure in the pilgrimage was about the style of worship or the number of people, then we may try and find something similar nearby. Keeping in touch with your fellow pilgrims by phone or e-mail is also a good idea especially in those early days of return.

We may do a great deal to bring the pilgrimage back home with us and to continue something of the life we have enjoyed and been enriched by, but at the end of the day we may also have to accept that the pilgrimage is over and that we have to face and again enter our ordinary lives. And God is in the ordinary as well as in the special times and places.

Churches Together in Britain and Ireland wrote in their book *Holy Land Pilgrimage* in 1992 about the value of pilgrimage and of the expectations of pilgrims coming home in this way:

The real worth of a place of pilgrimage is measured not in the visit but in the return to one's daily life. That worth is proved when one returns uplifted, inspired, challenged, moved and with a clearer vision of the tasks to which God calls. A journey which brings one home with no sense of commitment to, or solidarity with, the peoples among whom one has been visiting is not a pilgrimage. A journey from which one returns with no new vision of work to be done within one's own home community is not true pilgrimage either.*

Prayer at return home

Lord God, Lamb of God,
you have brought me home safely
through this time of pilgrimage
and I give you thanks.
I thank you for all you have done for me and to me during this time.
For your faithfulness while I have not always been faithful.
For your grace when I was not always gracious.
For your love when I was not always lovable.
But you are a mighty God whose nature is always to have mercy.
Keep me in the palm of your hand as I come home again.
Hold me in the shadows of your wing
while I pick up the threads of my daily life.
Stand by me as I start again to live my life,
as you would have me;
as you have shown me over this time together.
Holy Spirit, continue to renew my heart and soul
so that I will continue to grow closer each day to you.
I ask this through Jesus Christ, my Saviour and my Lord.
Amen.

* Churches Together in Britain and Ireland, Inter-Church House, 35-41 Lower Marsh, London SE1 7RL.

Checklist for returning home after a pilgrimage

Before we finish our pilgrimage we might think through the following questions, make a few notes, and try to talk them through with someone else before going home.

- What were our aims when we came on this pilgrimage?
- Have they been realised? And, if so, in what ways?
- Have things happened that we were not expecting?
- How has the pilgrimage experience changed us?
- What decisions have we made?
- How will these be put into practice?
- If these decisions affect other people, how will they be included and asked about them?
- How are they likely to react to these changes?
- If the pilgrimage has brought about repentance, how will this be displayed?
- If we plan to apologise to anyone, think through what effect this is likely to have on them and whether it will actually do them more harm than good.
- How will those being apologised to be likely to react?
- What other changes have taken place?
- How will we share our pilgrimage experience with those we live with?
- Who will we talk with about the details of the experience?
- Who will we talk with about the future changes that the pilgrimage will continue to have in our lives?
- Where do we envisage the pilgrimage taking us in the future?
- What are the best parts of the pilgrimage experience that we would like to continue with? How may we take them home with us?

Photograph: Barbara Butler

APPENDIX

Some Practical Pointers for Pilgrimage

Planning the Pilgrimage

Get the balance right

If we are a leader, there will be expectations from those who join the pilgrimage. It is wise to ask in advance what pilgrims want to get out of the pilgrimage. Are there special places they would like to see or activities they would like to take part in? We will have only a limited time to fit everything in, and some people are bound to be disappointed.

We should make sure, if we are on a pilgrimage to a special place, that we plan to have enough time there, both for public worship as a group and for private devotions. We should try to plan to encounter the place as it is today – its religion, culture and politics. It is important to understand what was going on through the ages, and at the time of any special events, but it is equally important to listen to the people who live there now.

Our pilgrimage may be focused on an issue or on meeting people, and, again, we will need to consciously plan to inform ourselves and our group about essential background preparation and reading, and to give sufficient time to our focus during the journey itself.

It is wise to invite everyone who may be interested to the planning sessions. Often it's those whom we least expect who decide to join in.

The wider we spread the invitations, the more likely we are to reach a desired number, though it is also important to recognise that, if the event is important, the number of people who join are the right number, no matter how many or how few.

Information evenings

We might –

- hold a launch evening when thinking about the pilgrimage

- hold a sharing and information giving meeting six months before setting off.
- hold a preparation meeting three weeks before the start date.
- consult key people in the church and community.

We should not offer lots of choices of dates, places to stay, and itinerary as this leads to confusion and can cause unhappiness when someone's idea is not taken up. We should be very clear about what is possible and keep in touch with people leading up to the pilgrimage with update letters, kit lists and new details, to maintain confidence and enthusiasm. It is vital to include the essential footwear in the kit list, especially if the pilgrimage is to be a walk, when strong boots will be necessary.

Some things that may go wrong on the pilgrimage
It is often helpful to discuss these during the preparation times, and then they will not be too difficult to face when they arise.

- leg blisters
- heat rash
- sunburn
- feet
- tiredness through lack of physical training or lack of sleep
- conflicting agendas of group members
- problems with the food
- disappointed expectations of some people

This list could go on, but, once we have set off, we can only take and enjoy each day as it comes, doing our best to make sure that everyone is as comfortable and fulfilled as possible. Serious health problems should always be referred to a doctor.

Everyone should carry their own
- sun hat, sun cream, etc.

- water in good water bottle
- food
- emergency food (not to be eaten unless there is an emergency)
- sweets, biscuits, crisps
- first aid requirements, including any necessary medication
- map and compass
- notebook
- full waterproofs (unless the pilgrimage is to a dry tropical area)
- extra warm clothes, especially socks

This list should be included in the kit list, which may also include optional items for the consideration of each pilgrim.

Some Pilgrim Routes and Pilgrimage Sites

Here are just a few pilgrim routes and pilgrim sites which we have chosen, but we also suggest books and sites on the internet which will give you a much wider view and opportunity.

A few pilgrim routes for walkers

- The St Cuthbert's Way – from Melrose Abbey to Lindisfarne. It is an easy walk which may be divided up into longer or shorter sections.

- The Pilgrim's Way – from Glastonbury to Canterbury. We have included a reflection on this walk in the section on 'Special Times'. It is a long walk, but very easy for people of all ages. For the Dunstan anniversary walk we invited blind people from the St Dunstan's Society, who were the strongest walkers.

- The Pembrokeshire Coast Path – from St Dogmael's near

Cardigan to Amroth, 170 miles long. It follows an up-and-down, round-about and zig-zag coastal route. It is ideal for artists who wish to pause and paint the dramatic and rocky coastal scenery, and also for those who are looking for a meditational walk, and will be content to live in the present moment at each step along the way.

- The Coast to Coast Walk – from St Bees Head in Cumbria to Robin Hood's Bay on the East Yorkshire coast, 190 miles long. It passes through three national parks and includes the famous Lyke Wake Walk. This walk was established by Alfred Wainwright and covers a wonderful variety of scenery, from the hills of the Lake District to the more rolling wild areas of the North Yorkshire Moors.

- The Pennine Way – from Edale in Derbyshire to Kirk Yetholm in Roxburghshire, 270 miles long. This is a difficult and for the most part a bleakly exposed walk along the Pennines which is best tackled from south to north. It is an ideal choice for those who wish to face a challenge of stamina and perhaps to develop a 'desert spirituality'.

A few pilgrim sites around the world
- In Egypt the pyramids of Giza, including the great pyramid, built around 2575 BCE, are a stunning and beautiful reminder of what was possible so many years ago.

- The great temple at Luxor, in Thebes in Upper Egypt, dates from about 1391 BCE. It is intricate and mysterious.

- In Zimbabwe the ruins of Great Zimbabwe are perhaps unique as large stone structures surviving from a society which mostly built in wood. The ruins are magnificent and puzzling, especially the great enclosure with its conical tower. The whole complex is thought to have been a trading and religious centre for the people who lived in that part of Central Africa between the tenth and fifteenth centuries BCE.

- In the Middle East the great city of Jerusalem stands out as a pilgrim place for Christians, Muslims and Jews. The main Jewish pilgrim site is the Western Wall of the destroyed temple, where Jews pray and also place prayers. The stronghold of Masada, where the Jews unsuccessfully resisted Roman conquest, is on the shores of the Dead Sea.

- The Dome of the Rock built in the seventh century CE is the third holiest place in Islam, after Mecca and Medina. The tradition is that the Prophet Mohammed ascended into heaven from the rock and inside the mosque there is a shrine containing a hair of the prophet.

- Christian sites in Jerusalem are many and include the Mount of Olives, the hill of Golgotha and the Holy Sepulchre. The present 'Via Dolorosa' includes the traditional stations of the cross.

- Petra is the rose red sandstone city in the Southern desert of Jordan, approached through a narrow gorge. The temple-like building at the end of the gorge probably dates from the sixth-century BCE Nabataean culture and is typical of many beautiful temples and tombs over a wide area of desert. There are also Roman remains from the time when the Romans ruled.

- Mecca is the holiest city of Islam. The hajj – the pilgrimage Muslims are challenged to make, if possible, once in a life-time – is included in the section on 'Pilgrimage in the Faith Traditions'.

- Ephesus, visited by St Paul and the place where St John is said to have died, is most famous as the site of the temple of Diana, one of the wonders of the world. Even the ruins are stunning.

- Santa Sophia in Istanbul was at one time perhaps the greatest church in the Christian world. It was converted to a mosque in 1475 when the Turks conquered, and it is now a museum.

- The pilgrim sites of ancient Greece are too numerous to list, but the Labyrinth of the Minotaur at Knossos is very special.

- There are many pilgrim places in Russia which are well worth visiting, including the great cathedral built to St Basil by Ivan the Terrible in Red Square, in Moscow.

- Rome is a centre of pilgrimage in Western Europe and we have included an account of one pilgrimage there. Some say that the early sixteenth-century cathedral of St Peter, with its dome designed by Michelangelo, is the greatest church in the world today.

- We have included a pilgrimage to Santiago de Compostela in northern Spain.

- The monastery of the Black Madonna at Montserrat is visited by perhaps 60,000 pilgrims every year. Its position is spectacular on the cliff edge. The Black Madonna is said to date from the fourth century CE and the Benedictine monastery grew up around it.

- Stonehenge is one of the most famous and representative of the many prehistoric sites in Europe. In spite of its being a tourist attraction, it does not lose its ability to enable meditation.

- Carnac in Brittany is the site of the largest number of standing stones in Europe, dating from perhaps 5000 BCE.

- Chartres Cathedral, built around 1100, is a famous and beautiful pilgrim church in France.

- North and South America and Australasia have many ancient sites from the time of the flowering of the indigenous culture and faith of the native peoples.

- In South America the site of Machu Picchu is high up in the Andes and very spectacular. It is the site of a city of the Inca Empire.

- In the Buddhist world of the Far East there are innumerable places to visit associated with the life of the Buddha. We include a short pilgrimage in the footsteps of the Buddha, which took place in India. The shrines of Tibet are sadly difficult, though not impossible, to visit now.

- Japan has Buddhist and also Shinto shrines. Some of the oldest Buddhist temples are in Nara. The huge Buddha of Kamakura, of the Amida school, is famous all over the world. Mount Fuji, the highest mountain of Japan, is sacred to Buddhists and Shintoists.

It is impossible to include all the Hindu caves, shrines, holy rivers and temples of India here. Varanasi is famous as the holy city of the Ganges. Hampi is associated with the stories of the 'Ramayana'. Orissa has very fine temples, not least the one dedicated to the Lord Jaganath at Puri.

Some of the pilgrim places of Britain are included in this book. Canterbury and Walsingham are perhaps the most popular places for pilgrims to visit. Others are listed below.

There is a complete list of Christian sites available on the Internet at the Catholic Encyclopedia site under 'Pilgrimages'.

It gives a brief history of the chief places of Christian pilgrimage, in early days, in the Middle Ages, and in modern times. These include the following from England, Scotland and Wales:

Canterbury, Kent
Chichester, Sussex
Croyland, Lincolnshire
Durham
Ely, Cambridgeshire
Glastonbury, Somerset
Holywell, North Wales
Iona, Scotland
Lichfield, Staffordshire
Lincoln
Oxford
Pennant Melangell, Montgomery
St Albans, Hertford
St Andrews, Fife
St David's, Pembrokeshire
Walsingham, Norfolk
Westminster, London

The site can be found at:
http://www.newsadvent.org/cathen/12085a.html

An Internet site giving Islamic pilgrimage sites can be found at:
http://www.al-islam.org/organization/dilp/html

An Internet site giving Buddhist pilgrimage sites can be found at:
http://buddhism.about.com/cs/pilgrimage/html

Two useful resources for pilgrim sites and places are:
The World of Pilgrimage: A Guide to the World's Most Sacred Sites, George Target (AA Publishing, 1997)
The Marshall Travel Atlas of Sacred Places: A Guide to the

World's Spiritual Oases, James Harper (Marshall Publishing, London, 1994)

Some Pilgrimage Organisers

• Christians Aware is an international and educational charity which organises visits, mainly to the developing world, which are pilgrimages in the true sense of the word. The visits offer opportunities for new experiences and insights, and sometimes for a new direction in life. Participants are challenged to be flexible and open to different ways of living and doing things; to be patient and sensitive, and to be happy to listen and learn as well as to give. Christians Aware also offers its members resources, books and a quarterly magazine, and opportunities to attend conferences and courses. Christians Aware, 2 Saxby Street, Leicester LE2 0ND http//www.christiansaware.co.uk

• McCabe Pilgrimages does far more than organise pilgrimages to a number of holy Christian sites around the world. It also runs a loan service for pilgrimage leaders – even if you're not using their service – an extensive Reference Library, a free mail service for fact sheets and a number of videos, audio tapes and slide sets, as well as having a bimonthly news-sheet full of articles and up-to-date items of interest about pilgrimages, the Holy Land, new publications, new books in the library, and so on. McCabe also has an educational Trust.
McCabe Pilgrimages, 53-55 Balham Hill, London SW12 9DR
Telephone 020 8675 6828

• The Nativity Walk from Nazareth to Bethlehem, included in our section on 'Pilgrimages for Justice' was organised by Guiding Star Ltd, PO Box 19421, 4 Al-Hariri Street, Jerusalem 91193

E-mail: rianne@guidingstarltd.com
It was booked through Alternative Tourism Group, PO Box 173, Beit Sahour, Bethlehem, Palestine

- The retreat to the desert was organised by Wind, Sand and Stars, 2 Arkwright Road, London NW3 6AD

- Soul of India, Revd Kenneth Wilson, 6 Westland Road, Wolverhampton WV3 9NY
  Telephone 01902 561485

Some Other Useful Organisations

- The Countryside Commission, John Dower House, Crescent Place, Cheltenham, Gloucestershire GL50 3RA

- The National Trust, 36 Queen Anne's Gate, London SW1H 9AS

- Council for National Parks, 45 Sheldon Street, London WC2H 9HS

- The Ramblers' Association, 1/5 Wandsworth Road, London SW8 2LJ

- The Youth Hostels Association, Trevelyan House, 8 St Stephen's Hill, St Albans, Hertfordshire AL1 2DY

- Ordnance Survey, Romsey Road, Maybush, Southampton SO9 4DH

It is wise to contact Ordnance Survey and to visit a good map shop before planning a pilgrimage. For pilgrimages in the UK the 'Landranger' series of maps is perhaps the most useful. It is wise to take advice about the most suitable maps for every journey, especially when the pilgrimage is outside the UK and maps and plans may have to be ordered.

A Few Extra Resources

Pilgrimage tokens such as earth and water from Jerusalem as well as oils can be bought over the Internet from a variety of sites including http://www.jerusalem-gifts-online.com/

Prayers in Latin – Michael Martin has a site on the Internet which gives a wide range of prayers in Latin. You can find them at http://unidial.com/~martinus/index.htm

Background to prayer, scripture, meditation, saints and contemplation. These all abound on a site with multiple links to other sites that is kept up-to-date well. You can find it at http://landru.i-link-2.net/shnyves/prayer.html

Some Relevant Books

Pilgrim Guide to Holy Island, David Adam (Canterbury Press, 1997)
A guide to a holy place by someone who loves it.

Forward to Freedom, David Adam (Darton, Longman & Todd, 1999)
The story of Exodus from a modern perspective.

St Cuthbert's Way Pilgrimage Book, Barbara Butler and Jo White (Christians Aware, 2000)
This contains Celtic prayers for morning, midday and evening worship, as well as a Communion service that could be used anywhere. The rest of the book relates specifically to the St Cuthbert's Way – a 100-kilometre walk from Melrose to Holy Island in the North of England.

Pilgrimage: Yesterday and Today, J. G. Davies (SCM Press Ltd, 1988)

Roget's Thesaurus of the Bible, A. Colin Day (Marshall Pickering)
An excellent way of finding themes in the Bible.

The Road to Canterbury: A Modern Pilgrimage, Shirley Du Boulay (HarperCollins, 1994)
The author has written about her walk along the Pilgrims' Way and at the same time reflected on modern pilgrimage.

Caught in Between, Riah Abu El-Assal (SPCK, 1999)
The extraordinary story of an Arab Palestinian Christian Israeli.

Going Home, Thich Nat Hanh (Rider, 1999)
A resource for personal spiritual exploration from a Vietnamese Zen master, poet and peace activist.

A Candle of Hope, Garth Hewitt (Bible Reading Fellowship, 1999)
A journey with the Palestinian people at the time of the Millennium.

Living Stones Pilgrimage: With the Christians of the Holy Land, Alison Hilliard and Betty Jane Bailey (Cassell, 1999)

The Pilgrims' Manual, Christopher Irvine (Wild Goose Publications, 1996)
Described as a manual for pilgrims travelling in the steps of the saints. It contains hymns, prayers, Bible readings and music samples.

Between Extremes, Brian Keenan and John McCarthy (Black Swan, 1999)
A journey to South America which was first planned when the authors were hostages together in the Lebanon.

Windrush: The Irresistible Rise of Multi-Racial Britain, Mike Phillips and Trevor Phillips (HarperCollins, 1999)
This book represents the many pilgrimages people around the world have made from one country to another, to a new life and hope.

Pilgrims, Stephen Platten (Fount, 1996)
An insight into the lasting importance of some well-known pilgrims across the centuries.

A Do-It-at-Home Retreat – Spiritual Exercises of St Ignatius of Loyola, Andre Ravier, SJ (Ignatius Press, 1989)

Glendalough. A Celtic Pilgrimage, Michael Rogers and Marcus Losack (Columba Press, 1996)
A journey linking the spirituality of St Kevin with the modern world.

A Pilgrim's Book of Prayers, Gilbert Shaw (Convent of the Incarnation, Fairacres, Oxford, 1992)
A classic collection which was first published in 1945.

Celtic Worship Through the Year, Ray Simpson (Hodder & Stoughton, 1997)
A useful resource for most occasions.

Celtic Journeys in Scotland and the North of England, Shirley Toulson (Fount, 1995)
This useful book includes eight journeys which are based on the journeys of eight people. There are useful maps.

The Celtic Year, Shirley Toulson (Element, 1993)
The author takes us month by month through the Celtic year, including the Celtic saints' days, and for each month she offers a pilgrimage.

The Celtic Resource Book, Martin Wallace (The National Society/Church House Publishing, 1998)
Contains some excellent ideas for practical Celtic activities as well as prayers and lives of Celtic saints.

Sacred Journeys. Paths for the New Pilgrim, Jennifer Westwood (Gaia Books, 1997)
A useful and attractive resource.

Photograph: Barbara Butler

The annual publication of the National Retreat Association deserves special mention. *Retreats* is available from The National Retreat Association, The Central Hall, Bermondsey Street, London SE1 3UJ. It includes articles, resources, details of quiet days and workshops, and the programme of events for more than 200 retreat houses.